JUSTIFIED BY WORK

Justified by Work

Identity and the Meaning of Faith in Chicago's Working-Class Churches

Robert Anthony Bruno

THE OHIO STATE UNIVERSITY PRESS | COLUMBUS

Library of Congress Cataloging-in-Publication Data
Bruno, Robert Anthony.
Justified by work : identity and the meaning of faith in Chicago's working-class churches / Robert Anthony Bruno.
p. cm.
Includes bibliographical references and index.
ISBN-13: 978-0-8142-1095-6 (cloth : alk. paper)
ISBN-10: 0-8142-1095-3 (cloth : alk. paper)
1. Working class—Religious life. 2. Working class—Illinois—Chicago. I. Title.
BV4593.B78 2008
277.73'1108308623—dc22
2008005335

This book is available in the following editions:
Cloth (ISBN 978-08142-1095-6)
CD-ROM (ISBN 978-08142-9175-7)

Cover design by Dan O'Dair
Typeset by Juliet Williams in Adobe Goudy
Printed by Sheridan Books, Inc.

∞ The paper used in this publication meets the minimum requirements of the American National Standard for Information Sciences—Permanence of Paper for Printed Library Materials. ANSI Z39.48–1992.

9 8 7 6 5 4 3 2 1

This book is dedicated to my mother, who asked me to always believe in something.

CONTENTS

ACKNOWLEDGMENTS

I HAVE TO be honest: writing about religion and working-class life did not come naturally to me. I'm not a religious scholar and I had no prior expertise in the sociology of religion. But I did feel inspired by the volume of steelworkers, postal clerks, nurses, food store employees, electricians, plumbers, and other hardworking folks who said that God was a part of their lives. What exactly that meant and how that was possible fascinated, troubled, and challenged me. Most importantly, the sacred that workers found embedded within their secular lives was a part of working-class life that I no longer chose to ignore. Getting started, however, and finding a respectful path to some deeper understanding of the meaning of faith in the lives of working-class Chicagoans depended on the good graces of a number of people. The horrid events of 9/11 complicated my desire to gain access to a Muslim mosque. As an American academic of Catholic upbringing wielding a tape recorder, I did not present an inviting invitation to chat about Islam. Fortunately, *Chicago Tribune* reporter Steve Franklin introduced me to people at The Council of Islamic Organizations of Greater Chicago. The Council's contact did not open up any mosque doors, but it did welcome me into a social setting where I could speak with Muslim taxi drivers. Finding a working-class Jewish synagogue was no less difficult. In fact, I never found an appropriate one. But Mike Perry of the American Federation of State County and Municipal Employees Council 31 did offer suggestions about rabbis who could help me with my research, and Jeff Weiss of the United Food and Commercial Workers

Union Local 1546 made a genuine effort to solicit Jewish workers from the people who labor in the retail food industry. Once I found people of faith to interview, the easy part was engaging them in conversation. The hard part was transcribing over a thousand pages of interviews into a coherent, accurate record of what was said. Fortunately for me, Linda Ellis was willing to sacrifice much of her leisure time and, with a patient regard for nuance, to help move the voices of my interviewees onto the written page.

Steven Warner, professor of sociology at the University of Illinois at Chicago, offered the valuable gift of his time and insight about how my work might fit within the sociology of religion. I am also indebted to the kindness and guidance of Elfriede Wiedam, who helped me to navigate some of the Roman Catholic parishes in the blue-collar neighborhoods of Southwest Chicago.

I was very well served by the contributions of the press's copyeditor Mary Read and the manuscript was nicely improved by the often humorous and always precise suggestions of Managing Editor Eugene O'Connor. It's important to note that while my wife, Lynn, is no expert in religious practices, she encouraged me to take a walk into this subject matter and not be intimidated by what I found. As usual, her faith was justified. Finally, I am most grateful for the pastors and reverends from each of the Christian churches who welcomed me into their spiritual homes and invited me to speak with their faithful. I offer to all of these folks a heartfelt thank you and a silent prayer of appreciation.

INTRODUCTION

The Unhallowed Many

AS A BOY I always walked to school. My navy blue or dark black creased pants, starched white shirt, and hooked-on skinny blue tie marked me as a Catholic. On the first Friday of every month, I attended church service along with other elementary school kids at St. Nicholas Parish. On many of those church visits I was chosen to read from scripture. It was always an honor to be selected. Teachers and school parents were so impressed with my ability to speak publicly from the Bible that they often encouraged me to consider the priesthood for a vocation. While I imagine that the school and parish staff proffered similar career choices to many of my classmates, my father's mother also never tired of telling others that I would make a good priest. Talk of a vocational life in the spirit heightened as I progressed from one Catholic ritual to another. In truth, I seemed to be a favorite of the order of nuns who ran the grade school. Once out of childhood, however, talk of my religious vocation mostly faded, as did much of any personal religious worship or thought.

By the midpoint of my college years I was having spirited debates with College Crusaders for Christ about the existence or nonexistence of God and the meaning of faith. They were always welcome in my dorm room because by jousting with them I could reaffirm what I no longer believed to be true. After countless Sundays of church singing and homilies I had concluded that if there were a God, it mattered little to how my life or anyone else's unfolded. Instead of holding on to my Catholic elementary school training, I was engrossed in my steelworking father's employment insecurity. Where Sunday masses had taught to me to celebrate God's goodness, I wondered why my mom always seemed so sick and in chronic pain. Undaunted, Mom did miracles night after night with potatoes and bologna, and Dad went in and out of work until he nearly lost his hearing. Neither of my parents were the kind of people to complain about their condition, and they were deeply upset over my transformation from church lector to doubting Thomas. But praying for better times and good health only brought silence. Who was I talking to? What was I expecting to happen?

Then in the late 1970s the steel mills in Youngstown began to close. When the mill furnaces went cold and padlocks went up on chain-link fences, many friends, neighbors, and family were crucified. People caravanned south looking for work, families were torn apart by depression, drinking, and abuse, and a whole generation of hardworking servants of God suffered a terrible loss of civic identity.[1] Most were believers in an all-knowing, all-powerful creator, but like my dad they were out of work and Sunday preaching was no better than salve on a wound. To be honest, Dad hardly went to church, but he insisted that his four boys go. Mom went, too, and she always made a point of reminding me that I needed to believe in something. Faith I had, but not in a god.

I believed that there were political and economic answers to why steel communities were devastated by powerful forces and why wealth congregated in the hands of the top 5 percent of Americans. I was also certain that I had a psychological answer to why my mother's yearning for a more satisfying life got projected into the near fanatical way she served her family and others. But for me nothing that explained the world as it was came from my Catholic upbringing or from religious influences. Not even from the pastor at St. Nicholas Parish, who, after reading a number of my commentaries in a local paper about community renewal following the first mill shutdown, wrote me a heartfelt letter appealing to me to rejoin the church. I coldly rejected the offer from a church which, in my youth, had been part of the neighborhood infrastructure and had been the faith home for countless steelworking families. Pastors had once walked the community adjacent to the church and occasionally stopped by our home unannounced to share milk and break bread.[2]

Even in the midst of economic panic, many Youngstown houses of worship, including my own, had joined together in an Ecumenical Coalition to try and uplift our community.[3] But in the end, religious belief and practice was no match for the love of Mammon. Mills were blown up and workers abandoned. They were sacrificed for higher profits to be drained from other working-class religious communities like those that baptized, confirmed, prayed, wed, and died at St. Nicholas Parish. So I denied God, and declared to myself that the faith that I had grown up with had lost its meaning. And my faith remained meaningless through family illness, marriage, the adoption of my daughter, and the start of a new career as a college professor. But after teaching labor studies to union workers in Illinois and other states for twelve years, I have reconsidered the meaning of spirituality and religious practice. More specifically, I have become curious about the relationship between religious belief and practice, the work a person does, and the use of faith to get you through the days after Saturday and Sunday.

Almost without exception my students professed a strong faith in God and had an unbroken affiliation with a house of worship. Their experiences strongly buttressed the national religious survey data that showed year after year that an overwhelming majority of Americans are religious or spiritual people.[4] But most of the people of Youngstown and the workers I have taught were not just faithful Americans; they were working-class believers. They went to work in mills, factories, hospitals, schools, and office buildings and went to give thanks for God's blessings in churches, synagogues, and mosques. Prayer and production happened daily. It was, as one Chicago-area pastor told me, as if they had "hearts to God and hands to work."[5]

One of my students with a heart as big as the furnaces she made was Lori Landers-Rippy. I first met Lori in 2002 while teaching a summer class on labor and politics. The class was part of an educational program for Illinois and Indiana members of the United Steelworkers union. I recall Lori as a vibrant, knowledgeable, and activist member of her Indianapolis-based local union.[6] But what I had not known about her at the time was that she possessed an unyielding Christian faith. However, in the summer of 2006, at yet another summer class, Lori told me of two unusual blessings that she had received from God that illustrate the way that many of my worker-students experienced their faith.

On April 17, 2003, Lori was diagnosed with breast cancer. She was forty years old at the time and had been working as a press operator for a company that manufactured home furnaces. But two weeks later, Lori underwent a radical mastectomy and had three cancerous lymph nodes removed from underneath her right breast. Eight months of agonizing chemo and radiation treatments followed. During her treatment period, she fought off numerous ill effects of the poison coursing through her veins in search of healthy as well as cancerous cells. The worst part, though, was the needles. Lori hated being stuck. And she hated missing a union-organized trip to Miami to protest globalization and the kind of government trade policies that were decimating the jobs of thousands of her union brothers and sisters. Chemo-induced pain and lost moments of union activism aside, by the start of 2004 things were looking brighter. With the ordeal mostly behind her, Lori embarked on the future feeling that God had spared her life for some purpose. She figured she would have plenty of time to find out what that purpose was. Until then, she was going bowling.

But to keep doing what she had loved doing for most of her adult life, Lori would have to learn to throw the ball with her left hand. The surgery had saddled her with a permanent five-pound lifting restriction when she used her right hand. On returning to work Lori had sufficiently mastered a non-press operator position, although it did require the generous assistance of a fellow employee. But at the hardwood lanes she would have to go it alone. Lori laughed that "It was a sad sight" watching her throw with two left digits jammed into a bowling ball. Despite her awkward form, Lori, her husband, Greg, and a few fellow workers from the company made it a routine to bowl after the day shift ended at 4:30 P.M. Usually the group ate dinner before bowling and Lori recalled that "one day in May of 2006 I hurt my back while twisting to hold open the door of a pick-up truck I was stepping out of." At the time she thought that she had pulled a muscle and later that evening bowled as she had done a thousand times before. Only this time she used her left hand and nursed a sore back.

The pain in Lori's back continued the next day and the next and the next. For a while she "popped ibuprofen to get through the work day," and participated in some back therapy. But one morning she woke up and discovered that she was in "incredible pain and could not move." At least four MRIs, multiple bone scans, X-rays, and blood tests later, Lori was told by her doctor that she had cancer—again. "They found a mass in one of the bones near the fourth lumbar." The cancer was attacking the bone and draining it of calcium. The news devastated her. "I went home and fell into an emotional tail-spin." What lay ahead for Lori were another twelve treatments of radiation and a monthly intravenous dose of medication for the foreseeable future. It also meant a lot of sharp needles. Her husband, Greg, said that "she cried something terribly when they gave her the first shot." The shots were still coming when in June of 2006 Lori believed that God sent her another gift.

Both Lori and Greg were to attend a union conference in Indianapolis at the Adams Mark Hotel. However, because Lori's father was being thrown a retirement party in honor of his working thirty-odd years as a welder for Amtrak, she would miss the first day of the conference. Greg and Lori made plans to meet up later that evening at the union conference when the party was finished. If Lori had been in the conference hall that morning, she would have witnessed something completely unexpected, modest in its effort and yet powerfully uplifting. The session opened, as they often do, with a prayer. A preacher and union member of Lori's local conducted the prayer. After giving thanks to God for allowing the roughly three hundred union delegates to gather, the union-preacher informed the congregation that Lori Rippy was struck for a second time with cancer. He then proceeded to ask everyone to pray for her and asked God to be merciful. When Lori arrived at the Adams Mark, she was besieged by friends, co-workers, and union members she had never seen before. "I was astonished. They were all praying for me, so many strangers keeping me in their prayers."

Lori had first experienced an outpouring of intercessory prayers from her local "union family" when she was diagnosed with breast cancer. The show of support was "God's first blessing." She was so moved by the response of her co-workers and local union to her health problems that she attended a Sunday morning union meeting to "thank the members for praying for me and making it possible for me to pay my medical bills." Now she was inflicted with another dangerous threat to her life. Again, her co-workers were praying for her and her union-negotiated benefits were paying the medical bills. That, according to Lori, was God's second gift of grace. "I have cancer, God loves me and I love him." Lori has still not determined why she survived breast cancer nor if she'll overcome the illness in her back, but she believes God still has a purpose for her. She has drawn strength from her favorite Bible passage: "For I know the plans I have for you, declares the Lord . . . plans to give you hope and a future. . . . You will seek me and find me when you seek me with all your heart."[7] Whatever that purpose is, Lori remains confident that "It will be revealed."

The overlapping affinities of the workplace, co-workers, labor organization, and church created a space where working-class individuals like Lori could experience God. National survey research on congregational affiliation has revealed that, although America's religious groups cross class boundaries, religious beliefs and practices can be correlated with annual income, occupation, and levels of education.[8] H. Richard Niebuhr wrote in his classic work *The Social Sources of Denominations* that "the divisions of the [Christian] church have been occasioned more frequently by the direct and indirect operation of economic factors than by the influence of any other major interest of man."[9] In 1987 Wade Roof and William McKinney compared members of Protestant denominations, Catholics, and Jews in terms of education levels, incomes, and perceived social class.[10] Christian Smith and Robert Faris opened their 2005 assessment of socioeconomic inequality by acknowledging that "American religion has from the beginning of its history been stratified by education, income, and occupational status."[11] One of the more intriguing if not unchallenged findings from the sociology of religion field was that social stratification is positively correlated with congregational activity but inversely associated with a spiritual religiosity. In other words, higher- and middle-income believers, as well as college-educated congregants, had higher participation rates in their congregations than working- and lower-class believers. However, believers with less formal education and from working-class backgrounds revealed a greater emotional attachment to their faith than upper-class individuals.

Eric Goode noted that the "lower the class level of an individual, the more likely he is to be spontaneous in the expression of his religious feeling," while the higher the class level, the more ritualistic or "cultic" religious expression becomes.[12] On the other hand, working- and lower-class belief can be seen as unfolding in a "practice," or "good works" dimension.[13] Certainly the owner of a large Fortune 500 company can be religiously zealous (I suspect many are) and if so, he or she offers prayers up for something. But my focus is not on the elite or college-educated believer, but on what the bricklayer, clerk, and truck driver prays for. To paraphrase one of H. Richard Niebuhr's more trenchant comments on faith and status distinctions, my attention was not on the "righteous few" but on the "unhallowed many."[14] It was how people like Lori and my parents put their faith to work that inspired me and renewed my own spiritual and intellectual journey.

The motivating questions behind this book are threefold. First, "How does faith inform the lives of working-class people?" Second, "How do working-class people use their faith to find meaning in their lives?" And third, "What influence does faith have on a person's daily work?" The country's preeminent sociologist of religion, Robert Wuthnow, has questioned whether the "fine points of belief, matter so much anymore." His research strongly suggests that "it's practice" and being in "some kind of relationship with God that matters."[15] How working people practice and establish that relationship to God is the subject of this work.

While I primarily address the religious views of working-class people, I appreciate that believers in the highest income and advanced education groups are equally challenged to put their faith into action. But this study will not include the voices of professionals, managers, executives, large or small business owners, doctors, lawyers, stockbrokers, or even college professors. It will include people who work for minimal or modest wages, have had intermittent employment opportunities, and for the most part have little or no college education. Many, but not all, own cars and homes and have earned incomes between $15,000 and $75,000. They are men and women of faith who, when they work, do so under the supervision of others and mostly put in steady eight-hour days, and in a few cases hold a second job. The work they do they self-define, with few exceptions, as a job and not as a career even though some have been doing the work for a long time. In most cases they view their material wealth as adequate, if not secure, but they hold little expectations for greater social mobility.

Their ages ranged from the early twenties to the early seventies and most were either married or divorced. In most cases the working-class folks I spoke with had been lifelong members of a particular faith, and many had grown up in the religious community they were now worshiping in. Nearly everyone claimed to be a "practicing" member of the faith and a regular attendee at worship services. Only two interviewees—both Jewish—said they were not practicing. When questioned about their self-imposed designation, these workers explained that they were not (but had been) members of a synagogue, or presently respecting all religious/cultural traditions or tithing a percentage of their income. However, in conversation with each of them, they acknowledged a belief in God and, more importantly, stressed that they had a relationship to God through the way that they lived their life. More will be said about these two people and all the other workers as they are introduced to the reader.

While only a few did volunteer work for their congregation, most had participated in one or two nonworship congregational activities. Their congregational status and regular attendance at worship services sets them apart from the majority of people who believe in God, claim a religious affiliation, sometimes attend a worship service, and are not members of any congregation. Mark Chaves estimates that roughly only 25 percent of believers attended weekly worship services in the 1990s and Michael Hout and Claude Fischer estimated that about 60 percent belonged to a congregation.[16] Believers included Caucasians of various ethnic backgrounds, African Americans, and U.S. and foreign-born Hispanic-Latinos. Nearly all were lifelong Chicagoans or had lived the bulk of their lives in one of the inner suburbs ringing the city.

They are people who belong to or attend, with one exception, houses of worship located in Chicago or within the city's inner suburbs. The Religion in Urban America Program at the University of Illinois has documented, among others, the rich religious denominational history that exists in Chicago.[17] From the concentrated wealth of the Near North Side to the deindustrialized South Side, the city of Chicago and Cook

County are home to at least sixty-three different faith traditions. A conservative estimate reveals that there are at least 2,346 denominations, including 307 Catholic and 778 mainline Protestant churches, 117 Jewish synagogues, and 46 Islamic mosques.[18] Historians and sociologists have described how life in the city's diverse ethnic working-class neighborhoods most often revolved around the community's dominant houses of worship.[19] Chicago's reputation as a working-class polyglot of national, denominational, and commuter religious groups makes it a fertile ground for a study of the everyday meaning of faith. The workers in this book are but a small sample of the city's religious groups, but they include believers from Mennonite, Lutheran, Christian Reform, Catholic, Evangelical, Unitarian Universalist, Muslim, and Jewish faiths. While only one of the congregations would fit Liston Pope's description of a "mill church," each has either a predominant or significant number of working-class believers (see the appendix for denominational descriptions).[20]

The conventional wisdom about a person's religious affiliation is that it influences how that person interprets and practices her or his faith. Surveys of congregants' religious beliefs have documented the influence of denominational identity. Christians from mainline to Pentecostal churches widely disagree on subjects like voting for president, affirmative action policy, regulation of business, the inerrancy of the Bible, evangelism as a personal responsibility, the actual existence of Satan, eternal salvation, that Jesus Christ was sinless, and even that God is all-powerful.[21] Differences among Jewish Orthodox, Conservative, and Reform congregations over "Jewish identity," values, culture, world outlook, the existence of miracles, and God's response to prayer have been equally well documented.[22] Islamic ideas about the prophet Muhammad, the status of women, the use of force, predestiny, concepts of good and evil, and God's methods of guidance are also contested among Muslims originating from different parts of the world.[23] In addition, different views on many spiritual and secular subjects are evident across religious traditions. It would appear, then, that denominational identity is—within limits—a fair predictor of a person's religious views.

But would religious affiliation still matter as much if congregational members were asked to explain how their spirituality actually informed their daily lives? What if the focus was not on conventional matters of theological concern or about correlating faith with voting patterns? Would denominational variation still predominate? The cumulative account of what is conventionally known about religious attitudes raised for me a compelling question: if believers' responses were correlated with a set of variables that would assign to each person a class status, would the way that denominational views informed their lives still be explanatory?

I suspect that efforts to understand religious meaning as a class phenomenon could be very threatening to many clerical leaders. Identifying the influence of class filters in understanding the word of God seems contrary to any religion's universal message, dominant theology, and accepted dogma. It might also challenge the position of the religious leaders as an authoritative interpreter of the faith. Certainly the explosive growth and popularity of Liberation Theology in large parts of Central and South America have demonstrated the impact that concrete economic, political, and social reality can have on how God's salvific power is understood and put into practice.[24] The United States' early-twentieth-century Protestant Social Gospel and Depression-era Catholic Social Worker movement, and the support that first-generation Jewish immigrants gave to constructing nascent labor organizations attest to our own experiences with a living faith sharply influenced by a muscular working-class component.[25]

The workers interviewed in this book were not handed a survey to fill out and were not quizzed about theology. Where they worshiped and what religion they claimed membership in was mostly for comparative purposes. My interest was not primarily in what Judaism (orthodox or reform), or Christianity (Evangelical or mainstream), or Islam (rationalist or traditionalist) established as correct views on anything. The focus here is on how a small number of Jewish, Christian, and Muslim working-class believers used their faith to inform their lives. Believers were all members of a particular congregation chosen to ensure an approximate representation of Chicago's dominant faiths. Congregations consisting of predominantly Hispanic-Latino and African American believers were also added to reflect some of the racial and ethnic diversity in the city. Individual congregations were selected through contacts made with Chicago-area religious leaders who recommended houses of worship with primarily or significant numbers of working-class members.

Identifying Protestant and Catholic churches with janitors, nurses, painters, secretaries, bus drivers, junkyard workers, and flight attendants was easily accommodated, but finding a suitable Jewish congregation proved rather difficult. I conducted a wide and comprehensive search among orthodox, traditional, conservative, and reform communities, as well as through numerous Jewish civic and labor associations. In the learned opinion of nearly every Jewish religious, civic, and labor leader I spoke with, Chicago was not home to many, if any, predominantly working-class congregations.[26] One of the more common responses to my inquiries among Jewish leaders was that my search was a generation or so too late. Early-twentieth-century first-generation Jewish immigrants to Chicago and other urban areas were among the country's hardest-working industrial workers. Jewish immigrants worked extensively in garment, textile, and meatpacking industries. But an unrivaled commitment to educational and social betterment, fueled to a large extent by European and American anti-Semitism, produced in a few decades a burgeoning entrepreneurial and professional class of Jewish descendants of butchers, tailors, and candlestick makers.

Large-scale studies of socioeconomic status and religious affiliation underscored the successful social mobility of the American Jewish community. Among the most well-educated Americans, more than 60 percent of Jewish citizens hold college degrees (compared to only 21.7 percent of Catholics) and the average Jewish household income is the highest among the country's top twenty religious denominations.[27] For that reason the Jewish workers featured in this book were either not currently members of a synagogue or of the same synagogue. They were, however, with few exceptions, all members of reform congregations and claimed to be religious Jews.[28]

Another exception to the one congregation approach applied for strikingly different reasons to Muslim workers. As a result of widespread government and civilian bigotry against Arab Americans since the terrorist attacks of September 11, 2001, I could not get permission from any Chicago-area iman to approach a Muslim congregation. Instead, I needed the assistance of active members of the Chicago Islamic Council to arrange for me to interview individual Muslims at a popular restaurant that caters to Islamic dietary preferences. Further reflecting a fear of public exposure, none of the Muslim workers would reveal the names of the mosques in which they worshiped.

My conversations with working-class believers amounted to over one hundred hours of discussion and their voices are prominently featured in the pages that follow. While the learned opinions of religious leaders will be evident at certain points throughout the book, it is not my primary purpose to assess what the congregational leaders think about faith and work. Surprisingly, based on the minimal scholarship on this subject, it appears that local religious officials spend very little, if any, time thinking about what Armand Larive calls a "theology of work."[29] The eminent Southern religious scholar and Christian pastor Tex Sample goes so far as to point out how irrelevant most church services are for working people. He challenges his pastoral colleagues to develop a "blue-collar" ministry that will speak more meaningfully to the needs and fears of parishioners who struggle to put and keep the bread of life on their tables.[30]

Larive's concern for working people and church ministry leads him to think deeply about "the importance of what they [workers] do and how poorly it is honored by the church."[31] What, after all, was a religious act?

Most faith traditions would recognize attending religious service, praying, reading from a holy book, tithing, and accepting sacraments as faithful acts. But Larive provocatively declared that "getting out of bed is a religious act."[32] At least it is when a fireman awakens from a midnight sleep to respond to an alarm or when a teacher rises early in the morning to get to school to make sure her classroom is ready for learning. If Larive is correct, then my non-church-attending, but God-believing, father was as religious as St. Nicholas's Father Gubser who liked to drop in on my parents to drink a glass of milk and read the Bible. Dad never failed when able to work; nor did Father Gubser. The two men worked in different places under different contexts and expectations. They used radically different tools and produced different end products. One was compensated by communal offerings of daily support, the other with union-negotiated wages. But both had worked in the conventional sense in common and, according to Larive, there is an underappreciated theology "in the way God is present with workaday activity."[33] It is the idea that the work people do constitutes an authentic religious ministry that informs much of the discussion at the core of this book.

Extracting the sacred from pipe fitting or lawn maintenance is not, however, the same as using religious beliefs and spirituality to sweat additional labor out of employees. A manipulative cottage industry has developed among Christian employers characterized as the "faith and work" movement. Books, articles, magazines, newspaper stories, weekend seminars, professional and business associations, Web sites, and blogs have touted the social and financial capital gains that can come from training a company's managers to motivate workers with the "relationship skills that Jesus used to train and motivate his team."[34] While I claim no special insight into the life of Jesus or Muhammad, I feel confident that their life experiences, no matter how cleverly distorted, were not about corporate team building or developing "marketplace leaders."[35]

In texts that commend the reader to link overt religious beliefs and evangelizing with employment practices, religion is primarily a tool for CEOs and supervisors and hence becomes a wickedly perverse strategy for workplace discipline and control. In addition to the dubious purposes of using the workplace to proselytize, so-called faith-friendly companies run a considerable constitutional legal risk when they impose biblical principle upon their employees.[36] Since 2000, religious discrimination complaints with the federal Equal Employment Opportunity Commission have risen more than 30 percent.[37] Attorney Angela Ekker successfully represented one group of employees in a religious discrimination case and noted that "there is a sort of religious fanaticism growing in this country, and as a result we'll be seeing more of these cases in the workplaces."[38] The pursuit of ways to use God to further denominational growth and the bottom line have unfortunately gotten considerable assistance over the past ten years from the United States Congress, which has considered legislation to allow greater expression of religious views at work.[39]

Larive's concern for the inherent sacredness in labor is further juxtaposed to conventional religious treatments of work. Christian churches, he notes, typically reduce the sacred value of work to opportunities to be kind toward others, for keeping the Ten Commandments, to make a personal witness, and to build a workplace ministry. Religious leaders are quick to talk of proper workplace ethics but hesitant to raise the issues precipitating a local workers' strike or the closing of a community manufacturing plant due to foreign competition. It's of course true that there are many Christian and non-Christian religious leaders who have condemned corporate greed and called their congregations to the defense of worker rights. Chicago is the home of the National Interfaith Committee for Worker Justice, which has led many ecumenical campaigns to benefit particularly low-wage workers. But these locally based religious leaders are the exceptions. I believe that in houses of worship all over the country the most common response to the need for a faith portrayal of working-class realities would be similar to the words spoken to me by a well-respected Chicago rabbi and a Catholic pastor. In explaining why he was not interested in talking about faith and labor, the rabbi undoubtedly incorrectly noted that "in the [Chicago] synagogue there are not workers and non-workers, only children of God." The Catholic priest simply rejected the idea by stating without any apparent irony that his mostly low-wage immigrant "parishioners don't have time to talk about work and faith, and besides they come to the church for other things." It seems the message to the believer is that secular activity has some value as a way to do service to others, but the work a person does possesses no inherent religious value. Sadly, believers come away from each long workday incorrectly thinking that God cares more for their soul than God does for their body.

A believer could be excused for elevating a metaphysical existence above a three-dimensional life of blood, bone, and muscle. Douglas Sherman revealed that out of a poll conducted with 2,000 Christians, 90 percent had never heard a religious sermon applying biblical principles to everyday work issues.[40] For example, Sherman noted that congregants were not familiar with sermons on health-care policy or on the need for a livable wage to ensure that "the laborer deserves his wages."[41] On the other hand, in 1997, Robert Wuthnow documented that 58 percent of church members "claimed to have heard a sermon about caring for the poor."[42] Now nearly 40 percent of the poor are competent workers without sufficient work or income, but a sermon on caring for the disadvantaged is effectively a message of Christian charity. It is not a message about an employer, government, civic association, or union acting to dignify work or make work pay in the way that God intended for an act of co-creation. And while Sherman does not mention it, I feel very confident that only the barest fraction of church members has ever heard the word "labor organization" mentioned alongside any of the Gospels. Sherman also surveyed religious seminars, prayer meetings, religious bookstore listings, and recorded tapes and concluded that the "Church has grown virtually silent on the subject of work."[43] A noted example of this absence is revealed in the most recent work of religious historian Alan Wolfe. A review of the index of Wolfe's book subtitled *How We Actually Live Our Faith* does not include a single reference to "work" or "labor." The table of contents does, however, address the topics of "doctrine," "morality," "sin," "worship," "tradition," and "witness" among others.[44]

Family, marriage, personal piety, morals, sacred traditions, biblical texts, and institutional needs typically make up the canon of professional preaching. In my own church-attending experiences I have also been confused by the narrow "playlist" of suitable topics. Even an uninformed reader of the Bible, Torah, or Qur'an would recognize the numerous textual references to economic justice issues. At best, a religious leader may offer his or her congregation an obligatory sermon or homily about the nobility of work on a Labor Day Sunday. Larive explains this lack of attention to work life on the dearth of training that church leaders receive on a theology of work: "One can search seminary academic catalogues in vain for any such course offerings."[45]

The absence of much formal training is all the more surprising considering the rather sizeable and significant public positions that each of the world's major religions have taken on the proper role for human labor. Catholic, Protestant, Jewish, and Islamic theologians have written about how their faith provides clear principles for respecting a fundamental religious truth that through work people share in the activity of the Creator. The neglect of work in the spiritual life of community religious institutions is inconsistent with every major religion's command to speak out on the value of work. While my discussions with workers were not designed to elicit the substantive knowledge of each person's faith or to discern a correct theology, I do refer to sacred scriptures and writings to support the way that Christian, Muslim, and Judaic religions embrace the dignity of labor and labor organizations.

Scholars like Tex Sample contend that work is absent from much official religious inspiration and education because churches, synagogues, and mosques have traditionally treated the working life as a distraction from the holy. Joanne Ciulla argues that for many people work "substitutes for the fulfillment we used to derive from family, friends, religion and community."[46] Instead of finding happiness in doing God's will or in social relationships, we have committed the fruitfulness of our lives to the "hands of the market and our employers."[47] Ciulla recognizes that human labor can provide discipline, identity, and self-worth. It can structure our time and impose a rhythm on our lives. Work can engrain us into various kinds of groups and social relationships. It makes possible improvements in living standards and provides for the collective needs of others. Remunerated work is also the means by which we provide for our material sustenance. Clearly the working life holds out much promise. But how does living in a capitalist society predicated on a production for private profit morality, with an increasing dependency on the fate of our employers, bring our lives closer to the image of God? Work, it seems, can easily betray a balanced life of spirit and sweat.

If our work is debilitating, humiliating, and valuable only as a means to survive, then traditional Christian views of work as a curse and punishment would seem to support a benign neglect of the labor we do. At best, attendees at religious services will come to know work as having only an instrumental and worldly value. And, most important, the work we do can never save our souls. Regardless of the bridges we build, the bodies we heal, the children we educate, the toilets we clean, the food we harvest, and the garments we mend, we amass no credit with the Almighty. Salvation only comes through "accepting the free gift of God's grace." But what if Greg Pierce of the National Center for the Laity is correct and "work itself is holy—not just a means to proselytize others"?[48] What if Larive is right that a person who does good work is like the "good and faithful servant," and that God delights in the work we do? What if "good works" included a well-painted house, a safely driven bus, or my father's nicely repaired roller in the 9-inch pipe mill? Can work, after all, be a Christian, Jewish, and Islamic path to God?

In searching for the relationship between the work lives of people and the faith they hold, my conversations with workers continuously revealed a few dominant ideas or meaningful narratives. While worker comments did not exclusively fit into narrow categories, five principal faith and work narratives emerged. The first was a narrative of *human suffering and healing grace*. A second life story evolved around how workers understood *God's will*. A third account stressed the *obligations of the righteous* to overcome injustice and sin. The fourth was embedded in a debate over the *genesis of work*. And, poetically, the final one centered on a story of *salvation*. Each of these narratives is briefly introduced below.

Human Suffering and Healing Grace

It was important to know how people have used their faith in meaningful ways. Asking folks to relate a story of where in their life faith mattered to them in a particularly special way enabled me to identify the real places, occasions, and inspirations that triggered a phenomenological religiosity. Hearing personal accounts of how people strongly felt when they believed themselves to be in God's presence introduced me to the importance of struggle and suffering in measuring a faithful life. The role that suffering plays emerges from these discussions as a fundamental condition of working-class spirituality. Pain is to be expected. Family members get sick, loved ones leave, and jobs are lost. Some jobs pay too little; others are, as Studs Terkel poignantly notes, "too small for the human spirit."[49] A human life is a temporary gift filled with all manner of treasures and dangers. The body, heart, and mind are capable of brilliant flights of knowing and creation. They are equally susceptible to injury, breakdown, and disease. In C. S. Lewis's words, the faithful "are never safe, but we have plenty of fun and some ecstasy."[50] In the discussions I had with workers, suffering is not always preordained, nor is it necessarily God's will. But significantly, it always strengthens the faith.

God's Will

Workers also described their God. The words, phrases, stories, and metaphors they used to characterize the object of their faith revealed the nature of the relationship that working-class people believed was possible with a transcendent figure. It also established the boundaries—if any—for what God was responsible for in the material world. Within that relationship was the opportunity for God to bless a person with a new job or a pay raise. It's also possible that God's plan could leave a worker behind. The people who spoke to me declared unanimously that God or Allah made all things and all things possible. But was God responsible for poverty, homelessness, hunger, and corporate greed? Was the lack of health care afflicting millions of Americans God's doing? If not, then what or who was responsible and did a person's faith help her to understand her economic status?

Obligations of the Righteous

Questions about God's will and the usefulness of faith to make sense of one's station in life underscored the relationship between a believer's faith and his sense of justice. Workers who turned to biblical readings and accepted Sunday preaching against immoral behavior had grounding for judging righteous action. But what did faith compel the servants of Allah, God, or Yahweh to do when they witnessed evil? And what was evil? By conservative accounts the marketplace is managed by a den of thieves and scoundrels. In 2005 the nation's poverty rate rose to a shameful 12.7 percent and nearly 46 million Americans had no employer-provided health care.[51] Pensions at large employers like United Airlines and major steel firms were dumped to free up cash for company executives with six- and seven-figure compensation packages.[52] Scandalous accounts of corporate theft and destruction of employee retirement savings at Enron Corporation, Tyco, Global Crossing, WorldCom, Adelpia Communications, and HealthCare South, to name just a few, seemed to define a marketplace rife with injustice.[53] But what does a faithful working-class Jew, Lutheran, or Catholic do about such things? When injustices exist at work and in the marketplace, does faith require the worker to walk a picket line, join a union, boycott an employer, stop shopping at Wal-Mart, participate in a demonstration, sign a petition, or vote for a particular political party? My interviewees reminded me that one could also do nothing and leave the unacceptable situation to God.

Speaking of evil required us to also recognize the existence of sin in the world. Sin, according to the Ten Commandments, the Qur'an, and the Torah, is clearly delineated and well understood by the workers interviewed in this book. But is it a sin to offer people work without health care or a pension? Was it a sin to close a factory and move it overseas to take advantage of cheap labor? Was it sinful to make products with prison or child labor? Workers admitted to knowing sinners and to being sinners, but the sins of the marketplace were not so obvious. It seemed that faith could be a redress for some offenses, but not necessarily for others. Sin required offending God, but as heart-wrenching as the demands of commerce could be, economic dislocation appeared to be a victimless act. No employer was willfully violating God's law when they laid a worker off. But if work was holy, how could it be denied and still preserve a person in the image of God or Allah?

Genesis of Work

If the market and the job a person does could be occasions for sin, then they could also be a blessing. Despite long hours and insufficient compensation, the majority of workers revealed that they are deeply committed to the work they do.[54] It is in the end not all about Mammon. But are workers called to do the jobs they do? Is this, too, where God wants them to be? The workers interviewed came to their labors from vastly different directions and they were not unanimous in whether they were led or whether they had simply chosen. Work for some could be a vocation, but for others "work ain't nothing but a job." The Greeks also thought of work as a necessary evil. Aristotle thought mechanical labor was enslaved to the needs of the body and among its many detrimental effects was to keep a person away from higher contemplative activities.[55] From the Renaissance came visions of work as creative expression; from Henry Ford came nightmares of work as mechanical motion. Martin Luther and John Calvin interpreted work in the book of Genesis as "God's commandments to us, not his curse on us."[56]

Work in the American civic imagination has always embodied a host of life-enhancing qualities. No matter that work was necessary for survival and that differences in power created one class of people who worked and another who lived off the labor of others. Our labor fulfills goals, is redemptive, and is a path to social mobility. My parents, my students, and my interviewees lived by a simple faith: labor really works. Philosophers like James Bernard Murphy, Al Genie, and others have written persuasively that work should be a means of self-realization and often defines a worker's sense of self-identity.[57] Simply stated, we are our jobs. But did God mean for work to be hard or delightful? Were there godly jobs or jobs that made a person feel closer to God? Is there a spiritual dimension to the way a person does a job and does the job you do "praise God"? And do religious working-class people really believe that Martin Luther was correct when he declared that "man is not justified by works, but righteousness must come from some other source than his own works"?[58] Dorothy Sayers thinks the church has sent too limited a message to people who work for a living: "The Church's approach to an intelligent carpenter is usually confined to exhorting him not to be drunk and disorderly in his leisure hours, and to come to church on Sundays. What the church should be telling him is this: that the very first demand that his religion makes upon him is that he should make good tables."[59] What work meant in the lives of each believer and how it was described was an important window into each worker's spiritual identity.

Salvation

Working for a lifetime is the American way. We expect it to make us productive individuals and citizens. But to a Muslim cabdriver, Jewish grocery clerk, and Catholic nurse, it cannot get you into heaven. Only the grace of God determines the soul's destiny, and Martin Luther and John Calvin gave structure to a Protestant work ethic that defined people who work hard as good and those who are lazy as immoral. According to Christian, Jewish, and Islamic orthodoxy, it was only through faith that a person could enter the kingdom of heaven. Salvation to each of my workers was a gift from God. But if belief alone was sufficient to attain everlasting life, then what does God expect from the lives we live? Is there nothing redemptive about the efforts an auto assembly line worker commits to in rotating eight- or ten-hour day shifts? St. Augustine and Luther conceived a high wall separating the domains of work and grace. But Miroslav Volf counters that Thomas Carlyle infused work with explicit religious overtones. Mundane work for Carlyle "replaced prayer to God and became a means of secular salvation."[60] Was work mere secular instrumentality or a salvific part of a life in the Holy Spirit? The question of human labor's contribution to salvation fully animated our discussions and significantly shaped the relationship between a worker's faith and occupation.

In conducting the oral interviews and reading through pages of transcripts, I was reminded of the last time someone encouraged me to be a priest. For many years before I finished this work, my late father-in-law, Donald Quackenbush, and I engaged in spirited debates about economics and politics. After a particularly prolonged assertion of my affirmative belief in the righteousness of workers, my father-in-law pointed out that I should have gone into the church. It was, he noted, there and only there where my "left-wing" views could actually be legitimately expressed. Apparently Don believed that church leaders were expected to "comfort the sick," "feed the hungry," "clothe the naked," and do full-time service for the dispossessed. It seemed to him that religion was best suited for such "do-gooding." It is precisely what working-class believers expected from their do-gooding that I set out to know.

CHAPTER 1

Suffering and Healing Grace

C. S. LEWIS grappled with the paradoxical reality of being a Christian and having to live with tragedy and pain. Lewis posed perhaps the most essential objection to Christianity and all religions: "If God is good and all-powerful, why does he allow his creatures to suffer pain?"[1] Since people did suffer and feel pain, Lewis reasoned that God lacked either goodness or power. He set out in the *Problem of Pain* to explain how an all-powerful, loving God could allow bad things to happen to "honest and decent people." At the heart of this question was a fundamental doubt that any such God could exist. It is a question even the strongest believers ask when the suffering is very personal. After the death of his wife from cancer, Lewis not only asked it, but uttered condemnations of God.[2] I have asked it many times myself.

I asked it when my brother-in-law Tommy died in an automobile accident. He had recently recovered from colon cancer and had just accepted a new job. In a diabolical twist of fate, on the day he was driving to the personnel office to complete his employment papers, Tommy was the victim of vehicular homicide. I also asked the question when my mother died of heart disease. She was a lifelong smoker who never got lung cancer. But she did get breast cancer, although that didn't kill her either. Mom died of a massive heart attack. Sure, she should have quit smoking, eaten better, and exercised some, but that prescription for health applies to thousands of people and they don't all die at seventy-four of heart failure.[3] Maybe that is unreasonable of me, but why would God allow the most Christ-like person I ever met to die in such a way? My prayers were bountiful, but "the thing didn't work."[4]

Lewis's explanation was straightforward; it comes with the territory. Since God made us human and gave us a fixed nature of matter that included a free will, there is a distinct possibility, though not a necessity, of suffering. Now, according to Lewis, God could "exclude the possibility of suffering," but to do so would be to "exclude life itself."[5] Human life includes suffering not because God wills it, but because our free will allows pain to enter through the choices we make. Biblical scholar Bart Ehrman knows the "free will" defense and all the others conventionally given to explain suffering and the existence of an all powerful, all loving God. But after many years of thinking and wrestling with the contradiction, he admits that he can "no longer reconcile the claims of faith with the facts of life."[6]. Ehrman recognizes the hurt in the world and poignantly reveals that "I came to a point where I simply could not believe that there is a good and kindly disposed Ruler who is in charge of it" (3). Among many other types, Ehrman sees "the pain of lost jobs, lost income, failed prospects," and is driven to ask, "Where is God?" (6). Mike Mason in *The Gospel According to Job* poetically analyzes the perseverance of Job and recognizes that the "only bootstraps in the Christian life is the cross." But, he adds, "Sometimes laying hold of the cross can be comforting, but other times it is like picking up a snake."[7] As suffering and human nature are inconceivable without one another, it seems also that true faith in a God of creation requires an acceptance of suffering.

Bill Kamp helps Americans to communicate with one another. He is an affable middle-aged man who prepares coffee for Sunday services at Park Lane Christian Reform Church in Evergreen Park. In truth, his coffee does help to open up conversation with a lot of church people, but Bill's primary communicative function is as a service technician for postage and mail handling equipment. He does his job mostly without complaint because it provides a living. But in 1999 he was without employment for a while and that is when he claims to have found out about being near to God. "If everything was rosy all the time, you would not feel like you needed God. It is when in times of suffering that you really know that God is there for you. Things happen and I was laid off for a while." What happened next reaffirmed Bill's belief that misfortune was an opportunity for God to nourish his family. Since he was unable to pay some bills, "some church couples took over our [family] payments for our car and medical insurance. That was nice until I got another job." Suffering is essential to knowing God because it is unpredictable and strikes indiscriminately. Bill admits that hardship can seriously shake up a person's faith, but when most in doubt a person should trust in the words of Proverbs: "Be not wise in your own eyes; fear the lord, and turn away from evil. It will be healing to your flesh and refreshment to your bones" (Proverbs 3:7–8).

Instead of needing suffering to realize the graceful characteristics of God, Bernice Feltz of St. Bruno Catholic Parish sees struggle as serving a more fundamental purpose. "People are charitable. Things are happening to them and they are able to get beyond that. That kind of strength is not just something that happens to everybody. I think that there are people who are able to get beyond it, are evidence that there is a God. That there is something working." Bernice contends that "unless you go through something traumatic," the inner strength of a person is never realized and it is precisely ordinary people enduring extraordinary pain that proves the existence of a higher power. How else to explain the human capacity to recover from tragedy or endure hardship? How else to explain how Bernice, a mother of three with nearly a quarter century of office work with the same Fortune 400 company, is able to speak with me? In Bernice's own life she buried a father "who was an alcoholic for the greater portion of his life." She also had a very painful marriage end and then lost a job because the employer relocated to lower labor costs. "No one in my family had ever been divorced. . . . I had three kids."

Bernice does not blame God for her difficulties and has no idea if it was part of some grand personal destiny. But she does see the possibility that her struggle has made her a more positive person. "I have been able to work things out with my ex-husband as far as working things out with the kids and to being involved in their lives." Bernice's ability to weather the breakup of her marriage and separation from her three children convinced her that she had not been forsaken. "I just always felt like that if everything else fell apart in the world, God was there. I assume that because things [have fallen] into place that something must be working." Bernice believes the "something" was promised to her in the book of Deuteronomy: "When you are in tribulation, and all these things come upon you in the latter days, you will return to the Lord your God and obey his voice, for the Lord your God is a merciful God; he will not fail you or destroy you . . ." (Deuteronomy 4:30–31).

"There is a reason for the things that happen to me and I should learn from it" is how Margarita Tellez deals with misfortune. Margarita is a prekindergarten bilingual teacher at a church-run school and recently began to attend St. Bruno Church. She has had her share of suffering, but defends God's willingness to let her struggle with life. "We have to trust in God that it is always for a purpose." Margarita, however, does not view faith as a way to passively accept hardship. For her, faith is both shield and sword. Margarita admits that in moments of duress she has clung to a faith in God's mercy to survive the blows. Hunkering down, until hopefully the crisis passes, is sometimes all a person can do. But Margarita's trust in God's providence is not just an expectation of a respite from struggle; it is a passage to a fuller life. In her life, the experience of suffering has served as a training routine or educational program with a real-world benefit. "I think there is a lot to learn from them [bad experiences]. Somehow, we become stronger and more knowledgeable."

Margarita's schooling began at home and has had a lasting influence. "I was born in Mexico and came here when I was five or six. My father was an alcoholic. When he was drinking, ever since I can recall he used to drink and it was a difficult situation. There was no beating but there was a lot of intimidation. My dad's alcoholism did put us through a lot." Margarita had initially shown interest in a nursing career, but her father had other ideas. Ironically, it was her father's condition that inspired her desire to become a nurse. "[But] my father had these very old-fashion ideas that a woman's role was to get married and have kids and stay at home and attend to the house. He would say that I was a woman and if I had been a son then he would not care." So Margarita accepted a different occupational trajectory and ended up working with children. She has never regretted the course of her life. "I could have been real good [at nursing] . . . but now that I look at things at my age, it was his alcoholism that made me who I am now. There is a lot of good that came after that." Margarita's explanation of the first unseen, yet slowly unfolding "good" in her life reveals the blessing that she believes God intends for suffering. "I have been able to help others because of my own personal experience with my dad." She eventually broke free of her fathers' addiction and felt called to the classroom. Margarita now believes that the suffering she experienced early in life made it possible for her to serve others. Her suffering was not wasteful nor without purpose. And from the first drink her father took to the last, Margarita remained steadfast in her faith "knowing that in the Lord your labor is not in vain" (1 Corinthians 15:58).

Labor may never be discounted by the Lord, but much of it can certainly be a source of significant angst. Lisa Augustyniak of St. Bruno Parish makes sandwiches for a popular national fast-food restaurant chain. She lives apart from her husband and children, and on a good week brings home a paycheck of $120. If you do the math, Lisa's work is leaving her poor. But poor with a job and a little money is still better than what Lisa had been experiencing. "Six months ago, I was not working at all. I used to work at Wal-Mart and I got into an argument with a co-worker." Lisa's abrupt firing left her feeling desperate and forsaken. "For a while, I did not even think that He [God] existed. Why did He do that to me? I was jobless, my sister is on the verge of throwing me out, and I have a car that is a piece of crap that is falling apart, not to mention that six months before, my husband walked out on me." Unemployed, nearly homeless, saddled with a broken-down car, and abandoned, Lisa was under siege. "I asked God if He thought He had already done enough to me in one year."

But in the darkest period of her life, Lisa dusted off her pride and heard what she believed to be God's answer. "I went out and pounded the pavement and put out my applications. Then out of the clear blue sky, [the employer] called me. [They] said that they had a couple of positions open because they were opening a new store. My first day at work was Christmas Eve. What more of an incentive do you need than that?" Starting a job the day before the Son of God was born was too coincidental for Lisa, a lifelong Catholic, not to see a divine hand at work. Lisa offered that struggles rarely come with a rationale for why they have been visited upon a person. "I did not quite grasp the reason then or now and I hated God for it, but later on I may learn what that lesson was." Until a purpose is revealed, Lisa contends that suffering can be alleviated if a person remains watchful. "You have to pick up the little hints and clues that He throws down at you every so often . . . it's like a slap in the face." Enduring a deep sense of spiritual rejection, Lisa decided to make sandwiches and surrender her anxiety to a God whom she believes is without malicious intent. "I feel that everybody has a divine purpose on the earth and it is not just to work your tail off and pay bills and taxes." Work we must and taxes for those who must work are inevitable, but according to Lisa, suffering is tolerable because God has bigger plans for us than a lifetime of hurt. "Therefore I tell you, do not be anxious about your life, what you shall eat, nor about your body, what you shall put on. For life is more than food, and the body more than clothing" (Luke 12:22–24). Lisa recommends that people need only to take the hint.

Laura Dawson is a forty-seven-year-old married woman with one child. She is a member of St. Denis Catholic Parish in the Ashburn section of Chicago. Laura has worked a number of part-time education jobs, most recently as an English as Second Language (ESL) instructor for Spanish-speaking children. She believes that people need to get closer to God through fellowship with others. In normal times living her faith is not a trial, but "trying to see God more every day in the common things in life, even the hard things," is the true test of faith. However, at the time of our conversation Laura's mother was very sick. In response to a request that she tell me about an experience when her faith was critical to her, she explained that her mother has "multiple melanomas diagnosed with cancer of the blood [which] affects the bone marrow." The disease has been a constant weight on Laura's energy, time, and emotions. Unfortunately, her mother's condition is getting worse. "We [recently] found out that she has bipolar disorder. So she has manic depression." Laura admits that as her mom deteriorates, it becomes a "real challenge to see the goodness and the mercy in the day-to-day things."

Seeing God in the midst of her mom's struggles does not come easy for Laura. She admits that she does not always "do so well," but "keeps thinking that things could be worse or that we have some blessings." But in fact, Laura points out that things have gotten worse. "We just buried my mother's mother a year ago and there were problems with that and I keep thinking, what if my grandmother was still alive?" Dealing with her grandmother would not have given Laura much relief. "She also had some type of mental disorder-obsessive compulsive disorder that caused her to collect tons and tons of stuff, like four or five dumpsters." Recalling the Herculean effort necessary to keep her job and maintain the health needs of both women allows Laura to find some affirmation in all of this sickness. With a hint of guilt in her voice she clarifies that "we didn't want Grandma to die," but that it was a blessing "that we did not have to be taking care of both her and my mother at the same time."

Through the ordeal with her mother and grandmother, Laura and her four sisters grew closer. But was it necessary for a person to suffer before he or she can get closer to God? To Laura "suffering can help a person get closer to God," but not if "one gets fed up and turns away from God" because of the pain. Suffering demands perseverance and no matter the bad times it is a choice whether to remain faithful or to become disillusioned. But either way Laura did not think that "God picks people to zap." There was no cosmic list with names of people who are "picked to suffer." But suffering could provide a person with the chance to "know some grace and goodness from God." The question Laura asks in all situations, but particularly during the most painful ones, is "where is God?" Faith demanded that Laura not forsake God during moments of distress but instead try and find the act of grace woven within the struggle. As Laura described it, suffering may not be preordained or even required of the truly faithful. But in her case it was an opportunity to tighten the relationship with her sisters and to demonstrate more fully a daughter's love for her ailing mother. To act selflessly in this way is to act more like Jesus and, consequently, get closer to God. It is a relationship Laura forged with God in the whirlwind of ambiguity and doubt.

> Behold, now is the acceptable time; behold, now is the day of salvation. We put no obstacle in any one's way, so that no fault may be found with our ministry, but as servants of God we commend ourselves in every way: through great endurance, in afflictions, hardships, calamities, beatings, imprisonments, tumults, labors, watching, hunger . . . as poor yet making many rich; as having nothing and yet possessing everything. (2 Corinthians 6:3–10)

The poignancy of a mother-daughter relationship also awakened Mertis Odom to the existence and grace of God. Mertis is a thirty-year member of Community Mennonite Church in Markham, Illinois. She has served as a rehabilitation counselor for almost as long. In Mertis's eyes her work and faith have been divinely inspired because she has a daughter inflicted with multiple sclerosis. A year before we spoke, Mertis's daughter got a flu shot. "Three days after the shot she has not walked since. She got the flu shot in the morning." Mertis fights back soft, flowing tears as she explains that despite the pain, she does not "do pity-parties." I am moved by the anguish reflected in her face to ask the following accusatory question: "Do you think that God is keeping your daughter in this condition?"

> Honestly, it makes me feel closer to God. It is painful sometimes, but I know that He is still there. I think that God intends for us to have some kind of challenge. Some are different than others. Maybe this is hers. Maybe it is our family's. We have a very close-knit family [husband and three other children]. We are very supportive of one another. I don't know if this is His way of keeping us like that. I don't know why this has happened but for some reason, it happened. You hate to see it but you see so many people out there, people with no legs . . . whole families, homeless.

Beyond the shock and grief caused by a child's inability to walk, Mertis has not grown doubtful. Admittedly she and her husband have posed questions to God, but Mertis points out that "I have never asked God if He did that to my daughter." As the father of a teenage girl, I wondered if I could be so resolute, so certain, so forgiving of any deity that I imbued with the power to make all things good. Mertis, however, finds solace in a God who visits her at the times when she could simply fall apart. In these moments a spirit touches her. "One of the special times He comes is in the wee hours of the morning. I get up when I cannot sleep and go to the den and it is just He and I together." In the cover of early morning dark,

Mertis gives God praise for all the things in her life. Good and bad, "thy will be done." And someday, "I still think that in His time that she will walk again. I really believe that." In Mertis's presence I can easily accept that all that I believe is not all that there is to believe.

Suffering may not be inevitable, but for people like Jeffrey Goldberg it does allow God to reveal the power of grace. Goldberg has been a union electrician for eleven years with the Chicago Transit Authority and a member of B'Nai Yehuda Beth Shalom Reform Synagogue in Homewood for twice as long. Jeffrey was raised in the Jewish faith and along with his wife, Sarah, who converted to Judaism, takes seriously being religious. But despite his upbringing, Goldberg recalls how he lost God by foolishly betting against the house. "There was a time where I was probably as far away from my faith as any single person could be." That time would be from 1996 to 2001 when he was addicted to gambling, blackjack particularly. "I think the only time that I used the 'God' word was when I asked 'God, please don't let the dealer pull a queen up.' Then usually there was a bunch of profanity after that." In those five dark years Jeff estimated that he easily lost over $100,000. Jeff struggled to break the habit, but failed time and time again. "The clouds of my mind were so cluttered up and I couldn't think straight." He was encouraged to use his faith to clean up his life but stubbornly held fast to his pain. "I was consumed in my own misery and reaching out to my God and my faith really was so far removed that it did not seem an option." But eventually he found his way into a twelve-step Gamblers' Anonymous program. "I got myself into recovery, and then I was able to see more clearly." What he claimed to see was how much pain he was putting his parents and friends through. Jeff also learned that his spirituality could be a source of strength and hope. "My faith was a big part of it. I believe that my faith had a lot to do with me realizing that there was a better way of life out there for me. All I have to do is just grab it." Jeff grabbed on so tightly that in addition to his full-time electrician's job he now volunteers every Sunday to answer a hot line for fellow gamblers. Despite being raised in a religious home, Jeff ultimately had to lose then gain back his faith to appreciate what the ancient rabbis claimed for the power of God's grace: "The attribute of grace, it was taught, exceeds that of punishment [i.e., justice] by five-hundredfold."[8]

Pat Glatz has suffered, too, and claims God released her from her agony for a purpose. After nearly twenty-eight years of teaching experience in Chicago, she was diagnosed with colon cancer that had spread to other parts of her body. A St. Denis parishioner since 1967, Pat explained that it was "a stage three tumor, I was on chemotherapy for an entire year, and here I am today." The cancer finding scared her, but amazingly she never missed a day of work. Pat was fortunate to be put into a study group at Oak Park Hospital and knows "definitely that the chemotherapy obviously played a part" in her survival. For Pat it was not the fear of a painful death that revealed the workings of God through suffering. She "knew that this illness was not going to get the better" of her, but that there was "some purpose, that there was something that I needed to do or be doing." Pat is certain that she was saved for a reason. But, I challenged, "What purpose did suffering serve to make possible?" "I don't think there is one thing," Pat answered. She then added, "Just do what I can do, so that is what I try to do."

In Pat's life, to suffer and be released is to be saved in order to do God's will. Suffering is like a wake-up call. It confirms to a person that your life has meaning. Suffering for Pat reaffirmed the value of her life. It was in effect God's way of telling her that she still had a contribution to make to the world. During the extreme moments of her illness, Pat prayed. She also prayed when after her divorce "finances were extremely tight." Her three children needed new shoes and books for school and the car insurance was overdue. She wondered how on a special education teacher's salary she could possibly provide for her family. Pat acknowledged that when "money was very, very tight, you tighten your belt and just do the best that you can." Doing the best for Pat also meant praying for relief. "But how did prayer help?" I wondered aloud. "Did it provide you with food or money?" Pat's answer was brief: "It made me stronger to endure."

Whether it was fighting cancer or scraping up the nickels and dimes to pay her bills, Pat understood suffering not as a curse, but, as the Bible states, a path leading to "endurance and hope." Hope that the days will become brighter and that faithfulness will be rewarded. Not just in heaven, but here on earth. It was Pat's belief that somehow "if you simply believe [in God] and pray you are going to come out of this squalor condition." Pat is not a reader of the Bible, but her beliefs show a confidence in the words of Samuel: "In my distress I called upon the Lord; to my God I called, from his temple he heard my voice, and my cry came to his ears" (2 Samuel 22:7). As a cancer survivor she could not claim otherwise. After all, she was here today.

Katie Jordan has been doing God's work ever since she came to Chicago in 1960 from Hot Springs, Arkansas. She is a legendary figure in the Chicago labor, civil, and women's rights movement.[9] Katie is also a communion minister at Holy Angels Catholic Parish in south Chicago. Situated in the "Bronzeville" area of Chicago that is 94 percent nonwhite, the parish is nationally recognized as having the largest operating African American Catholic elementary school in the country.[10] Bronzeville was once known as the "Jewish Gold Coast," but by the early twentieth century was hailed as the "Black Metropolis."[11] The church was also the context for a 1980s television feature film. Along with her parish affiliation, Katie is also a member of Holy Angels' gospel choir.

As a retired thirty-three-year textile worker and pioneering figure in the city's labor movement, Katie has seen firsthand her share of physical and psychological suffering. Much of the suffering she has witnessed has been in the form of the abuse of workers. Katie was the first black woman to work as a fitter in the Litton garment shop on the corner of State and Jackson Streets. Eventually her acumen at helping other women contend with various factory floor problems brought her to the attention of city garment and textile union officials. Katie actively participated in a successful campaign to unionize the shop and thereafter was chosen to be a union steward charged with protecting the rights of workers at Litton. Katie's workplace leadership eventually elevated her to the presidency of the United Needletrades and Industrial Textile Employees Union, Local 5.

Once unionized, the female workers at Litton expected to get a raise in their pay. The increase did come, but not without some disappointment. Katie noticed that the contract listed lower salaries for the women performing "Ladies Alterations" and higher pay for men doing similar work as "Fitters." But women were also now working as fitters and they were upset about the discrepancy. Katie indignantly recalled that "everyone was talking about equal pay, but we were getting less than the men were getting, yet we were all fitters. It was bunk." She led a collective effort to have the union equalize the pay for the same work done. While in her long career she confronted many cases where workers were mistreated, Katie's proudest moment of stewardship came on behalf of a woman who had lost her job and was now living near the edge of poverty. Katie explains below how she alleviated a sister worker's frightful situation.

> She was not retirement age at the time, but she had a vested pension. But then she reached retirement age. Unfortunately her husband was very ill and she said he could not work and that she was babysitting for the kids because the little social security that she got just was not going to take care of everything. I told her that she had a vested pension through the union and did she file for her pension? Well, her English language skills were not very good. So she hadn't, so I got her an application and sent it to her. So she filled it out and sent it back to me. I took it over to the union hall and two months later my friend calls me and was crying.

The tears were of joy and relief because the woman was now receiving a pension check. Katie was certain that the "young woman had prayed to God for some help and that He sent it to her through me."

Katie's co-worker was like so many workers who are "prevented from accomplishing the things they are capable of accomplishing." They are held back because they "can't send their kids to college and because we live in a world of plenty." She rhetorically asked, "Why is it that everybody cannot have equal benefits that will make their lives good?" A good life to this working-class Christian woman would include "decent wages at your job, healthcare and fair treatment at work." It was the fight for providing workers with the means to accomplish what they were capable of, or in other words, what God had made possible, that justified suffering in the world. For Katie, economic struggles "affirm that God is in it all." But, I asked, "If God is in it all, then why does God permit so many to go without food, shelter, healthcare, and education?"

Katie's response to my question reveals how suffering connects each person to one another and also to God's tolerance of human misfortune: "Here is something that oftentimes we forget. What would this world be like if everybody was rich and had everything? There would be no need for God to have anybody doing his ministries. But when He allows it, he gives others the opportunity to help that person over there. There are opportunities for all of us to make things better for the person for whom things are not so well." Suffering works here to connect human life; to form a community. Katie's understanding of the role of suffering underscores the religious idea that the only hands God has are the hands of each person. Katie's helping hands ministered to many women toiling long hours in garment shops. Her efforts ensured that "he who plants and he who waters are equal, and each shall receive his wages according to his labor" (1 Corinthians 3:7–8).

Todd Macdonald comes from a family of union painters. His father was a painter for about thirty years and he and his brother also work as painters. Todd is a graduate of Chicago's once prominent Washburn Trade School and a member since 1980 of Local 194 of the District #14 Allied Painters Union. Painting work, like other craft occupations, can be very irregular. When there have been plenty of jobs to do, Todd's wife and two children have been well provisioned. But when the work dries up, as it has for at least eight to twelve weeks each year of the twenty Todd has painted, it has been a real struggle to make the Macdonald family ends meet. Todd remembers a five-month layoff that almost unhinged his sense of security and well-being. "I was married and we just had our first kid. We were living on food stamps and it got to the last month that we had to move out of our apartment and we moved back with my parents. Man, it was very bad." In other layoff periods Todd was fortunate enough to collect unemployment benefits. Many American workers are not so fortunate. Historically, only between 31 and 41 percent of people out of work are eligible to receive temporary supplemental wages.[12]

But even with some financial aid Todd regularly wondered about his plight. "I always prayed and asked why this was happening to me. It scares me a lot of times." His response was to pose a question. "Sometimes I ask the Lord if I am in the right profession." Depending on the answer, this slender, soft-spoken, grey-haired member of Family in Faith Lutheran Church in Glendale Heights asked a followup. "If I'm not, could you lead me to the way to the right place where I'm supposed to be?" Being in the right place also meant finding a sacred space to worship. Todd found comfort in a new Lutheran congregation resting on a bluff along a busy road. Formed "as a prime location for a mission congregation," Family in Faith was established in an unconventional manner. Church leaders "formulated plans for the planting of a mission with a unique seeding strategy." Local residents were contacted by phone and asked about the "interest in a church and a possible name for the new congregation." After a "phone blitz" the community affirmatively embraced reopening a vacated church facility and christened it "Family in Faith." Following a large community mailing, the church "opened its doors for worship" in October 1993.[13]

Like many people similarly situated, Todd's struggle for economic security challenged him to reassess what he was doing for a living. But his faith added an additional qualifier: was he in the "right place where I'm supposed to be"? Struggling in this case caused Todd to monitor his work for signs that it was not what God wanted. As Todd and his family suffered with recurring bouts of unemployment, he turned his worries into an assessment of God's intentions. Should he "go work for McDonald's" or "just keep doing" what he and his father have always done? Suffering forced Todd to stop and consider whether he was doing what God wanted for him or if he had simply chosen the path of his earthly father. At the time we spoke, Todd had not been given an answer. He chose, however, for now, to keep painting when there was painting to do. Most important to him, he would remain attentive to God's voice. In doing so, Todd responded to his struggles as the biblical prophet Micah once defiantly did: "But for me, I will look to the Lord" (Micah 7:7).

Michael Morman has been employed for the last five years as a union bus driver for the Chicago Transit Authority (CTA). His fellow parishioner Rebecca Danforth was employed for over twenty years as a secretary for a Chicago-based telecommunication company and now does some volunteer work. Both are members of Holy Angels Parish, although Rebecca is a recent convert. Rebecca and Michael have both been through numerous work and personal hardships. Rebecca has suffered for many years with arthritis and degeneration of the discs in her lower back. On some days she is so unsteady that she can "not get off the regular bus" and is forced to ride "transportation for the disabled." Michael's struggles typically ride with him at work. While he takes great pride in driving a bus and believes it is "good to see a person that is smiling at you when you get on the bus or wishing you a good day when you get off," he admits that CTA is "making it hard to stay there." Michael runs through a series of grievances that workers have with the transit authority that adds up to a concerted effort to downsize the workforce. He is certain that CTA wants to eliminate all full-time drivers and replace them with "part-timers, at part-time rates."

Michael's struggles at work present him with a dilemma. He is a working-class Christian taught to love those who would do him harm, but he is also a unionized bus driver being exploited by his employer. Michael pondered the possibility of a strike against the CTA. Would being disobedient to the employer by refusing to drive your route be consistent with being a Christian? Imagining he had the chance, Michael thoughtfully responded that "what I would tell God was that they [i.e., the CTA] started to fight and I am trying to turn the other cheek, but I am going to have to push back a little to let them know that we [the workers] are not going to take this as well." Struggling sometimes is a product of human greed or indifference and in those cases, Michael contends, faith does not command mere obedience to fate. Michael acknowledged that "the Christian way would be to meet them [the CTA]" and negotiate something fair, but since the employer was "one-sided" in its objectives, the struggle sanctioned an act of defense. God was not responsible for the troubles faced by city bus drivers, but, to Michael, living in the Holy Spirit meant resisting "the Devil in a person that is doing wrong." From Michael's perspective, the struggle of bus drivers to protect their jobs was a call to cleanse the modern Temple of the money changers.

Rebecca Danforth had more internal demons to fight against. Her health had once left her depressed, but she was now doing much better. "I no longer feel sorry for myself and I just live with the condition." Rebecca relies on medication that sometimes affects her mental acuity. However, because she wants to "function mentally," she sometimes skips the medicine. Rebecca has learned that she can "endure so much pain." Her inspiration is the Mother of Jesus. Rebecca explained the relationship between Mary and her suffering in the following extended exchange:

REBECCA: You want to be perfect, but if we just keep Mary in mind and remember that she gave up her life to do what God said. He said come and she did. So if we could do that we can make it.

What do we make?

REBECCA: You make it in life and over the really difficult things that happen. You remain spiritual. Each time we walk out this door, there is always a possibility of something happening to us. If you are spiritually gifted you will be able to handle anything that confronts you when we are in the real world. I am just saying that if you are gifted with the love of God and spiritually endowed, then you can almost overcome anything that confronts you.

For Rebecca, suffering was used to invoke the power of the Holy Spirit. Miroslav Volf has written that it was the Spirit that made possible a "union of human beings with the Son of God."[14] Suffering led Rebecca not to despair, but because of her spirit-guided response to pain she had a renewed commitment to life. Suffering strengthened her just as "Samuel took the horn of oil, and anointed him in the midst of his brothers; and the Spirit of the Lord came mightily upon David from that day forward" (1 Samuel 16:13).

Arthur Reliford teaches biology in a Catholic school. He starts each class day with a prayer and does not believe there is any contradiction between science and the biblical account of creation. Arthur is a very warm, studious-looking black man who explains that "I am talking about my belief in God and to me there is really no difference in the way I present scientific facts and then the way that I present my logic as being a believer in God." He has been attending Holy Angels Church since before the original edifice burned down in 1986. Once rebuilt, the church became one of the most recognized and active religious institutions on the city's south side. The parish has been a leading spiritual and social institution within a black community that had been for decades ignored, patronized, and subjugated by Chicago's machine politics and terrorized by racist white civilians.

Unlike his two older siblings, Arthur attended Holy Angels elementary school and proudly points out that "the best thing that I had going for me was the education that I received from the nuns and priests." Despite his lifelong engagement with the church, when we spoke, he nervously flicked at his short salt-and-pepper beard and revealed that he was "in a crisis of faith."

Arthur's struggle was grounded in his disagreement with how the parish was now conducting community organizing. He wrestled with the relationship between the parish's social activism, which he supported, and its spiritual mission. In a city where few black parishes were growing, Holy Angels was ministering to over five hundred families and eight hundred parishioners, and had become a leading force for community renewal in an impoverished area. As we talked about that duality, Arthur shared stories of his ancestors who migrated to Chicago from Arkansas and Louisiana. "I am aware of some of my ancestors who were slaves. I am aware of how they lived and some of their sufferings." It appeared that Arthur's current self-doubts about the parish were finding currency with his ancestral legacy. He spoke of his mother's father, who was nearly lynched for allegedly stealing a cow, and his great-grandmother, who was a "very vigorous woman who loved life and was a very proud woman." Plowing through the past while speaking of his present confusion compelled Arthur to acknowledge that "my ancestors, when I appealed to them they have helped me through some very difficult times." What was the connection between Arthur's "crisis in faith" and his ancestors, and what did it imply about suffering?

When I asked Arthur to talk more specifically about the links between past and present, he drew from a deep well of collective African American memory and spiritual connection. "They delivered me just like the Israelites when God delivered them from slavery to the Promised Land. I used to struggle about time. What is the time issue? I think that is our most severe limitation which is we go through a crisis of faith and cynicism because we are stuck in time." Arthur compared his modern impatience with bad times to the Israelites and black slaves' despair that a savior would not someday come and set them free. "We cannot see the future and we do not appreciate the past. We are just living in the present and the present seems bleak and then we give up. But then my son graduates from college and I'm overcome. I'm overcome because I think about the suffering that my grandparents and parents went through and again I was overcome because his graduation was a culmination of that suffering."

Arthur's son graduated from New York University during a beautiful outdoor ceremony in Washington Square Park. To the son the event simply marked the beginning of a single career, but to the father it was the fulfillment of the biblical exodus prophecy that repeats itself generation after generation. Just as the ancient people of Israel and the chattel slaves of the plantation Confederacy were freed from slavery, Arthur and his son are rewarded for their faith and hard work. Arthur drew this lineage in the following way: "I find I am most humbled when I refer to the suffering of my ancestors. I am least humbled when I think about the triumphs. I have to connect it with my suffering more now than ever." To struggle today with spiritual doubts, physical pain, or economic hardship is to recall the ancient Hebrew and African American faith in God's saving acts of mercy. During times of trial and tribulation God promised to restore the faithful to a promised land. Arthur's comments reveal the affinity he perceives between his working-class Christian life and the black slave experience in America, as well as the Hebrews of the Old Testament.[15]

As Arthur suffers, he uses his faith as a tool of earthly emancipation and as a way to advance the social progress begun by his ancestors. Arthur's great-grandfather may have been a slave, but his great-grandson may one day be a doctor. If so, Arthur is confident he will hear again God's promise of deliverance: "I have heard the groaning of the people of Israel whom the Egyptians hold in bondage and I have remembered my covenant. Say therefore, to the people of Israel, I am the Lord, and I will bring you out from under the burdens of the Egyptians and I will deliver you from their bondage" (Exodus 6:5–9).

Craig Rutz plays the guitar once a week during mass at Family in Faith Lutheran Church in Glendale Heights. Going to church is more meaningful to Craig when he brings along his guitar because he feels "it's the main talent that I have." His day job for the past twenty-three years has been as a neighboring village policeman. In his job Craig has confronted the deaths of strangers. Craig notes that these last moments of a person's life are the times when God's presence is most felt. "I think the times when I feel most close to God is when I am dealing with someone who is dying in front of me or someone who has just died or the families who have just lost someone." The severe trauma of a person's death and the "bizarre things that happen on the job that make you think that it can't be a coincidence, it has to be guided for some purpose even though I cannot imagine why," give Craig reason to believe that God is in the plan. The threats of death or serious injury are things Craig regularly struggles with. "Yeah, dealing with death, it is something that is always there."

It is a cliché to say that fear of death is part of a law enforcement officer's job, but handling that fear is uniquely personal. Craig does not try and figure out why bad things happen to good people. He cannot "imagine why"; he can, however, trust that God has "guided it for some purpose." Believing this allows him to do his job and it is a job he feels that God has blessed him to do. Thus, he has been at peace with being a police officer for a long time. Unfortunately, when we spoke, that ease of mind was threatened by a legal clash with the village government. Craig explained that he was "very conflicted" and "in a bad situation—the work situation is very bad."

The source of his struggle was an age discrimination lawsuit he filed against village officials. Craig alleged that he was demoted after whistle-blowing the possible misappropriation of six to seven million dollars in village funds. He feels that the police department has been vindictive. "I was put on foot patrol for a year, if you can imagine that, I'm the highest-ranking guy there and I am foot patrol." Craig likened his predicament "to a 1950s B movie." He recounts all the further ways "they [village officials] are doing everything they can to force me to leave." Fighting against job harassment has forced Craig to balance two Christian principles. "You are always supposed to forgive people, but you are also supposed to pursue justice. By suing I'm not forgiving those people at work, so I am wondering if I am doing the wrong thing on the basis of my religion." Craig's religious beliefs have created a dilemma: "It's like the law comes in conflict with faith." In pointing out the questionable expenditures, Craig feels as if he "had to sacrifice everything." He questions his suffering because if the Bible says to forgive those who hurt you, but render to Caesar what is Caesar's, then what does his faith command?

Craig is resentful at "being treated like a bad guy" and now seriously questions his continued work as a village policeman. But he also believes that by challenging an injustice he is "doing what every Christian is supposed to do and say 'that wrong is wrong.'" In Craig's case, his suffering was brought about because he waved an accusatory finger at his superiors. He could have chosen to simply ignore the situation and go on with his job. Instead, he acted in the ways of an Old Testament prophet and scolded the village kings to "cease to do evil, learn to do good; seek justice, correct oppression" (Isaiah 1:16–17). Craig insists that he is "very much an average person" and is not "a person called to condemn authority." Perhaps his lawsuit and charges will ultimately prove groundless. Nonetheless, Craig deals with his suffering by believing that he is following the dictates of his faith. "It is that simple, there is nothing more to it."

John Schiavone now regularly attends services at Family in Faith Church. But for most of his work life, spent as a computer data entry operator, he was not a Christian. Not that converting at forty was at first very important. John admits to at first "just sitting at the campfire." He was good at saying that he believed "Christ died for all my sins and that He is my one true savior," but really just "said that I believed because that is what they wanted to hear." John also hated his job and felt stuck in a dead-end position without any hope of escape. On top of his miserable job he suffered from herniated discs and very painful kidney stones. Then he got religion. John decided to take his faith seriously. He began to pray, attend church, and read the Bible. Why the real conversion? "Because it is really what got me over the edge." Suffering turned John into a Christian.

As he explains it, "the thing that I wanted to deny and felt was wrong" now convinced "me to let my yes be yes." Suffering from poor health and a job that was only a corrosive vehicle to pay the bills, John made a confession. "Never having prayed before as a young man or thinking that God was the way out" caused John to feel stuck in a job that he hated every day. But John's difficult work situation eventually brought him to a realization that he needed God. His growing desperation triggered a "crying out to God" for help. That assistance came not in the form of a new job; John still prays that God will show him where "I should be, to help me find the right job." In this case, John's faith changed *how he viewed his work*. "Now that I am a Christian, it is not as hard as it used to be." Mounting data tapes and typing in a few commands on a computer is still not very satisfying to John. But neither is it any longer a penance. Suffering compelled John to take seriously the belief in a forgiving God. Faith of this sort did not transform the material world, but it did provide John with a new perspective on work. His more hopeful bearing confirmed John's belief that God's "word is a lamp to my feet and a light to my path" (Psalm 119:105).

John's wife, Donna, admits that she does poorly with suffering. Unfortunately, in her line of work she feels it a lot. Donna works as a massage therapist. Pain is the reason Donna has a job. She has worked providing pain relief for over a decade. Some weeks she may do as many as fifteen or twenty treatments. Familiarity with suffering, however, has not made it any easier to understand. Donna shakes her head slowly when she explains that she does "not understand why this person has to have this illness." As a therapist she has seen "a lot of illness and disability," and "it is chronic and will never stop." The suffering Donna places her hands upon is the worst kind of human nightmare: pain "for the rest of their lives." She admits that with most of her patients she cannot permanently remove their pain. But as a Christian she can do as Jesus once did. "Whatever I can do to help people stay calm, centered, and focused and have a life that is not all pain and stress, then that is a good thing."

While Donna does not claim to have any insights into why some people hurt so much, she is certain that it has nothing to do with whether they are believers or not. Suffering is not for her a reflection of a lack of faith. It is not God's punishment of the unrighteous; "God does not spite the non-believers." Yet Donna is very moved by her clients who pray that they will be freed from their pain. Moving beyond pain, however, takes more than just faith. "The clients that I see who are in bad pain are remarkably inspiring to me." Donna points out that "they have two choices. They can sit and cry about it and say 'Oh woe is me' or they can let it build their character." By building character Donna refers to finding a way to manage your pain and not surrender to its control. Part of that pain management process can get you closer to God "if you cry out to him." Donna believes she has seen it work, but acknowledges that she does not fathom how it works. It's not that her worst clients suddenly can walk or bend again without pain. No hands-on, tent-revival miracles here. But Donna firmly believes that through therapy and faith people do get better with living with a chronic physical problem.

Like her husband, John, Donna does not see faith as transfiguring geometric space or the human body. But because suffering can bring a person into a personal relationship with God, it can help a person endure a complex human existence that is part blessing and part decay. Both John and Donna's patients pray that God will "bring me out of my distress [and] consider my affliction and my trouble" (Psalm 25:17–18). In truth, they have found more often than not that when God answers, life simply "is not as hard as it used to be."

Angela Blunt, however, praises those times in her life when she experienced extreme duress. "I feel that we all go through the wilderness." Suffering is never solicited, but according to Angela, a member of the Church of Our Lord and Savior Jesus Christ, God "plans every step that you take every day." Her steps have not always been well chosen. "I was going out partying every day, even though I had two good jobs I was blowing my money. I had nothing to show for my money." Then God stepped in. "He took it all away from me." Angela believes that God pulled her away from those things that she mistook as important and subjected her to a revolving wilderness of unemployment and poverty. Angela's financial profligacy culminated in a series of events which found her without a home. Why, I quizzed, would God do this? "He is bringing me back to where I need to be. He takes us through these [painful] processes to make us stronger." Angela is describing a cleansing kind of suffering that shakes off the ashes of a materialistic life driven by the need to exchange money for useless acquisitions. The more she worked, the more money Angela made; and the more money Angela made, the more wasteful her spending; and the more wasteful her spending, the more distant she was from God. So God allowed suffering to enter her life—not to punish her, but to bring Angela back to "church, to faithfulness." Angela now works as a customer service representative and, as a result, "He gave me a better place each time."

Cheryl Lawrence also attends the Church of Our Lord and Savior Jesus Christ and understands this wilderness journey as a way to add to a person's life through subtraction. "I agree that God allows suffering, but I believe He allows it because sometimes He has to take away for us to learn." Cheryl had recently found a new job as a customer service representative after unexpectedly losing a part-time position with the Chicago Public Schools. But it was the death of one of her children that inspired Cheryl to emotionally explain how suffering had taught her to trust God's plan. "I think the things that we all go through—that I go through—happen in order that I can walk the walk that God wanted me to do." The pain involved in burying a child was not random, nonsensical, or the sign of a vengeful God. "He had to take me through certain things so that I would understand what someone else is going through." Suffering here becomes a way to feel connected to others, to strangers. Feelings of loss, pain, fear, and confusion have properties that can apparently make a person less singular in their worldview, less self-absorbed, and more relational. Cheryl contends that God allows her to suffer because through suffering she can become a better person. "So sometimes you have to lose a job, you may lose a child, you may have to lose everything that you have, but it is not because you did something wrong, it's just so that He can get you to grow into the person that He wants you to be and do the work that He is preparing you to do."

Church of Our Lord and Savior Jesus Christ pastor Reginald Earle McCracken explains that suffering is not always deserved, but it is always an experience that strengthens us to live more faithful lives. "You don't have to be doing anything wrong. Job was not doing anything." According to the biblical text, Job "was blameless and upright, one who feared God, and turned away from evil" (Job 1:1–2). But as McCracken notes, "God pointed out Job to Satan and Satan gave Job hell—he gave him pure hell." McCracken is a part-time preacher and the religious leader of a small group of working-class evangelical Baptists who have recently formed a "storefront" church. McCracken would appear to be the right man for the job. He is employed with the University of Chicago and is a member and steward of the International Brotherhood of Teamsters Union, Local 743. His workplace leadership experience has more than a passing relevance to organizing a new congregation.

The Church of Our Lord and Savior Jesus Christ was formed by McCracken and others who were coming together from different congregations to experience a more high-voltage, ecstatic relationship with God. At the time of my visits the church was temporarily housed in the unfinished upstairs' quarters of the Bethlehem Star M.B. Church on Cottage Grove in Chicago. This house of God was a simple room of white walls decorated with silver laminated stars. A drop ceiling with remnants of past water damage hung above rectangular windows with wire meshing. In the winter three large visible radiators would keep the room warm, but on this hot summer morning a giant circular fan blew a cool breeze over the floor's slightly frayed thin green carpet. This place felt like a space that Jesus would prefer worshiping in. No stained glass, no large statues, no ornate wood carvings, no booming sound system or jumbotron screen. Nothing but people and a small cross cut into a wooden podium that only barely hid a padlocked door.

These modest accommodations, however, did not appear to suppress anyone's enthusiasm for worship. Services began with believers standing in a circle, eyes tightly shut, holding hands and swaying back and forth, while singing God's praises. Once the worship continued people did not stay seated for long. Each congregant was called by the pastor to "stand and read the word of the Lord." Here is a church where all use their voice to "come to God."[16] Preaching is unquestionably the pastor's job, but his words just get things started. Once God's Word is released the congregants move the worship service through a crescendo of shouted "hallelujahs," "amens," "thank you Jesus," and cries of "yes" and "alright now" to statements of faith.

Pastor McCracken explained that at first Job's suffering was not patiently endured. Here was a faithful man at the height of his physical and intellectual development stricken with all nature of ghastly afflictions. "I loathe my life," Job said, and wondered how the Lord could "count me as thy enemy" (Job 7:16 and 13:24). McCracken likened Job's reactions to how most people today are quick to feel victimized by the difficulties in their lives. But Job eventually stopped complaining when God asked him, "Will you condemn me that you may be justified?" (Job 40:8). In McCracken's interpretation, the Lord said, "I am God and will do what I want to do when I want to do it and how I want to do it." From then on, though, Job's life improved and he was eventually rewarded with greater blessings than he had known before his trials. For Pastor McCracken, there is a lesson in Job's story and in our own suffering. "The Bible says that all things work together for good for them that love the Lord. Every time Satan throws something at us, God himself is right there with us. He turns the negative into a positive." So what is a sufferer to do? "We learn to trust God more, so if you are without a job, you learn to pray more."

But do not expect to secure good fortune by staying on bended knees. All the believers I interviewed were certain that God's healing power demanded hard work and effort from the sufferer. Allah or God could heal in a nanosecond and no one is equipped to understand or predict when miracles will happen. But healing or release from struggle usually required active partnering with God. Yes, wanting a new or better job meant praying to God, but it also meant attaining new skills or education. It might require taking a more proactive political stance or becoming a union member. The point was cleverly made by award-winning author John Feinstein in his biography of legendary pro basketball coach Red Aurebach. As recounted by Feinstein, Aurebach once asked the Boston Catholic bishop Fulton Sheen whether making the Sign of the Cross actually helped players make a foul shot. The bishop replied, "Oh yes, but it helps if they can shoot."[17]

Not all suffering is created equal. The pain brought into someone's life because she ignored a traffic signal and crashed the car into a light pole is caused merely by human error. Working-class believers spoke knowingly about the kind of suffering a person experiences because of stupidity or poor sense. This pain was earned pain. It was, on the other hand, the suffering caused by unexpected job loss, an illness without a known causal agent, or an innocent's death that called God's grace into existence for some and into question for others. This suffering was undeserved suffering. It was not something any of the workers I interviewed claimed to understand. In the end, the way that most of them dealt with undeserved suffering was summed up in the following Bible passage: "Not that I complain of want; for I have learned in whatever state I am, to be content. I know how to be abased, and I know how to abound; in any and all circumstances I have learned the secret of facing plenty and hunger, abundance and want. I can do all things in him who strengthens me" (Philippians 4:11–13). Cheryl Lawrence had a particularly prosaic way to express what it seemed was every congregant's belief about the relationship between suffering and faith. "You go through the hurt to know God's grace."

Once he or she has gone through the pain or hard times, a person can pause to relish the small miracles of life. Kim Vargas has learned not to sweat the absence of better times or bigger treasures. She attends Family in Faith Lutheran Church and is married to Gerry who works two clerking jobs at a nearby hospital. Kim takes great pride in her ability to stay at home and to take care of her three children. But she understands that it comes at a price. Gerry puts in a lot of work hours and that means that Kim and the children spend a fair amount of time without their father present. Long working hours and multiple jobs have become the norm for working-class families. The average weekly working hours for American families has increased by 11 percent over the past few years.[18] Kim and Gerry are among thousands of American households who depend not only on longer working days, but also on two or more jobs to pay the bills.[19] The need for multiple paychecks can be explained, at least in part, by a national minimum wage that has failed to adequately keep up with the cost of living index and an inability of workers to organize into unions to negotiate higher pay.[20] Work is still essential to live a civil life, but for a majority of earners, a job barely pays.

Kim and Gerry struggle to balance the needs of a growing family and spiritual life, and an omnipresent life of labor. Gerry is out of the house by 7:30 A.M. and does not return until after 9:00 P.M. His children are primarily raised by their mother and he painfully admits that "one of [the] things that hurt me the most is to not spend as much time with them as I would like." Gerry recalls the times that his four-year-old son has adhered himself to the front glass door and cried over Daddy's leaving. "That is the one thing that broke my heart and I have prayed and asked the Lord about what I should do." But what could he do? "Right now," Gerry's stresses, his "job is to pay the bills." While Kim lovingly assumes her primary caregiver role, she is not naive about the family's condition. "It is kind of a vicious circle because neither of us completed college. Then once you are married and you have kids, you do not have time to go back [to college] nor do you have the financial resources to go back. So basically you are locked sometimes in a certain bracket." But they do not complain or curse the economic and political system. Nor do they cry out against the fortunes that God has laid upon their table.

Strengthened by their trust in God, Kim and Gerry have found the blessing of self-sufficiency through the daily challenges of simply making the family's ends meet. Kim toughens herself up against the difficulties of raising a family in an unforgiving economy because she "always remembers that the Lord is the one that provides everything." When times are stressful, Kim has a way to find solace: "you lean on the Lord." And after a dozen years of marriage she feels wealthier than any millionaire who sits back and watches the money roll in, but who does not have a personal relationship with God. Kim's extended remarks on the purpose of human struggle and God's healing grace express her preferred desire for spiritual riches.

> We are more blessed than some people who have a lot of money. Because of our dependence on the Lord we have the ability to see the little miracles; the bills being paid when they have no business getting paid, we can see that and appreciate that because we have to depend so much on Him. That in itself is a great blessing. When you think about it, two people who have not graduated college, we have no business even owning a house when you think about it. To be able to have a house. To be able to stay home with the kids. I know that Gerry works an inordinate

> amount of hours, but we have grown in the Lord, which is the biggest blessing of all. We take comfort in the Bible verse that says "Don't store treasures on earth where they can get moth eaten, but store your treasures in Heaven." Every weekend we sit here, we read the Bible, and we get the Bible dictionary out and we both look at it. We discover things together. I tell you, that's the greatest blessing of all. There are people who have a lot of stuff, but they also get lost within the things that they have. They fail to see the blessings that the Lord gives them on a daily basis. The little miracles. I think we are tremendously blessed, just not in a materialistic way.

Kim and Gerry go so far as "to thank God" for their adversity. In struggle and doubt, in pain and suffering they find comfort in God's Word. Life's struggles and sufferings are not curses to wail over but opportunities to know God's mercy. One of the Bible passages that Kim and Gerry take great comfort from sums up the undiminished faith that they both have that the Lord has provided for their needs. Kim recites it word for word: "Therefore I tell you, do not be anxious about your life, what you shall eat, nor about your body, what you shall put on. For life is more than food, and the body more than clothing" (Luke 12:22–24).

Andy Schutt worships at Parklane Christian Reform Church in Evergreen Park. He has driven a cement truck for nearly forty years. For many of those years he handled his rig with two badly damaged knees. Eventually both knees had to be surgically replaced. He also offers thanks to God for his and life's many infirmities. Andy speculates that the pain and suffering people experience in their lives may be a strategic way to serve God and others. "Many times some of the hardships that we go through could very well be for someone else's benefit. We just don't know." By Andy's perspective, personal suffering is not a test of faith or a way to know the grace and presence of God. It is instead the basic ingredient to bringing life and comfort to others. Simply put, we suffer so that someone else will not. Andy has described a very parent-like approach to living with pain and struggle. It is commonplace for second-generation, working-class parents of kids like me to commit to a lifetime of hard work in order to make possible a better life for their children. My parents worked and suffered through steel industry layoffs, strikes, injuries, bank loans, forgotten personal dreams, and ill health and when I asked why they tolerated it all, the answer was always "for you." Andy solemnly points out that God "used His own son for our benefit and you can't get much better than that." So in life we suffer. As Andy sees it, "Sometimes God needs us."

Azmat Ali has also celebrated moments in his life when sacrifice and struggle darkened his existence. Ali has driven a cab for many years since coming to this country from Pakistan. His faith, nourished from daily prayers, visits to the mosque, and readings from the Qur'an, has bolstered his sense of blessedness during moments of trouble. He admits to having many human frailties, but being disrespectful to Allah is not one of them. "What the Islamic faith gets for you during the harsher times is to be thankful during hard times. Once you turn to Allah during hard times, that is the only thing that you need." Ali has an unbreakable faith that the suffering in his life is actually a gift from God. Undeserved pain is not purposeless. Allah "tests us" with misfortunes; it is one way to determine the righteous from the idolatrous. But no matter how difficult life becomes, a true believer in the Islamic faith is not abandoned to cruelty. "You must tell Allah that this time is a hardship." Ali believes that Allah is listening and that some day, in this life or another, the righteous believers who bore their pain in good faith will be rewarded. By the Qur'an, Ali contends it can be no other way:

> And if God visits thee with affliction, none can remove it but He;
> and if He desires any good for thee, none can repel His bounty;
> He causes it to fall upon whomsoever He will of His servants.
> He is the All-forgiving, the All-compassionate.[21]

Edward Bartoszek has spent a good deal of his adult life repairing telephone lines. The work provided a good living, but it also sensitized him to a world full of failure, decay, and trouble. Ed's talent was overcoming the physical broken downness of the world and he took great pride in his accomplishments. Nonetheless, this bighearted telephone lineman was never so certain about the redemptive quality of gracefully bearing the agonies of life. Despite being raised a "religious" Catholic and a member of St. Bruno's Church for over fifty years, he is hesitant to credit a divine meaning to human suffering. Claims of miracle healings and God's interventions come "much easier from somebody else's lips than it comes out of" Edward's. But he has known the kind of struggle that gives way to feelings of remorse. "When my parents were older and having [health] problems I would somehow too often think about how it would be if they were gone already. That they would be out of my hair. I did not really hate them, but I would be thinking that it was not my job to turn them around. Or really be able to take care of the thing that is behind their problems. I would just think about my selfish side."

Edward regrets his less than heroic approach to caring for his aging parents, but he never viewed the responsibility as a spiritual calling from

God. Yet Edward's faith inspires him to approach his work as a way to heal the world. "[Jesus] went through learning the trade of carpentry and then took it as His job as well as being an itinerant preacher. I don't know where the tie comes in, but I often recognize that there is work to be done here. There are problems in this life. Life is not going to be a bowl of cherries." But fixing a telephone line has its rewards because "I am able to take part of that goodness of God." No one knows the cycle of brokenness and loving care better than Edward. He has once again been thrust into the role as a major caregiver for an Alzheimer-inflicted brother. But this, too, is not perceived as any test of faith. "God, why me?" he has pondered at times, "but the feeling does not stay that long." Still, Edward's faith does make it possible to bear the weight of others' misfortunes without resentment. "I realize that helping my brother is what it is all about and Christ died in a terrible situation for all of us." What then is the lesson of Christ's sufferings for addressing the hurts of mere mortals? "We have to do our share."

Gwen and Chuck Kozlowsky have done more than their share. They have been married for nearly fifty years and are faithful members of the Community Mennonite Church in Markham. In 1991 Gwen had surgery on her right eye. Five years later, after more than thirty surgeries, she lost her left eye to cancer. Chuck is a Vietnam veteran who has worked long stints for a trucking company and the postal service. He has suffered two strokes and admits to occasional psychological pains from his tour in Southeast Asia. Gwen's battle with eye cancer never shook her faith in a loving God and she used the occasion of our conversation as evidence of God's grace. But Chuck traveled a different spiritual trajectory. It was Gwen's illnesses that brought Chuck to God and caused a rebirth to occur.

> CHUCK: I feel that our religious belief or whatever you want to call it is our life, our whole being, what we had before was terminated and a new us began to live.
>
> GWEN: I think our faith got stronger again with my surgeries. I believe that. And I think that is when you started to have some faith in the world.
>
> CHUCK: But we got . . .
>
> GWEN: Well, you could have turned the other way at that point and really gone the other way.

But instead of rejecting faith, Chuck and Gwen used their fear and suffering to develop a bond with God through prayer. Gwen and Chuck have prayed together for many years. Mostly they recite a rambling collection of warm and thankful praise to God, but one formal prayer they have always said together at meals: "Come on Jesus, be our guest and let these thy gifts to us be blessed. Amen." Through all their tribulations they have accepted a simple fact of life. Gwen states it plainly: "There for the grace of God go I because there's always someone a lot worse off than we are." The Kozlowskys' self-awareness and approach to earthly struggle, like that of other working-class congregants I spoke to, were as practical as the lives they endured. "Just take a look around and stop feeling sorry for yourself."

Larry Hill makes a living caring for those who no longer suffer from temporal afflictions. He attends St. Denis Catholic Church and for more than two decades he has worked in a cemetery. He believes the job was God's way to reassure him that "after we leave the world people are cared for and nurtured by God." There had been times when Larry had reason to doubt. In 1986 his mother suffered a massive stroke. Her heart attack followed exactly six months from the date Larry's aunt died from heart failure while attending church. Larry, a devout Catholic, was distraught and badly confused. "That is when I asked, where is God?" His answer was slow in coming and, besides, he had to decide how to care for his mom. Doctors had recommended nursing homes, but Larry opted against institutionalization. "I brought her home and I took care of her."

During the working day Larry hired a part-time caregiver to help with his mother. In the evening he learned to nurse and to care for her. "She started out in a coma where she was hardly responding at all. I grabbed every tool that I could and read all of the material I could." After roughly two years of frustrating personal care, his mother began to improve. "We were redefining what normal was," and along the way Larry began to see God's merciful hand. He considers his six and a half years caring for his mom as a miracle. "At the time, how could a forty-six-year-old guy who works six days a week know how to accomplish this? I had no medical experience. We started out at ground zero." Larry's stewardship of his mother's health seemed to invite one miracle after another. Four days before his mother was supposed to leave the rehabilitation center, Larry realized he had a big obstacle. "How are we going to get in the washroom [at home] with the size of the wheelchair?" Larry needed a special chair. While waiting one afternoon in the medical facility, he felt someone grab at his neck. Another miracle had arrived. "It was a friend that I had worked with years ago who had just started working that day at the rehab center. I told him I needed a [special] wheelchair. He told me that he had his grandmother's and that she had just passed away. So I had a wheelchair that afternoon."

Larry's mom died in 1995, but he is still amazed at the years they spent together after her stroke. It was not a joyful time of mother-son reminiscing or long carefree chats. Mostly it was reading about how to care for a stroke victim and sitting at his disabled mother's side. But there was more. Here was a chance to be a servant, to heal the sick, and to comfort the afflicted. Larry's personal suffering was mirrored by the inexplicable tragedy he confronted on the job. "I see this every day, where we are burying a seven-year-old or the parent of a nine-year-old dies of a brain tumor. At times you just don't understand it and I have stopped trying." But his mother's illness and a long line of seemingly senseless burials taught him a valuable lesson. "I think that sometimes you just have to let go. Most of my life I was a control freak and I had to learn to let go of things and let things happen." When Larry "let go," he claims that he learned what God wanted him to learn: "To depend on other people. That took a while for me to do."

His mother's death drove Larry into a huge depression. Nearly five months went by without the capacity to face his loss. "I would not answer the phone, I would not go outside. I felt like banging my head against the wall." To add to his wounds, Larry had nearly been financially wiped out by his mother's illness. But his "darkest times" began to brighten when after carefully being nudged and pushed by his friends, Larry got better. He believes that God was working through his friends, and once he accepted help "things were falling into place so much that it was alarming how things were working out." Larry credits those friends and "some type of a spiritual or a force higher than us" for his ability to not only comfort his mom but live with her absence. He cites Psalm 34 as a Bible passage that reflects his journey from suffering soul to grateful son: "I sought the Lord, and he answered me, and delivered me from all my fears. . . . This poor man cried, and the Lord heard him, and saved him out of all his troubles" (Psalm 34:4–6).

Larry's intimate and regular association with death has also transformed his idea of God. "I was raised in the old church where God was this kind of 'going to getcha God.' He was just waiting for you to make a mistake." But Larry has spent too many years staring down at freshly dug graves to believe that anymore. "Because of my work I saw a more merciful God and a God who would be there for people." Suffering was a challenge to his faith, but ultimately it proved to be a prism that permitted Larry to see God with fresh eyes. Through pain came an opportunity to know a more merciful God; a God who offers a final loving resting "place where people are together again." How or in what form people are reunited remains a mystery to Larry, but learning to care for others and overcoming the separation of death was certainly God's doing. "How else," Larry whispers, do you explain that "it was just me and my mom?" He smiles like he knows something. Now when Larry buries the dead, he knows that they are not alone.

CHAPTER 2

The Ghost of the World

IN A NATION where 85 percent of the population claims to believe in a Supreme Being, cultural and personal notions of the Almighty are as numerous as the believers themselves. America's predominantly Christian affiliation has manufactured a mountain of Jesus images on icons, billboards, movie screens, stages, radio programs, hot air balloons, T-shirts, and bumper stickers. Stephen Prothero also points out that the "Library of Congress holds more books about Jesus than about any other historical figure."[1] In Chicago, Web sites are dedicated to Muslim worship and knowing the sacred words of Allah and Muhammad. Muslim-owned restaurants like Chicago's Kabob Corner feed the stomachs and the souls of cabdrivers faithful to Islamic traditions. Jewish reform and orthodox synagogues, schools, businesses, newspapers, and civic organizations project an image of the ancient Israelites' God into the Windy City. Despite the conventional wisdom that religion is not a suitable or safe topic for conversation in a bar, God is a popular subject of curiosity and debate just about everywhere. Everyone who believes (or doesn't) has an opinion.

I have had many. When I was a child, I believed that God was the creator of everything. Frankly, I don't recall even hearing the name of Charles Darwin until I finished the eighth grade and graduated from St. Nicholas Elementary School. In high school God was still the arbiter of souls, but while attending college the Lord became a silly ruse. Since college my views have gravitated from hostile disinterest to teaching Sunday school at Glen Ellyn First Methodist Church to what religious scholars call the "scared at the center of existence."[2] The evolution of my own thoughts brought me to the realization that however I described God or the divine reflected also what I believed God's will to be. In other words, to describe God was to make God accountable or responsible for a set of human outcomes.

The material demands on the 44 percent of people classified by the Department of Labor as working class can be a significant challenge to their spiritual commitment.[3] What, for example, is the relationship between "knowing God" and unemployment or a loss of health care or a retirement income? God in the house of worship is one thing; God in the streets is another. It is not a question of putting faith into everyday practice, but how believers do it. More profound for the men and women of faith who slog off to work every day is the realization that they do so created "in the image of God" (Genesis 1:27). But what does it mean to live as a working-class human being created "in the image of God"? Where is human life heading and what, if any, is our destiny? The connection between what a working-class person believes about God and what a working-class person expects from God helps to explain the nature of the relationship that working-class people believed was possible with a transcendent figure. As I embarked on this line of conversation, I heard Walt Whitman's voice whisper in my ear: "I hear and behold God in every subject, yet I understand God not in the least."[4] Shortly after beginning my interviews, St. Bruno Catholic Parish member Mira Sojka Topor rephrased Whitman's sense of mystery by calling God the "ghost of the world."

Denise Wilson of Community Mennonite Church in Markham did not believe in ethereal projections, but to her God was no less real for being unseen. "Like the air and the wind" was the metaphor Denise composed to tell me of God's existence. Metaphors were common ways in which Christian, Jewish, and Muslim believers described God. "And," she added "when people are kind." The other preferred way that believers described God was to attribute extraordinary and positive human characteristics to a divine being. But what happens to God's presence and, more important, His character when people are mean? Denise does not doubt God's existence or unconditional love when the world is a terrible farce: "It's just the way that the universe is, [it's] so bad."

Nothing in the American experience has been quite as bad as racial prejudice, and as an African American woman Denise feels the hurt of discrimination. "I have always felt that the majority of white people . . . are privileged. You do reap the benefits of your ancestors and I, in turn, reap the benefits of mine, which are not all that wonderful. But I do have a chance to turn that around. But the fact that, especially with my sons being black males, is that they have to start out way down here. I will see kids that are the same age [twenty-two] working on a construction site because their dad or their uncle or their cousin got them the job or because they are white they will get the job very easily. Making $20 or $30 an hour. My sons have to go and get a job starting at minimum wage. That kind of aggravated me."[5] But as bad as discrimination is, Denise says that God is neither to blame nor ever absent. Despite the insidious contradiction of discrimination, God remains "all forgiving, infallible, a superego in the sense that He gives us the ability to choose to do right or wrong." In Denise's way of understanding God's teleology, the human ability to make choices is the source of worldly problems. "God gave the ability to think. But I am truly just in awe and disappointed in the mess that we have made of what God has given us."

Denise's concern for her sons' economic opportunities underscores her realization that it is not always the fault of the person who suffers from a sinful world. She has worked for more than fifteen years as an intensive care nurse. She has seen her share of heroin, alcohol, gun, car crash, cancer, and cardiac-related disease-driven emergencies. Many of her patients have gotten better; many have died. God, she believes, determines the fate of her patients. "I believe that if it is God's intentions that you be healed, then you shall." Her explanation left me with a troubling question: why would God not want someone to be healed? Denise hasn't a clue but trusts in God's will. "Should I pray that a person be healed or allowed to die? When you're born, you are going to die; nobody lives forever. Maybe it's just time." At some time each of us will be admitted to a moment when life hangs in the balance. Some will come out of that moment with more days to live while others draw a final breath. One will look as deserving of life as the other. One will have his prayers answered. But as far as Denise knows, only God understands what was best for both.

Exposure to people who struggle with physical or mental handicaps can be a powerful lesson of life's burdens and blessings. For those working with the disabled, an unflinching acceptance of God's intentions can be put to a mighty test. Donna Logisz of St. Bruno Catholic Parish worked mostly part-time for nearly thirty years as a nurse in a rehabilitation center. Her short grey-speckled hair accentuates a woman who has worked long enough to ruminate on the origins of life and death. Just a few weeks before we spoke, Donna decided to quit the job. Despite regularly witnessing patients who had suffered through traumatic and physically damaging experiences, Donna never questioned God's existence or essential character. While working, she attended worship services three times a week and prayed for "the good health of patients, family, and friends." No matter the cause of a person's hardship, God was always "understanding, sympathetic, kind, and nurturing." Donna came to know God metaphorically as "kind of like a mother."

God as mother allowed Her creations to freely act in the world but ultimately took care of the pains Her children suffered. But God as mother would not always make all the bad go away. "In life people die, a miracle recovery" does not always happen. According to Donna, God, as mother, is all powerful and could prevent bad things from happening to people, but "God gave people free will." I was curious whether She gave free will to also do bad things? Donna was unequivocal: "yes." But free will must also allow individuals to perform affirmative acts, so is God responsible for the good in the world? Donna figures her matronly God is a lot like her own flesh-and-blood mom who did not interfere in her life, but who prepared Donna to act responsibly. "Here on earth people make the good things happen as well as the bad. They [good things] would not happen if people did not do them." Donna can no more blame or give full credit to the divine for all of her life's experiences than she can to her own birth mom. However, Donna does believe that some divine inspiration has called forth her marriage and five children. Nonetheless, she graciously insists that her station in life is not proof of her own mother's existence, nor is it of God's. To Donna, God as mother wills only that Her children be safe, happy, and inspired to live a deeply meaningful life. But how that happens is up to the children.

Donna has also relied on an understanding of the Son of God to inspire the work she did at the rehab center. Jesus, the earthly son of Joseph the Carpenter, was not a member of the ancient aristocracy but "was just an average man." Jesus' working-class status was important to Donna because He was more familiar that way, more realistic, more accessible, and more like her father. "My dad was a truck driver, so yes, it humanizes Him more." *Jesus as working man* is a metaphor that positions God as an advocate for the less fortunate and "gives hope to the hopeless." The image of a savior born into a blue-collar trade who journeyed across a hard land to serve people of humble origins suggests to Donna that God "favors them [working people]." Of course, Jesus as working man also lent a healing hand to the rich and powerful. So, too, did Donna. "I don't know many people with privilege unless I have taken care of them in the hospital. That is an equalizer. I have taken care of some very wealthy people." So is it possible that her work as a nurse may have been part of God's will for Donna? The thought had never occurred to her, but now: "In looking back on those days, yes." At fifty-one, Donna now expresses a comfortable realization that she has more often than not lived up to the loving expectations of her divine and earthly mother.

Mohammad Abdullah has been driving a Chicago cab for the past seven years. He is a carefully spoken, slenderly built man who reluctantly offered his insights on the nature of a Supreme Being. After all, he protested, he is not an expert or a holy man, but a Sudanese-born thirty-year-old cabbie of Islamic faith. "There are high up people who can give you a better understanding." Still, he is certain of one thing: "Allah is everywhere all the time." Abdullah knew an Allah who was responsible for life itself and, therefore, was ever present in life and death. This was a Supreme Being who was also a demanding rule-giver. With creation came a code of conduct that guided how a person should live and work. Abdullah stressed that "you have a covenant with Allah to obey the rules and guidelines." Allah did not simply breathe life into being, but handed down a set of behavioral rules for people and societies to follow. Being born meant agreeing to live according to a covenant of faith. To be a faithful Muslim meant "trying to live by these rules . . . obeying these rules is a requirement."

Even the work you do has rules. Omar Ali knows that it is against the law to drive a taxi while drinking, but he would not work in a liquor store because he believes it violates a Muslim tenet. "A liquor store is a place that can hurt a human being. You should not work where it is bad. You have to be clean." Ali explains that it is important that work be "done honestly and you are doing the right thing." If the rules are not clear, "Allah will punish us." In Ali's understanding, if you are not abiding by the religious laws of Islam, then your earthly existence will be bleak. The will of Allah can subject you to suffering or misfortune. "People make mistakes of course" and are not punished if they are "a true believer in Allah." But is Allah responsible for the life situation a Muslim inhabits? By Mustafa Ali's account the answer is yes and no.

Mustafa Ali is the married father of an infant. He asserts that his ability to work, the job that he has, and the money that he earns all comes from Allah—but not because Allah determined that he should be a taxi driver. "It is not that it is what Allah wants me to do. It's something like what we call luck. Whatever you get." The essence of Mustafa Ali's and other Muslim descriptions of Allah is not of a God who dictates personal fortunes, but one who favors those who live rightly. Each of Mustafa's fellow cabbies added that Allah also rewards those who help themselves first. "God changes not what is in a people, until they change what is in themselves."[6] It was an idea that resonated with Christian and Jewish believers as well. No matter the job or situation, Allah has prescribed rules of behavior that, if followed, can secure a believer's peaceful time on earth. But if the guidelines are ignored then problems will follow, for as Mustafa Ali reminds me, "I have to account to Allah."

Sherwin Epstein believes in a God but frankly admits he is not sure why. And to be honest, he is no more certain now than a few years ago when he was a member of Beth Judea Congregation. Sherwin has not always been a synagogue member, but he has worked thirty-five years as a union meat cutter and credits God with watching over him. His faith in a watchful God is practical and confident. "I get up and go to work and the day is good. When something happens that is not supposed to be and I don't understand, then there is a reason for it. He has a reason for what He is doing or whatever is happening to me." Sherwin attended Hebrew school as a child and carries forward from those years a very benign view of what a deity does for people or demands from their lives. In Sherwin's mind, God is less about making particular things happen and more about letting things happen. "If you were to lose a job God isn't responsible for that, but he gives you the confidence to go on. Instead of mourning about it or just feeling sorry for yourself."

Sherwin acknowledges that some people always "carry burdens while others are always successful." His eighty-three-year-old mother is one of those unfortunates who have been badly burdened. She suffers from extreme depression and Sherwin is her only hopeful lifeline. But his mother's burden, and in truth Sherwin's also, is not God's doing. "He doesn't pick anybody to have depression. It just happens." Sherwin is so gracious to a God who by the nature of being supreme could heal his mother of her mental and emotional condition that he even refuses to petition for divine assistance. Why? "I just don't have time to think about it. I just have to take care of what happens in the situations that arise. I sometime talk to God about taking care of Mom and my dad and daughter, but that's it." Sherwin figures that if God let his mother be depressed then who is Sherwin to question why.

When Sherwin is not caring for his mom, he spends a large chunk of time cutting meat. Seven-day and fifty-hour work weeks are not uncommon. The hours are long but Sherwin has never complained. He counts himself as one of the fortunate ones who have never been out of work. His steady employment has made it possible for him to own a nice car and to support his twenty-four-year-old daughter's educational interests. Work for Sherwin has been a blessing. The company, distraction, and security that work affords him have eased the disappointment of a failed marriage. But that does not mean that work is a pleasure. "I don't think there are too many people in grocery stores today that are happy doing their job because they are kept under the thumb of management. They [managers] watch every move that we make. Management writes you up for almost everything; especially if you take a breather, they accuse you of 'stealing time.'"[7] Burdens on and about the job are probably the most common kinds for people to carry, at least for those lucky enough to be employed. The intensification of work through omnipresent supervision is a characteristic of many labor markets. Sherwin hates to see what has happened to his work, but he understands that significant changes have transpired in the economy. He assumes that the Lord tolerates the changes, but does not "think God has anything to do with that."

Nor does God create the long lines at the unemployment office. Never having experienced a job layoff, Sherwin has avoided the social indignities of being economically dependent on a "handout." Being out of work is enough to make some working-class believers angry at God and others to fervently pray for help; but not Sherwin. Just because people lose their jobs "does not mean that God is not looking out for them." But, I insisted, "Can't a person's faith explain why he or she is without a paycheck?" "No," Sherwin quickly answered. "It is just something in life that happens and they have no control over it. It is mostly luck." More luck than the work of an Omnipotent Being. God is there, God is aware, God cares. But "something in life just happens" and it's up to Sherwin what happens next. If fortune smiles it's because he worked hard and caught a break. No matter the fallout, God's intervention seems unlikely to Sherwin.

Heaven and hell exist for Sherwin, but he never thinks about either, and contemplating God's judgment of him hardly raises the hairs on his head. He has a "heart-to-heart" relationship with God and while more time in synagogue may, by his own admission, make him a "good religious Jew," he believes he knows what God expects. "It's important that I treat everybody well and that I show respect. That is all that anybody can ever ask or that God could ever ask of me." In turn, Sherwin asks very little of God and credits the Creator with even less: "Everything is foreseen by God, but the right to choose is given to man."[8] Good or bad.

Jeffrey Goldberg considers himself a "practicing" Jew who does not readily explain life by pointing to an interventionist God. At least he does not justify his life that way. His conception of God, however, is drawn from a frank acceptance of his own limitations. "My God pretty much says, 'Jeff, I'm not going to ask you to do much because if I do, I know you better than you know yourself and I know that you will let me down.' So my God says that I should just try a little bit harder today to be better than yesterday." Jeff's God wills no more than Jeff can imagine doing.

But how does God want Jeff to "be a little bit better"? Surprisingly, it does not require much theology at all. "I should be more compassionate, a little more understanding and tolerant. I think that ultimately God wants everybody to be the best that they can." God wills only that people be all they can be? (We joked about the classic Army recruitment jingle.) Jeff answered yes, but then offered a supple and challenging meaning of personal fulfillment. Being the best you can means "touching upon all of the characteristics which makes a person human." God is not expecting saintliness or devoutness or adoption of a creed. Instead, Jeff believes God is at work in his life by inspiring him to be kind, understanding, forgiving, welcoming, tolerant, accepting, and a little more helpful. "God has basically said to me that here are the tools and I am giving you everything that you need to sustain your life—everything to be a good humanitarian—to be a good person—a good Jew, now what you choose to do with this will be your choice."

Jeff chose to be an electrician, or at least has worked as one for a dozen years. Not surprisingly, he does not see his craft or station in life or anyone else's for that matter as part of some grand plan or divine design. In fact, it is unlikely that God is responsible for much history at all. In Jeff's personal faith, God has little incentive to be involved in the daily workings of human life. Expressing a view contrary to those typically held by religious conservatives, Jeff asserted that "I don't believe that God wants me to live my life for Him." But who else would a person of faith live for? "I believe I live my life for the betterment of mankind, and if I do I have lived my life better. God has everything that he needs. He certainly does not need Jeff Goldberg falling on his knees saying 'God, whatever you want of me [I'll do].'" According to Jeff, God is not giving people marching orders or willing human sublimation to a King of Kings. God's will is more a hope and a promise for a life lived with dignity and love. "I am being held accountable to God to deal with life on life's terms. Does He have His hands in everything? I believe so, but I don't believe that He controls things—not the weather, not anything. It is not what He does." After all, Jeff quips, "God can only do so much and He has an entire world to look after."

Goldberg's and Epstein's comments describe a God who's content to let human beings live out their lives the way they choose. God is the creator of life, but after Adam and Eve's transgression human beings are solely responsible for what happens next. At the center of Jeffrey's and Sherwin's Judaism is a keen emphasis on the individual's responsibility to the world. God is not the architect of our pain or pleasure, but God does judge how our behavior brings hurt or healing to the world. Nor is either man overly reliant on prescribed religious formulas to fulfill a divine plan. Both these working-class Jews put more weight on their own autonomy than God's intervention to determine the earth's fate. They figured that in a blink of an eye God could choose to change the world, but until then living in God's image means taking responsibility for how we live. What is perhaps most striking about Goldberg's and Epstein's thoughts is that by raising the importance of human sovereignty, they describe a Jewish faith that serves as an ethical guide to behavior. In other words, for these two men being a "good Jew" meant acting ethically. While they never said so, Sherwin and Jeffrey came very close to expressing the Kantian view of human reason as the source of moral authority and not God. The bottom line for both believers was that God made life possible and gave human beings what they needed to live righteous lives. It was not God's will that fortune or misfortune be visited upon a person but instead the unfettered free will of human beings that determined the nature of their lives. Rabbinical teachings strongly stressed that a "man can act virtuously or viciously," and although God allows people to choose "the way in which a man wishes to walk, he is guided."[9]

Barry Blaustein, too, has an idea of God's mission for humankind and also what is required of a person who wishes to live in God's image. He has studied these topics for a good deal of his twenty-six years as a member of Sherith Yisroel Orthodox Temple. Barry even dedicated seven years of his life to rabbinical college to enrich his life as a self-defined "religious observant Jew." An important element of his Judaism is his current work as a supervisor of a kosher kitchen and deli (*mashgiach*) at a large Chicago food store. When we spoke, Barry had served less than two years in that post after working nearly five years as a union deli clerk.[10] To Barry it seemed that God did not allow life to happen without a script and the "plan" most assuredly came with God-given moral laws.

Barry's God was immanent in the world and was very near to all who sincerely called on Him. God's will is mysterious but not everything was a guess. "The concept of our faith is loving your friend and your neighbor like you love yourself. Everything else is commentary." Barry is a devout Orthodox Jew with enough rabbinical and theological knowledge to substantiate a firm grounding in Judaic commentary and interpretation. No one I interviewed was as intellectually religious as Barry. But as he relayed to me a nonstop detailed lesson in Judaism, Barry revealed a surprising personal belief about what God wanted from people. "In essence, God wants us to have a relationship with one another more so than He wants us to have a relationship with Him." I never expected this portly, energetic, slightly gray-bearded man to say such things. Here in a modest older home, across a wooden table cluttered with stacks of papers from the synagogue, sat an Orthodox Jewish man trained in rabbinical studies telling me that my relationship with him was more important to God than my relationship to the Creator. So the lesson went on. "There is a need for everybody. We are a finite concept but God is infinite. He is forever.

Everything is important but these are the fundamental values. Most of the [Jewish] law is based upon 'do unto someone what you want them to do unto you.' God created individuals and God created the world. The point is that we interact with another. Working together and helping each other, that is how we are able to really satisfy God."

If God's will is first and foremost that people build loving relationships with one another, then we must have been given tools to get the job done. Yes, Barry assures me, they can be found in the system of Jewish behavior codified in the *Halakhah*. David S. Ariel quotes rabbinical texts in declaring that "*Halakhah* is the historical expression of what the Jewish people believe is God's will."[11] But then I addressed the obvious: how do we explain the Holocaust? "God is only good . . . there are things that God does that we do not really understand." It is an answer that working-class people of faith will tell me over and over again about monumental acts of cruelty and tragedy. This time it annoys me. But Barry has a reply. "Professor Bruno, we see things in one dimension, but God is many dimensions. My father, he is a Holocaust survivor. He endured it and he survived it. I am my father's son and we come from different worlds. I was born here in Chicago—baseball, apple pie, hot dogs, and Chevrolets—and my dad was a person who lived through Nazi concentration and labor camps and he saw the near-complete annihilation of his family. His community and his people are broken. It is unbelievable how a person can survive like that. So, and through all of this my dad is a deeply religious man."

By what act of faith is that possible? "Many people, Jews I mean, asked how could God do this to us? What did we do? Six million people were treated worse than dogs. It was beyond logic. My father was fourteen years old when the Holocaust came. My father came to America. He was a broken man. There is tremendous inner strength and courage to do something like that." Yes, I agreed, but surely the Holocaust is nothing if not one of the greatest human failures to love one another. It seems to me that if God wants us to embrace one another, then God has also failed miserably. Upon hearing this Barry's eyes sparkled and he leaned closer to me. "But look what my father produced . . . five children, thirty-five grandchildren. Who would have thought that when he was in Germany? Every day was a miracle that he survived. This was also divined. God wanted [him] and these people to survive. There was reason. We cannot judge God." From the vantage point of German concentration camps, the future in Chicago does indeed look like a miracle. Barry's father chooses not to judge God, and the son believes in a mission for everyone. "Yes, there is a reason why I am here in the world. Maybe it's to be a *mashgiach*, maybe something else. We don't know. But we try to be a good person and help other people. Mitzvots[12] [i.e., doing good deeds] are important. That is what I feel is our mission. Every person makes a difference in life." Some people preserve religious dietary laws, others survive death camps and father children, and there are those who even write books about it all.

"Somebody had to dream all of this up. Somebody has to be in charge of it. Somebody has to oversee everything that happens." When asked why she believed in God, Jewish food-store employee Sylvia Wald answered that "all of this" [i.e., the world] needed a "somebody." Sylvia is an unguarded, friendly inventory control clerk of a Chicago-area supermarket chain for thirty-five years. She is clear about her belief in God, but explains that she left the synagogue a few years ago because it was becoming "too expensive" to remain a member. She has, however, always been a worker, and along with her job Ms. Wald has committed considerable time to caring for her ill mother. As we spoke, tears filled Sylvia's eyes and her voice cracked as she recalled the last moments of her mother's life. Hospital ridden and surviving by means of feeding tubes, Sylvia's mother clung to life for three days. "I realize that we buried her body, that her body was just the packaging that God sent her to this earth in. But what bothered me is that I forgot to bring a pair of socks to bury her in, so I was worried for the first six or seven months that her feet would be cold. It bothered me tremendously." It seemed to me a sad end, but Sylvia demurred and claimed that "it is all part of a master plan." "I think all of the pieces of the jigsaw puzzle fit . . . we are not at Disney World right now."

Sylvia interpreted all the events of her life much as she did her mom's death. Life is mostly propelled forward in turns and twists that leave no discernible pattern. But nothing is left to chance. God's hands are invisible yet unmistakable. "There are very few choices that we make that are not predestined." Sylvia believes in a God who is everywhere and is all knowing, and most important, deeply implicated in the fortunes of everyone. But If God is willing the universe, then what happens to a person's free will? "I don't think that you have free will. I think that it is all kind of predetermined. If you are in the wrong place at the wrong time, it is all supposed to be there. It's actually not being in the wrong place at the wrong time. You were supposed to be there." For Sylvia, being with her mom and being at work were intricate threads in her divine tapestry. But it was not what she envisioned for her life.

> SYLVIA: I always envisioned the two children and the car in the garage and the little white picket fence and the whole American dream, but that is not what I ended with in life.

Is that because God had other plans for you?

SYLVIA: Yeah, at this point of my life. I would also say it was because my parents got divorced after thirty-eight years. My dad got remarried and passed away right after that. For the past ten to twelve years, my mother and I lived together. I guess I took care of her. I guess that was part of my plan. She always used to go around saying that she felt like she was a burden. I told her that she should never feel that way. I guess it is just part of the plan.

Did you ever feel cheated by God for being put in that situation?

SYLVIA: Good things come to those who wait.

Are you waiting for something here on earth?

SYLVIA: I don't know.

But you are waiting?

SYLVIA: I guess.

Waiting for something good?

SYLVIA: We don't know that.

She's right of course. Even the most devout believers admit to only the certainty of death and, if God wills it, everlasting life in heaven. What happens while we live may be inevitable and consistent with God's plan, but none except the delusional claims to know the future. Whatever it turns out to be that Sylvia is waiting for, she is not anxious about the mystery. Sylvia sees no point in worrying over what God has already done. "He made me the person that I am."

"I don't think God is an old man with a long white beard." That was the benign image St. Denis Parishioner Laura Dawson saw painted on a church wall when she was a child. When many years later as the mother of a small boy she saw that same image, it deeply upset her. "I went into my son's second-grade classroom and there was a guy's picture on the board that looked like that. . . . I thought it was Santa Claus without the cap, but then I realized that it was a picture of God." Laura (a white woman) was dismayed by the image because she no longer held to the idea that God was a white man. "It is pretty limiting to see God as a male and white." After all, weren't we born in the image of God? Laura allowed that God may have masculine qualities, but "there is a feminine side of God." What is God's feminine side? Laura's answer came with a twinkle in her eye: "I hope it is the side that helped create me." She then added that a feminine God, as opposed to merely a God with only masculine traits, would have "some understanding of what women go through."

Women like Laura have always been "nurturers in the family" and by all accounts are still overrepresented in the health and, like Laura, teaching professions.[13] "My grandma and aunt were nurses," and "they would take care of people and their needs, physical and emotional." The work that Laura and her female relatives have done produces a God that is not only feminine but also a healer. It also shapes a respect for a particular type of Jesus. Laura had always closely associated with what she called Jesus' "ministry of touch." It was "Jesus' ability to touch people, people that are ill" that most impressed her about his life. The Jesus who cared for the sick, injured, and lost informed Laura's religious life away from Sunday mass. To her, God existed because the sick were "made well" through the caring hands of mostly female nurses and teachers. But could God also be responsible for the sickness in the world? What happens when someone, like my mother, does not get well? "I guess I seem to be telling you that God is responsible for positive stuff, but not the negative stuff." She admits that she "is still working some things out."

Laura has also found confirmation of an acting God through her favorite biblical passage, the Sermon on the Mount (Matthew 5:1–12). "The words are so simple, but there is so much depth to what each blessing says" about the world that God expected Her creation to honor. In the Beatitudes, Laura finds a God who "has a special place in Her heart for the poor and needy." Laura concludes that being a teacher allows her to construct a relationship with people, which mirrors her relationship with God. Laura's nurturing God created her as a woman with expectations that she, too—like Jesus—would nurture others within a "different kind of community." Taking care of children in a special education class is how Laura sees to it that "Thy will be done."

For the past fifteen years Kenneth Cooke has been a teacher of the mentally handicapped. He grew up in Los Angeles and spent time in Louisiana, but in 1989 moved to Chicago and found work in a South side workshop for people with severe disabilities. After relocating, Cooke attended a variety of Chicago-area churches before eventually settling in at Community Mennonite in Markham, Illinois. In North America the majority of Mennonites are white, suburban, and middle class. But the

Mennonite congregation I visited and interviewed at, located sixteen miles southwest of the Chicago boundaries, was anything but typical.[14]

In 1955 the church gathered Mennonites and other believers who had relocated out of Chicago to the near south suburbs. The congregation chose a site on Kenzie Avenue, a major north-south thoroughfare, to construct a new church. In 1957 the small church was chartered and a sanctuary was constructed. By the 1960s the city of Markham had become predominantly African American and the departure of many white families left the Mennonite church with a core of only thirty people. The initial congregation was made up of many white bricklayers, electricians, and plumbers who leveraged mostly free labor and $30,000 to build the church. But the introduction of black Christians caused an exodus of some Caucasian blue-collar members. Faced with the choice of either rolling up their spiritual walls or inviting the "new neighbors to participate," Pastor Ron Krehbiel (1957–1961) and the surviving members chose an inclusive ministry.[15] Spirited by the "call of God" in the Apostle Paul "making the two one people," the church decided to be racially integrated.[16] Choosing a way that embraced social change, Community Mennonite Church of Markham embarked on the path to "be a refuge, a place of reconciliation, a door of hope for all who enter—black, white, Hispanic, blue collar, professional, mentally ill, single, divorced, addicted, homeless, abused, doubter, idealist."[17] Unlike conventional Mennonite congregations in the United States, African Americans now represent 60 percent of Markham's seventy-one members.[18]

When Kenneth and I spoke, this gracious black man was forty-one years old, but he recalled that God's will was made known to him at a very tender age. "My mother, when I was growing up, she was always going out a lot and drinking vodka. I saw how God touched her life and changed her from being that kind of person to a Christian person. To a person who did a complete turnaround. That was the first evidence that I had that God existed and that my prayers had been answered."

Kenneth also chuckled about the prayer he had answered that kept him from having to repeat the eighth grade. "I got my report card and I was devastated. I cried the whole summer. I was afraid to go out in the neighborhood. I was embarrassed that I had to repeat the eighth grade. But when I got to school at the beginning of the next year they had made a policy that everyone in the eighth grade had to be promoted." In his life God has always existed as a generous benefactor. "I would describe God as a lot of forgiveness, as somebody that you want to have as your friend. Somebody that is like a real good friend that always would be there to care for you." A God who answers a child's prayers most certainly has a plan for the universe. Kenneth believes that God's will unfolds in the fortunes of people. "I think that God has chosen people. There are those people who cannot take care of themselves and God has chosen other people to be put in their life to take care of them." Providing for others includes more than just people who suffer from mental illness. "I think that some people are made to be poor. God blesses some people to be rich and some to be poor." But Kenneth insists that an earthly balance is also part of the divine plan. It is God's will that sickness travels with doctors, the uneducated are sent teachers, the unemployed find good-paying jobs, and the homeless are comfortably sheltered. We can hold God accountable for the good because it relieves the bad. And we can hold God accountable for the bad because it calls forward the good. In Kenneth's faith everything from poor report cards to a mother's destructive behavior is the merciful will of a supreme friend.

Florence Joseph curls up with God. "He is comforting, merciful, and loving." Florence is a sixty-two-year-old widow of two grown children. Before recently retiring she had worked for a bank and now serves as an usher at the Church of Our Lord and Savior of Jesus Christ. Her God has been an active force in her life. "I believe that God is always directing me because if not, I would not be where I am today." God's directions have not been delivered through lightning bolts or hard shoves from the back. Florence has often known what she was meant to do because "God was tugging at me." Did God tug as an impatient teacher or a scolding parent? "No," she said with a warm smile, "as a companion." Soft and gentle is the God Florence knows.

St. Denis parishioner Pat Glatz teaches special education to children and she usually pictures God sitting with young people gathered around him. A second less warming image includes "children and the crucifix." God is sometimes nailed to a cross, often embraced by kids but never "sitting on a throne," and he is always in a human form. God, according to Pat, is "nonjudgmental, forgiving, open, and comforting." As described by Pat, God is not capable of vengeance or assigning the wicked to eternal damnation. What happens to the unbelievers and people who do evil is not for Pat to say, but a forgiving God does not forsake any soul. Instead, the image of a man captivating the attention of children suggests a God who is trying to guide others. Pat claims it's not about "retribution or punishment," but instead "attempting to keep us on the path that he intended for us." Yes, there is a plan for everyone and Pat "assumes that there must be an accounting at the end of our life." But it's not "something that I dwell on or consider consciously."

What Pat does think about is how Jesus "brought out a lot of courage to do things in people." Imagine "the apostles, leave your family, leave your wealth, give everything away and come with me, no questions asked." Jesus asked the impossible. "If somebody was around today and asked people to do that, I would seriously wonder about them, are they insane?" But Jesus made it possible for tender women like Pat and others to do the magical. The Son of God was crucified and "he didn't stop it." Jesus "ultimately did what his father wanted him to do and by going through this, it was a part of a plan, God's will." According to Christian eschatology, over two thousand years ago a man fully human was brutally murdered on a wooden cross and today Pat Glatz can do the miraculous; she educates emotionally and intellectually challenged students. By sticking to the plan, Jesus made it possible for people "to do good." What then of natural disasters, wars, poverty, her own illness? Pat saw no role for God in such things. People do harm with the goodness they are given. Pat, on the other hand, paints a beautiful picture of what God is responsible for: "Sometimes when I am coming over the overpass on Pulaski [Skyway] at a certain time of the afternoon and I look out at the sky and the cloud formations and the colors, I am just in awe of what God does." Pat's proof of God's handiwork or "kingdom" is less like a planetary shift and more "like a grain of mustard seed" (Matthew 13:31).

Katie Jordan has always felt guided by a higher power. Her years of union leadership and civil rights struggle seem to her like a scripted walk of faith. "I will tell you something and this has been true all my life, in the mornings when I get up I have prayer time. What I say is that I do not know what is going to come today, but please God lead me in the right way and the Christian way." Following the "Christian way" first meant confronting the religious elders. "One of the things that I did not quite understand was the church. I was one of the appointees that [Joseph] Cardinal Bernardin made when he appointed a coordinated team for the African American community. Sometime when they would be talking about things of importance to the church, I would bring up some social justice issue and it was like if I was not just talking about the Holy Spirit . . . no one responded to any social justice talk." Katie also felt the Spirit call her to oppose the Vietnam War and found another ministry within the Chicago Office of Peace and Justice. But her greatest service to God's calling was forged in the workplace, where Katie committed over four decades of her life to union leadership.

In each of her ministries Katie was comforted in knowing that "God was in the plan." "I just thought that I had to leave it all up to the one who makes all possible." The theme of possibility, opportunity, and a chance to do God's work is again recurring. But to do godly work requires more than a wing and a prayer. "You have to ask for things and you don't just sit and expect God to help. That's what I always believed, is that He is there for us to ask." From social justice work to anti-Vietnam activism to worker rights, Katie has moved through life with a purpose. Her sense of what God wills is revealed in the exchange below:

Is that purpose to die and go to heaven? Is that God's plan?

KATIE: No, we find God here, we find God in each other.

How do we do that?

KATIE: To serve you is to serve God. To minister to you is to minister to God. If you recall the scriptures where Jesus quotes about being in prison, for being sick, for being hungry and if you do this to my people then you have done it to me.[19] Each purpose might be different and sometimes we go through a lot of different changes before we actually recognize our purpose. I firmly believe that we are here for each other, not just for self because God tells us that whatever gifts we have are not for us but you give to others to help somebody.

To "be here for others" is a clear expression of what Katie believes God commands. It sounds a lot like "You shall love your neighbor as yourself" (Mark 12:31). More significant, Katie's achievements attest to a Christian belief that by honoring God's will, a person can reach a deepened fellowship with God: "Truly, truly, I say to you, he who believes in me will also do the works that I do; and greater works than these will he do" (John 14:12).

Family in Faith congregant Todd Macdonald was proud of being a good painter. He had learned the trade from his father and developed a special appreciation for patiently doing a job. Where did Todd's talent to paint come from? "Maybe from my father, but also the Lord helped me get better." Notice that here God is not the source, but the opportunity to fulfill a talent. "The Lord saw that I was getting into this trade." God did not choose painting for Todd. However, once Todd committed to painting, "God helped me by seeing that I wanted to get ahead in that field, so helped me get better as I practiced." Again, we have an image of a God who guides, teaches, supports, and makes possible. But what does it mean when Todd is laid off? I asked him if he thought God could be withholding support. "I guess he could be telling me that I should be doing something else. I don't know. I think he would probably be happier if I stayed working."

Whether Todd continues to paint or not, he expects God to lend a hand. Todd recognizes God as "a person that is trying to help people. He wants you to be good in life." And Todd believes that material success and earthly rewards are also part of the Creator's plan. But not, he warns, without doing acts of mercy and selflessness. God "wants you to get ahead in life where you are helping people." Making your living by doing things that help others is important to Todd's sense of how God wants him to live. Todd referred to Jesus' public ministry. "He cared for people, tried to help people out as much as he could." Working-class members of faith communities return to the concept of help over and over. Todd accepts that God "knows how people's lives are going to go in this world," but in the end, doesn't "know if He is responsible." God is not a puppeteer, but a great helper who plans for us to be great helpers. Todd's conception of God's will suggests an image of God as a co-creator and companion that is conveyed by Jesus to his disciples: "No longer do I call you servants, for the servant does not know what the master is doing; but I have called you friends, for all that I have heard from my father I have made known to you" (John 15:15). To a working-class Christian like Todd, Jesus, a peasant carpenter with little formal education, was a friend and co-worker.[20]

Jesus the carpenter was like others who work for a living, but to Steve Kennedy Jesus' brief public life was about perseverance in the face of resistance. "How he went out and everybody scorned him but he still walked with his head up." At age eighteen Steve's own head was braced skyward as he tried to leverage his part-time catering job with a large food store to pay for college. Steve's New Testament readings during service at the Church of Our Lord and Savior Jesus Christ had impressed upon him the "stick-to-it-ness" of God's son. "He did not back up," even when ignored, chastised, and threatened. Here was a savior on a mission. It was a mission, according to Steve, "to die for all of us." Steve was inspired by the stories of thousands who had heard Jesus preach and witnessed the miracles, yet "He kept going no matter how many people He had following him." For Steve, God's will was to liberate the world from sin and since Jesus' death upon the cross, everything that has transpired since then has followed a trajectory allowing each person to have a "relationship with God."

It was a suffering God who inspired Church of Our Lord and Savior Jesus Christ congregant Angela Blunt as well: "He died for my sins." The death of Christ is a paramount event in the living faith of working-class Christians. The significance of the Crucifixion to working-class Christians can be understood as a way to read how Angela and others came to define God. "Imagine knowing," Angela whispers, that you are "perfect within yourself?" She means that Jesus was without sin. "Can you imagine having that burden on you or never doing anything wrong and God looking at you as pure?" But purity aside, God's purpose for his Son was clear. "Can you imagine," Angela quietly repeats, "just walking like that and somebody saying that just because of that [being without sin], they are going to hurt you?"

Jesus was so aware of his pending suffering and painful death that in the garden of Gethsemane he prayed to God to be released from this burden, "if thou art willing" (Luke 22:42–45).

Angela was transfixed by Jesus' acceptance of God's will. Here was the greatest of all sacrifices. God's only son would suffer an excruciating death not because he was guilty of any transgression, but because he was the strongest sacrifice the Lord could make to redeem the world. Jesus was an innocent; but according to Angela Blunt, Steve Kennedy, and Cheryl Lawrence, they are not:

> ANGELA: He thought of me instead of Himself.
>
> STEVE: He died for my sins . . . he endured all of this pain and it should have been me.
>
> CHERYL: Jesus allowed these things to happen to Him just because He wanted to save us.

The working-class men and women attending the Church of Our Lord and Savior Jesus Christ, like other Christians I spoke to, interpreted the life and death of Jesus as a sacrifice. He lived in order to be killed for the sins of generations past, present, and yet to be. Here is a conception of faith deeply imbued with a sense of awe, appreciation, obligation, and guilt. Pastor McCracken explained that Jesus' physical and spiritual abuses are meaningful to Christians today "because it should have been us who suffered. He died for my sins." To McCracken and his church members, the death of Christ not only represents a second chance at salvation, it lightens a path for faithful living. The Teamster turned preacher sums up the message of the sacrificial offering by stating that "we are called to be repentful servants who live according to his laws." Cheryl Lawrence pauses over the things which have happened in her life and admits that "sometimes I feel like I don't do enough to say that I appreciate the sacrifice." Steve Kennedy simply bows his head and whispers, "I feel grateful and I'm thankful."

What Church of Our Lord and Savior Jesus Christ members are attesting to is their belief that God's will begins and ends with the sacrifice of his son in order to "prepare the way of the Lord" (Mark 1:3). As they interpret their faith, Jesus' life and death redeemed them from the world's sinful rejection of God and enables them to now have a merciful relationship with an all-powerful God. Trying to otherwise account for God's particular handiwork in the world, whether of apparent good or bad consequences, detracts us from the primal fact of Jesus' crucifixion. God's will, in other words, is best understood as the sacrifice necessary for eternal life. All the fire, brimstone, and world history that follows is in some way just a further working out of God's *essential* will. It is in multiple forms a continuation of the sacrifice at Golgotha.[21]

The question of the will of God or what God is responsible for is something every working-class Jews, Muslim, and Christian paused over. Perhaps to the dismay or pleasure of their pastors, reverends, rabbis, and imams, it was not common for believers to credit every worldly act to God. Many simply humbly cited their incapacity to know whether God is responsible for this day's rain or tomorrow's plane crash. But most knew of "free will" and the concept seemed to leave human beings in charge of their own existence. Nonetheless, as my interviewees reminded me, the capacity to autonomously choose a course of life did not happen without God's foreknowledge of what would indeed come to pass, or significantly, what was contrary to God's design for the universe. God remained the supreme architect. Somehow this pre-creation knowledge before the fact of a life fully lived also fit into a "plan" for each person, and most important, the world.

Judging the accommodation of free choice and determinism in theological terms is beyond my expertise or the purpose of this book. However, it is important to acknowledge that the workers I interviewed were very uncertain how to make sense out of a God responsible for *everything*, but not for every *particular* thing. With few exceptions, working-class believers did not believe that God killed innocent children or caused hurricanes or terrorist bombings. But everyone interviewed believed that God not only knew all this would happen, but preordained such things precisely to ensure that "His will be done." All of "it" was part of God's grand doings, but while He/She allowed "it" to happen, He/She did not make "it" happen. Rare was the case of Church of Our Lord and Savior Jesus Christ member Lamont Harrison, who, when asked to explain his view of God's will, simply and singularly answered, "I think just living everyday is doing God's will." Florence Joseph, also a congregant of the church, added a sly parting comment: "It's that free will that is what messes us up every time."

Arthur Reliford recalls that as a sixteen-year-old kid he accepted the "established" concepts of God. "You know, a Caucasian with a beard." Heaven was where your soul went when you died, if God judged you worthy, and salvation was earned by following the word of God. But as a fifty-year-old black man, Arthur's views have changed in important ways. "What I have developed over the past few years is a sense of heaven and God as a place where my ancestors reside." Heaven for Arthur is a family space in the company of God, but importantly, it is a place apart from all the souls of the dearly departed. In other words, it is not the same place that my mother believed she would go upon her death. Arthur's emphasis on spending eternity with his ancestors is more than just a desire to be reunited with family. It is family that compels Arthur to live an inspired life. "I feel that my ancestors are the ones that I have to answer to. Based on their cumulative suffering and getting me to where I am today, that group is who I answer to."

Arthur believes in the God of Genesis and is partial to Paul's letters and the prophet Isaiah. But I wondered out loud, "If God created the world, is God responsible for all that came after the seventh day? And is it all unfolding as part of a master plan?" Arthur's answer took me by surprise. "No, I think we are responsible for each other. For example, if poverty exists where there is extreme riches, then it is us. It is us being greedy or it is us being insensitive. God's plan is that we live. By his offering life and offering the ability to live from the fruits of our labors, I think that is sufficient." Once again God offers an opportunity, a means to live as fully human beings. According to Arthur, the Lord knows the efforts of people but is not the architect of a plan we simply follow or reject. But if there is not a plan for Arthur, there is a model. In describing God, Arthur answered, "My great-great grandparents, my great-grandparents, as my mother and father, their memory and care, their concern for me and how I conduct my life, that is how I would describe God." Here God is parent-like, acting as a wise guide. God is not a lawgiver, nor a judge enforcing a set of ideological and behavioral requirements. Satisfying God so as to be rewarded with a "blessed next life" is also foreign to Arthur. And there is no reconciling of sins at a last judgment. There is instead a God of sacrifice, hard work, grace, and wisdom embodied in those we loved and lost. Some of Arthur's favorite biblical passages come from Paul. I suspect Paul's reference to Jesus as "the wisdom of God" (1 Corinthians 1:23–24) best applies to Arthur's ancestors and his faith.

Craig Rutz has worked twenty-three years on the police force. It's a job he loves and freely chooses to do. But has his work as a policeman been consistent with God's plan for him? "I have always believed that God provides and if you do what He wants you to do," things just seem to work out. Craig is uncertain what else God is responsible for in life and admits "that I don't know why God chose to allow me to have the things that I have." Craig also frankly acknowledges that his faith does not provide much help in understanding his or anyone else's economic status. "In Jesus' time there were very wealthy people and there were poor people. It's not so much that my faith tells me that; it is my understanding of the historical record. It's okay for there to be different classes." Craig's belief in God's generosity toward him does not translate into a God who is responsible for rich and poor. "It's not possible for there to be society where everyone is at the same level."

Craig's reluctance to hold God accountable for much beyond creation is subsumed in his disbelief in a hell and uncertainty about a heaven. "I first came to the empty hell issue" years ago and while "I presume that there is a heaven, I'm not sure, but if so, I hope my dog is there." In Craig's theology, dogs may go to heaven but it is nothing for people to worry about. "The important thing is not whether the Resurrection really happened but that we are here, that earth exists." So what does God require of him? "I just know that I should do good things for people in thankfulness for being created." The act of creation imposes on Craig the one and only Christian obligation. "The comfort that I have allows me to be helpful to people and the important thing is that God promised us that he would take care of us. He created us and provides for all our needs. All we have to do is our best to fulfill whatever we are supposed to do." Craig is a believer without a long list of beliefs that he must commit to or else face eternal punishment. His faith focuses instead on becoming a good person with the gifts that he has available. God has given life and provided a way to sustain it, but in doing this has not required of us that we believe in miracles or resurrections. Craig's Jesus was not a teacher principally of what to believe or how to behave, but a teacher of "a path to transformation."[22]

Craig does not subscribe to a grand God-plan where our lives and our deaths are preordained. But yet, when I pressed him about the meaning of his faith, absent a judgment day, Craig mentioned a plan.

> I know that death is there for all of us. I am not afraid of it and I have had [as a police officer] a few close calls. If there is a heaven, that's great, but there doesn't have to be. You have already been given so many good things in life, so many things to be happy about in life, that if this is all there is and everything ends, that doesn't mean that God does not exist. That means that is the way that the plan was made and it doesn't matter . . . as long as you're doing the right things, for the right reasons, if we lived our lives in the way Jesus did.

According to Craig, God's plan consists only of our birth and death. Now in between we have the life of Jesus to guide us in how we should treat one another. The plan does, however, have a purpose. "The purpose is to do what [we] think right . . . that is, trying, like Jesus." Craig, like other working-class believers, projects God as our guide, but not as our judge. He provocatively states that if there is a heaven, then certainly Adolf Hitler must be there, too. And when Jesus speaks of God as one who "makes his sun to rise on the evil and the good, and sends rain upon the just and unjust" (Matthew 5:45), it seems he has a point.

On the other hand, John Schiavone thinks that a person strays from God's plan at considerable risk to their body and soul. John stresses that it is important to live as a true Christian. To do so requires accepting Jesus as your savior and having a personal relationship with God. To live otherwise is dangerous. "If you are saved, it could affect your life," and earthly riches may come your way or sufferings may be avoided. But "not being right with God and it could have a direct connection" to your prosperity. John's God has a definite plan and has given clear directives for right living and right thinking. For him, God is easy to discern. "A description of God is nothing more than knowing the Bible and the better you know the Bible the better you might be able to say that God is your judge as well as your creator." As judge, God is responsible for a person's fortune. A person may not understand why something has happened, but make no mistake about it, God's will is always done. He is troubled that there "are a whole bunch of people who created God as opposed to believing that God created them." The results are Christians who suffer in life because they "aren't right with God." For John, Jesus' message about his relationship to God serves as a warning: "Truly, truly I say to you, he who hears my word and believes him who sent me has eternal life" (John 5:24).

But Donna Schiavone does not buy her husband's religious fatalism. "No, I don't think it's black and white—not that automatic." Where John interpreted a person's fortunes as a reflection of their faithfulness, Donna saw no direct relationship. "It's not like God is mad at you and he is going to make you lose your job." Not only is God's will not manifested in every human action but it is never punitive. Living according to God's word may be good for the soul but it does not accrue worldly profits. Donna puts it this way: "I do not think there is a direct relationship between being right with God so I am going to have more clients this week." Donna's work as a massage therapist could always use a boost. When she prays, "sometimes I get more clients, sometimes I don't." But either way God is not recruiting the ill and the lame to seek her out. Donna does "not even pretend to know how God works."

Donna could sit home and "wonder why this other massage therapist has clients and I don't." Donna is a faithful woman, but there have been times when her "schedule for the week is empty and someone else's, a person not even a Christian, is full." What explains the difference? In this scenario there are likely many possible reasons for Donna's lack of work, but "being right with God" is not one of them. God is a "presence, security, and love" and Donna does not believe that the Lord is micromanaging her work schedule. But like her husband, John, Donna also subscribes to her own fatalism: "I think that it is just the way it is." While John sees God's judgment at work, Donna embraces a Creator who permits just enough randomness in life to leave us subject to chance.

Gerry Vargas, on the other hand, does not see the world as a giant lottery. "Everything is under his [God's] control." Gerry is a warm, gracious man who works one full-time and one part-time job to support his wife, Kim, and their three children. Both Gerry and Kim attend Family in Faith Lutheran Church. Though tired from yet another twelve-plus-hour workday, Gerry found the time and energy to deconstruct God's handiwork for me. On this occasion he saw an angry God of justice. "We just had the disaster in Florida with Hurricane Charlie. There were a lot of innocent people who lost their homes and some lost their life. Then September 11th happened. Many other things have happened, whether it is nature or whether it is done by human beings. How many times does the Lord have to give us a wake-up call? We as a nation are morally lost."

Notice Gerry refers to innocent life lost. He does not believe that God punished these particular people for being sinful. But Gerry admits that "God can't stand seeing the sin of the world and of the nation." So what happens when God grows disenchanted with the "sin" of a nation? "When God punishes, he does it in a very, how can I put it . . . in a bad way or in a good way, you take your pick." Either way, Gerry sees God as just. It may not be the Lord's will that humans commit sin, but Gerry is confident that nothing happens to us, good or bad, that does not have God's imprint. And, in the end, Gerry simply trusts that whatever happens is part of a grander plan for each of us. God's wrath could, however, be avoided. "If people would just do as God commands and love one another as you would love yourself . . . if we do that then this nation would be a much better nation."

Gerry obeys an impartial God who is capable of great punishment as well as incredible reward. It all depends on human choice; as Gerry quoted from the apostle Paul, "For he will render to every man according to his works" (Romans 2:6). Kim also had her favorite Pauline biblical passage that reflected her willingness to accept God's grace under any circumstances. "I will all the more gladly boast of my weaknesses that the power of Christ may rest upon me. For the sake of Christ, then, I am content with weaknesses, insults, hardships, persecutions, and calamities; for when

I am weak, then I am strong" (2 Corinthians 12:8–10). When considering the question of what personal or earthly events God is responsible for, other working-class believers addressed the theme of spreading God's word in times of struggle. Some members of Chicago's historic Mexican American Catholic Parish, Our Lady of Guadalupe, had very strong opinions about associating certain tragic events with otherworldly intentional design. The parishioners at Our Lady of Guadalupe lay claim to a special appreciation for the workings of the divine. Masses in Spanish are now offered in at least 110 churches throughout the Chicago archdiocese. In many of those parishes, shrines to the patron saint of Mexico, Our Lady of Guadalupe, have been constructed. In addition, annual festivals celebrating the miraculous appearance in 1531 of the Mother of God to the peasant Juan Diego Cuauhtlatoazin take place in nearly all of the heavily Hispanic-Latino populated churches. While many churches in Chicago honor the Virgin of Guadalupe as the foundational figure in their ministry, on September 28, 1928, George Cardinal Mundelein dedicated Our Lady of Guadalupe Church as Chicago's first national parish to give collective voice to the spiritual and social needs of Mexican immigrants.

Despite (or perhaps because of) the hardships caused by post–World War II economic dislocations, the church congregation of approximately 1,500 families (95 percent Hispanic-Latino) remains a vital force in the community. What began as a religious sanctuary for Mexican laborers working in the steel mills has continued to welcome new working-class entrants from Puerto Rico, San Salvador, and Colombia. While parishioners no longer make steel, they continue to support a full schedule of worship services in both Spanish and English. The church's National Shrine of St. Jude has become a famous spiritual site for people from all over the country and in 2004 celebrated its seventy-fifth anniversary. "Shrines generally you think of as out in the country, beautiful places in the open air, plenty of grounds around it," explained Reverend Mark Brummel, director of St. Jude, "but this is an inner-city shrine." The shrine and the parish have endured because, as Brummel proudly notes about St. Jude, they both serve "a real need in the community for people who need hope in their lives."[23]

Jimmy Estrada is a forty-something union bricklayer living on the south side of the city and he is also vice president of the church's married couples group (Matrimonios Unidos De Sur Chicago Nuestra Señora De Guadalupe). Jimmy and his wife, Marisela, pondered the eternal question of "why bad happens to good people." He admits to being confused about certain painful life occurrences. "As far as natural disasters, I always wondered why God lets this happen, especially in third world countries where they suffer so much already." But he hazards a guess at God's intentions. "Maybe it is for the other, wealthier countries to realize that it could happen to you also and that you should help out other nations." Marisela believes that "God created the earth and it was perfect," but as people harm God's creation the "Lord sends a signal" to get everyone's attention. Jimmy realizes that people never expect tragedy to strike them, but they should not be so confident. "I think these bad things can be signs that you need to change your ways . . . it comes from the Bible, all of these disasters that have happened." Bad things are not part of God's will, but if people are living sinful lives and they are not repentant, God will allow evil to strike. As Jim notes, God has done it before.

Our Lady of Guadalupe parishioner Manuel Murillo also thought he saw God's workmanship in the evil that exists in the world. Manuel works as a union laborer in a demolition yard collecting scrap metal for resale. He believes that it was because of the bad that people do to one another God inserted himself into the affairs of people. His thinking reflected a kind of cosmic balance: good (God) and evil (Satan) coexist. But if people "only lived their Christianity," then a divine hand in our affairs would not be necessary. God in this way is also a last chance emergency relief service. God's plan is for everyone to prosper, but when destructive ends occur in the course of a lifetime it is God "speaking" to the world not only of their wicked ways, but also presenting a way to be forgiven. But, contrary to Manuel, fellow church attendee Ana Valtierra held God strictly accountable only for the "happiness in the world." Ana spoke of a kinetic spirit that she believed was God's presence in her life and within her body. "I feel happy because God is in my life and inside me." Yes, there is sadness, too, but Ana does not equate feelings of disquiet with God's design. Instead, "people are responsible for their unhappiness because they have misused God's gifts." Tornados, car accidents, unemployment are not God's doings. But are they proof of an evil in the world? The parishioners of Our Lady of Guadalupe agreed that evil was real, but not always the cause of tragedy or unhappiness. And what that evil should be called brought no agreement.

Naming other positive consequences of God's power was much easier. Reyes, president of Matrimonios Unidos, was treated to an awe-inspiring spectacle of God's workmanship everyday. "I believe and feel the presence of Him on my daily journey." Mateo's journey takes him from his South Chicago bungalow to industrial locations around Midway and O'Hare airports. He is a salesman for a scrap yard and spends much of his time on the road and in the car. Traveling throughout the city's more industrial areas, he is struck by the enormity of the landscape. "Just a big mess of steel. I know that people did that (i.e., constructed airports, buildings, etc.) but only through the grace of God because He put up this world and it is for us to proceed." Mateo leaves no doubt that God has built the foundation. God has created the canvas and human beings are the painters, sculptors, carpenters, builders, welders, electricians, plumbers, ironworkers, sales force, and on and on.

Paula Castro attends Our Lady of Guadalupe and echoes the foundational quality of a divine role in our lives. She acknowledges the role of science to explain how the world evolved, but then notes that Darwinism has its limits. "Did we come from monkeys and cells and what began everything? Yes, I believe in science but at the same time I believe God was first. That's all. He created everything. You have all your other explanations, true, but God gave us everything." To Paula, God is the answer to the question of what came before the "big bang."

At their core, Mateo's, Paula's, and Marisela's views of God's plan for humankind begin and end with the creation story in Genesis. In six days the world was created and on the seventh, God rested. What happens next is still part of a divinely inspired plan, but according to Daniel Weinberg, human beings now have a creative function. Daniel is a sixth-grade science and social studies teacher at McCracken Middle School in Skokie, a northwest suburb of Chicago. He is also a member of one of the oldest Reform Jewish congregations in the Chicago area, Temple Beth-El. Strictly honoring the Sabbath and exposure to rabbinical religious education are important features in Daniel's spiritual journey. He notes that the will of God is a subject of multiple interpretations in Jewish texts. While he often goes to a rabbi for help in understanding the way that Jewish laws should be applied in contemporary situations, he needs no assistance in recognizing where God wanted human beings to focus their energy. "The focus is how we live on earth. There are all sorts of things that the [Jewish] traditions say that future time will look like and what will happen to the world. But I think our focus is how we live here on earth." Daniel explains that it is God's plan that we live a certain way on earth and not be obsessed with what happens when the body decays to dust. Something likely unfolds after death, but God created man and woman to fulfill a mission on earth. "Our goal is to repair the earth. God created the world in six days and the rest is up to us to get to that seventh. We are working to get to the time when the world will be complete."

Tikunolam, or "repair of the earth," is the creative obligation given by God to everyone. It is also, as Daniel sees it, a creative power that everyone possesses. As a middle-school teacher Daniel uses his creative power to advocate for his students. "I am doing my part to make the world a better place by creating responsible citizens and intelligent adults to go into the world." I questioned what happens if you follow God's law and help to patch up the earth's holes. "If I am a good person, then it will sort of come back to me; that nice guys don't actually finish last." A lifelong Chicago Cubs fan, Daniel is eternally hopeful that the "good" will eventually come.

Sometimes, though, God's plan is more than a platform for human endeavors but also includes a mild intervention to help people do things the right way. Gabriel Padilla, a parishioner of Our Lady of Guadalupe, has a story to tell about what he believes is an act of divine will. Gabriel works for a salvage company and runs a crane that crushes battered cars. Usually this process goes off without any incident, but there was one time. "Once while I was picking up a car the claw of the crane actually narrowly missed someone standing nearby and I realized that it could have been very dangerous and that God was showing me that I could have taken somebody's life. From then on I knew I had to be more careful." Gabriel believes that God provided him with a near-fatal accident experience to alert him to the dangers of his job. God in this way acted like a workplace safety expert. What is unique, however, in the lesson that Gabriel draws from this divine intervention is not that he was saved *this time* from killing a person. The intervention was that by showing how dangerous he could be at work, God allowed Gabriel to become a better and safer worker, and therefore would no longer pose a *future* risk to others in the workplace. God, according to Gabriel, "was watching me do a good job and gave me the insight that something bad could happen at work."

Work performance is a subject that Linda Schutt also believes reflects an inspired godly hand. Linda has been a nurse and conducted staff education for over twenty years in a long-term nursing facility in Tinley Park. She attends Park Lane Christian Reform Church in Evergreen Park, along with her husband and three daughters.

Park Lane was formed on May 27, 1953, when 383 people were accepted as charter members.[24] The new congregational members were largely young white families that had fled from the nearby and emerging black Englewood to Evergreen Park in the early 1950s. At the close of the charter meeting, emeritus Evergreen Park pastor Reverend Albert Jabaay "said he felt the thrill of bring an expectant father, one who had to step out of the room due to strain."[25] Ground was broken for the new church on April 17, 1953, and construction was completed in the spring two years later. The church was designed in a "modified Colonial style with a steeple rising to 64 feet" and featured auditorium seating for 520 people. The gallery was capped by high arched ceilings designed "to give a lifting and inspiring feeling toward God."[26]

Linda expresses a devout commitment to Jesus Christ as her savior, but does not hold to a deterministic theory about human fortune. God "has a plan" but apparently is not the grand puppeteer pulling on the earth's strings. Nonetheless, God does reward certain acts. Likewise, the Lord punishes some. "I do think there is a relationship, because God talks very clearly and in numerous places in the Bible how He honors working and working hard." Perhaps Linda had the following biblical passage in mind when she spoke of God's will for those who do honest labor: "They shall build houses and inhabit them; they shall plant vineyards and eat their fruit. They shall not build and another inhabit; they shall not plant and another eat; for like the days of a tree shall the days of my people be, and my chosen shall long enjoy the work of their hands. They shall not labor in vain. . . ."[27]

If God is responsible for the blessing of a new house built or a car purchased from wages justly earned, then what about the person in need of a home who is physically and mentally able to work but has made no effort to earn a living? It turns out, Linda notes, God is not so helpful to those who do not honestly help themselves. "How he detests sloth. So poverty that may come from sloth He would find unpleasing [and not reward]." Sloth is bad, but importantly, "that doesn't mean that because a person is in poverty that they were slothful or that they are not right with God." If and only if a person has freely chosen to be poor is Linda comfortable believing that he or she is "not right with God" and, therefore, the person would likely suffer the unfortunate consequences of God's displeasure. By Linda's reasoning, God could punish the self-destructive, lazy, and wasteful, but barely getting by on a meager income is no indication that God has taken offense. In fact, according to Linda, it's much more likely that God has favored the working poor and hard working. "God loves people and blesses people who are poor in financial ways. He gives them other riches. But without a doubt, God blesses and rewards hard work." Just not always in the pocketbook.

Andy Schutt, also a longtime member of Park Lane Church but no relation to Linda, knows what God is responsible for in his life. Andy's understanding grows out of his sense of who God has been throughout his life: "God was a real provider." I asked Andy to give me an example of when God provided for him and he reached back into his childhood. The following story he tells, however, is one passed down from his mother.

> ANDY: My mother was telling me a story about during the depression time. My parents were just out of money. There was also about three years of drought in the early 1930s. So money was out of the question. We had a cow to provide milk and my folks ran out of feed. They were praying people and my mother prayed and she was the one who took care of the money. She kept it in a drawer in the top of the dresser. One day she went

to get it and there was no money. She looked a second time, nothing, then a third, and still she prayed, not knowing what else to do. The cow had to be fed and on the fourth time that she went back, there was a five-dollar bill in the draw. She couldn't explain it. It was just there.

Is this a miracle?

ANDY: We would say a miracle. That was one incident.

The account may have been apocryphal. A reassuring story a loving mother tells to a little boy to help him get through difficult and confusing times. But nonetheless, Andy believes the tale and has seen the $5 experience repeated in his own adult working life. "I worked on construction first and there were always slow times in the winter. So I'd go out and look for a little work. Somehow or another, I always managed to get something. A lot of time it was hard, nasty work, but I could make a little bit to keep us [his family] going. I tell you, there were always some means that just happened to open up and help provide. So many little incidents happened where we could feel God's presence in helping us through situations." Andy spent most of his working life driving a truck as a member of Teamster Union Local 786. It is not surprising that it is his working life and the economic pressures caused by intermittent spells of joblessness that represent the times when Andy most felt God's presence. He acknowledges others, but most are tied to basic efforts at sustaining life. To Andy, God's plan included making available provisions for human life, family, and community. Full-time driving as well as part-time construction jobs came from God. Andy said he was always ready and willing to make an honest dollar, but frankly, so were a lot of other guys who often had a harder time finding work. While he does not think that being raised in a "prayerful family" made him more deserving than others, Andy quietly admits there were benefits. "I was favored, kind of, just because I think of my relationship with God."

Repeatedly working-class adherents to different faith traditions defined God as a provider. God was the one who gives spiritual and material life. They also primarily praised God for the blessing of work and for the gifts of hard toil. Good and bad jobs, and what wages could purchase were gifts from God, and with each new workday God's divine hand was present. In the life of Park Lane Christian Reform Church congregant Tim Goudzwaard, the will of God redirected him away from a dead-end unsatisfying job to a way to do good works every day. Tim thought that computer science would be a worthwhile career choice. He actually invested two years of college studies in the field. But Tim grew disenchanted about computer work and something "got my attention totally turned around through a variety of situations." Speaking about a "feeling of uneasiness," Tim explained that he was pushed into another occupation. "I wanted to be dealing more with people, not be tied down to a computer and I then found myself put in situations with people with disabilities." Computers had been difficult to understand, but children with learning handicaps did not intimidate Tim. So Tim reoriented his life and became a special education teacher for a Catholic elementary school.

Tim credits God with moving him away from what was hard to understand toward what seemed natural. God's plan for him was all about directional change. But what about Tim's first, less satisfying occupational choice? Was it preordained? "No, I don't believe that God creates bad circumstances. I believe that God uses the circumstance in our fallen world to help us to grow and to provide us with the things we need. It may be a change in direction." Tim believes that God intervenes in the world because the Lord is forgiving of human beings' past transgressions. "He is forgiving but He expects us to confess to what we have done." The record of poor stewardship over the earth and over each other is replete with examples of human abuse and indifference to one another. "I see those as consequences of the fall. That is the effect of sin in the world." But despite the sin, God has directed people to change their ways. Tim's message of change allowed God to use him for good. "So my response to the sin is that if God has put me in a position to where I am able to change something or to help somebody out, then I need to do that whether it is financially or using skills to do something for others." It is an all-loving God who offers people new opportunities to do something meaningful with their lives. In Tim's way of seeing things, when a person positively changes the direction his or her life is going, God is being merciful not only to that person but also to the world. By Tim's accounting, God is responsible for putting all of us into positions of redemption and creation. "I think that God calls me to do what I am able to do."

CHAPTER 3

Missing God's Best

Obligations of the Righteous

QUESTIONS about God's will and the usefulness of faith to make sense of one's station in life underscored the relationship between a believer's faith and his or her sense of justice. The values and morals that each working-class Muslim, Jew, and Christian ascribed to his or her religious influences came bound with an accompanying sense that God would strike down evil and right all wrongs. The God of either the Christian or non-Christian faithful was first and foremost a deity of justice. In his Pulitzer Prize–winning *God, A Biography*, Jack Miles interprets the Lord's missives to Moses "to reveal as eloquently as possible that he is a God who attaches supreme importance to justice and will be utterly relentless in its pursuit."[1] Workers who turned to holy book readings and listened to preaching against immoral behavior had grounding for judging righteous action. Sin and immoral behavior had been defined. But what did faith compel the twenty-first-century servants of Allah, Yahweh, and the Father incarnated in Jesus Christ to do when they witnessed evil?[2] What did God have in mind for the post-9/11 globalized economy of just servants and disobedient fallen? More important, how should a faithful Christian, Jew, or Muslim respond to acts of injustice?

Before engaging in a discussion with working-class believers about what their religion compels them to do in the face of sin or social injustice, it is worthwhile to point out that many scholars find religion to be more status-quo oriented than a force for radical change. In 1996, for instance, Stephen Hart identified some of the popular beliefs that often discouraged religiously active people from engaging in political behavior targeted at reducing socioeconomic inequality.[3] Despite heroic historical instances of faith-based political resistance against the day's forces of evil, congregational quietism on civic matters is the norm. According to Mark Chaves, congregational life in America is much more about cultural expression than it is about social activism or political activity. Chaves has documented that "the overall extent to which congregations engage in politics is rather meager."[4] While there would seem to be sufficient theological support for any religious denomination to encourage an activist worldview, "politics remains, for most congregations, a peripheral activity."[5] Despite the contemporary high-profile examples of Catholic and Evangelical churches that have used the pulpit to encourage particularly partisan electoral outcomes, the relative paucity of parish or congregational political activism remains the norm.

In addition, sociological studies of the relationship between Christian religious beliefs and either individual or collective participation in acts of protest against social injustice have not evidenced any significant linkages. The general consensus of researchers is that religious affiliation and theology have little direct impact upon whether a person speaks out against injustice. Rory McVeigh and David Sikkink have noted that while there are significant proportions (81.6%) of Christians who believe that they should use their faith to "change American society to better reflect God's will," only a fraction (9.4%) have ever participated in anything that remotely resembles an act of social protest.[6] In an examination of the relationship between congregants' concern for God and their potential concern for society, Evan Curry and his colleagues were struck by the "virtual absence of any effect of religious involvement on attitudes toward economic justice."[7]

Despite doctrinal differences, the world's three major Abrahamic religions all share an unyielding and unforgiving commitment to social justice. It is theologically inconceivable that a person could be rendered a faithful Muslim, Jew, or Christian if he or she is not an advocate for an egalitarian and just society. Each faith also demands that followers not only believe in justice but that they act justly. Withdrawing from the world's "brokenness" is not a legitimate faith-based option. Jim Wallis, founder of the progressive Evangelical religious group Call to Renewal, rejects twentieth-century ideas that faith is a "personal matter and a private affair."[8] Instead, Wallis embraces a vibrant prophetic approach to constructing God's kingdom on earth. "The prophetic tradition," he argues, "insists that religion that does not manifest itself in action for justice is false religion."[9] Justice is to be practiced on earth and is always related to the real material conditions that people find themselves locked into. In other words, acting justly means feeding, nursing, housing, clothing, educating, caring for as well as loving one another, excusing debt or not lending at usurious rates, and making peace not war. Yes, loving a monotheistic God is also paramount, but from this list of what justice demands of good Jews, Christians, and Muslims, it should necessarily follow that some societal and personal actions are beyond the pale of righteous behavior.

Murder, theft, taking the Lord's name in vain, adultery, bribery, greed, vanity, pride, idolatry, not following the dietary codes, drinking alcohol, borrowing money, child abuse, sexual depravity, and pornography are all sins of the common sort understood by people of one or more of the dominant faiths. Depending on a person's interpretation of God's message, some believers would go so far as to add homosexuality and dancing in public to the list of forbidden behaviors. But while Jesus, Muhammad, and Yahweh all proscribed immoral behavior between family and community members, they also sternly condemned abuse in the marketplace. So how does a working-class Catholic, Mennonite, Baptist, Lutheran, Muslim, or Jew define outrageous behavior in the world where Mammon is king? Is the average Standard & Poor's 500 chief executive's $11.75 million in annual compensation a sin?[10] Is it a sin when you take into consideration that such pay is approximately three hundred times greater than the average worker's paycheck?[11] When IBM CEO Samuel Palmisano is scheduled to earn an annual pension of $4 million upon retirement even though the company cut employee pensions in 1999 and 2006, and intends to further freeze all workers pensions in order to save up to $3 billion through 2010, has a sin been committed?[12] What about shrinking wages, poverty, illiteracy, homelessness, unemployment, inadequate or no health care, disappearing retirement accounts, exploitation of cheap labor, and violating workers' rights on the job? Are these sins or not? Mennonite congregant Paul Mares tends to see social inequality as the "faults of society" that become sins if they are the result of people who are selfishly disinterested in "our brother and sister." And if they are sins, then what are the obligations of the righteous?

Oil tanker driver Craig Doornbos has never been a social activist, but he knows what sin is: "corporate irresponsibility." A congregant at Park Lane Christian Reform Church, Craig believes that people with riches and power have been given a serious obligation from God. "More is expected from people with power. Getting rich doesn't allow you to skate." Craig bitterly commented on the loss of jobs in America due to outsourcing and he became very agitated when talking about the reduction of health benefits for millions of workers. He also referred to the wide and growing disparity in pay between the average American worker and CEO. A study of the Federal Reserve Bank's analysis of wealth distribution combined with data from the *Forbes* 400 wealthiest families reveals a "dramatic picture of how intensely wealth has accumulated at the highest rungs of America's economic ladder." According to the study, in 2004 America's richest 1 percent of the population held $2.5 trillion more in net wealth than the country's bottom 90 percent.[13] Conspicuous wealth accumulation among the nation's richest people (undoubtedly many of them very religious) is shamefully accompanied by the 7,837,000 workers living in poverty (undoubtedly many of them very religious).[14] "It is a few that want to make it good for them and give them the power to ruin it for the many." Craig is angered by the greedy anti-Christian behavior of people with the means to help others, but he is equally frustrated by the behavior of the flock. "The many will not come together to fight the wrongs because they are all looking for their own little piece of pie. If people cannot come together with one idea and unite as one to march forward, then there is no strength."

While Craig has not been on any recent marches for economic or social causes, he still has a passionate opinion about why poverty and inequality exist. "We cannot all come together and that is why companies spend so much time busting up the unions because once they get everyone going forward, suddenly they cannot get what they want. So the companies go to other countries and prey on those people over there." The cost to workers in the United States of exporting production jobs is profound. Rick Wolff, a professor of economics at the University of Massachusetts, describes the consequences of workers trying to compensate for falling wages in terms that are diabolical:

> In one "solution" to counteract the problem of shrinking real wages, many families sent more members out to work more hours. Part-timers switched to full-time positions or else multiplied part-time jobs to secure more income. Full-timers took second or third jobs. While this helped, in part, to offset the real wage problem, it also disorganized family and household life. Time with spouse and children was cut. So too was the energy and attention adults could devote after work to cope with family problems aggravated by lengthening work times for family members. Rising divorce rates, intra-familial difficulties and abuse, and indices of psychological depression became signs of the costs of this partial "solution."[15]

As sinful as the effects of exploiting cheap domestic and foreign labor are, it does not go unnoticed by God. Craig is humbled by the idea of a just God who ultimately will dispense eternal justice. "To sin against Him and openly defy him, He will hold you accountable." When? I asked. "When He comes again." Craig has no clue as to when that time will be, but he is certain that no one "skates away" unjudged. "While you are here on earth you have the chance to know God. To grow up and mature your faith so that when you get to heaven you are ready for it. You have made your choice." But what of the wealthy sinners who failed to feed, clothe, heal, and befriend the stranger? Craig saw only one dreadful outcome. "Satan was in heaven and He chose not to stay there." Businesses leaders should beware; "it is the responsibility of the rich to help take care of the poor." Craig is remindful that "[f]or the love of money is the root of all evils; it is this craving that some have wandered away from the faith and pierced their hearts with many pangs" (1 Timothy 6:10). Choosing fortune instead of Christian service to others is a sure-fire way to "cross Him" and if you do, Craig whispers, "you should be afraid."

Marilyn Vanden Bout has challenged plenty of injustice in her fifty-odd years of life as a Calvinist. She attends Park Lane Christian Reform Church and has worked at mostly secretarial jobs. She admits that she has "been a rabble rouser for a good long time." Marilyn spent a good part of the Vietnam years signing petitions and marching against the war. But "ours were very quiet and respectful. It was at a time when marches were becoming rough." Marilyn has since faced many situations in her life that she believed were unfair. She has approached each problem just as she did when the nation was at war in Southeast Asia. Her faith has encouraged her to "speak the truth in love." Marilyn has always been mindful of opposing injustice because "we live in a fallen world." Sin, she sadly notes, is everywhere. In her mind "not doing what God wants" is sinful, but Marilyn mostly laments the evil in the world because it is wasteful. Sin is a case of "missing God's best," or "not valuing the people who have been giving their best." She acknowledges that an employer who cut workers' pay to beef up the company's stock market prices would be "missing God's best." Marilyn knowingly adds that this is the kind of evil in society that "builds prisons."

Some people warrior-up against evil, others act kindly in the presence of sin. "I would not stand on a corner and demonstrate," St. Bruno parishioner Lisa Augustyniak explains, because "I don't think I have the gumption to do that." But she has been poor and is certain that poverty is a sin. Lisa has been faithfully bringing her sins and prayers for forgiveness to St. Bruno Catholic Church for many years. In their 2000 study, the Religion in Urban America Program at the University of Illinois at Chicago identified at least nineteen major Catholic institutions on the Southwest Side of Chicago and St. Bruno was the largest parish.[16]

The location was once a classic blue-collar, white-ethnic area very often referred to as a "village" by the person speaking about his or her neighborhood, or section, or parish. While still sporting a blue collar, the area is now much more heavily populated by Hispanic, Arab, and African American residents. Neatly embraced by "small brick bungalows in the middle of Archer Heights," St. Bruno Catholic Church, school, and rectory have been home to countless first- and second-generation immigrant families.[17] Founded in 1923 by a dozen Polish laymen, the parish built its first modern church in 1955 and then added additional buildings twenty years later.

God surely does not abide by a world condition characterized by shameful differences between the haves and have-nots. Lisa's confidence in God's anger at an economically predatory society is confirmed by her favorite spiritual petition, the Lord's Prayer. She silently repeats it numerous times a day while working at her fast-food counter constructing specialty sandwiches for lunchtime customers. Her attraction to the prayer is poetically woven into the verse, "give us this day our daily bread." Donald Spoto, the author of *In Silence, Why We Pray,* understands the powerfully obligatory force of the prayer's seven words. "The gospels are clear that Jesus of Nazareth, who fed the hungry and healed the sick, took human need seriously and sought to alleviate want and suffering," and, most important, Spoto continues, "our daily bread includes everything that people require for sustaining life—not just as individuals but as a community, aware of one another's needs."[18] So how does a faithful Lisa Augustyniak provide "daily bread" to others?

> First of all, I think that He is upset that there are not more people out there helping each other instead of saying me, me, me. If you stop to think about what it means when you help somebody else, I think it all comes full circle. When you help this person, that person will help another person and it is going to turn into a chain of thoughts. You could have started that chain twenty years ago and it could take twenty or thirty years to come back to you. But no matter what you do, everything comes back to you and full circle. If you help that person then somebody down the road is going to end up helping you when you need it. Last summer I was out driving with my girlfriend and there was a guy there with a baby who said that he would work for food "to feed my child." We were stopped at the light and my girlfriend told me to leave him alone because we did not know what kind of a person he is. I told her that he had a baby. I want to give him something. If he uses it for drugs or alcohol or whatever, then he is the one that is going to have to do the

answering [to God], not me. So I called him over and gave him $5. He was so appreciative. He went right to the Burger King and got his kid a sandwich. Come to find out, the guy lives two blocks away from me. He always saw my car parked out in front of my house. A couple of weeks later, I go outside to go to work and there was a note on my car door. I opened the note and it was from him with the $5 that I had given him. He gave me back the money. So it came back to me full circle. I think that God's divine plan is for everybody to help each other.

Some of the faithful would become part of God's plan by politically organizing to advocate for the poor. "The polity in the United States is perceived as a human-made 'fabric,'" according to David Gutterman, "and it is the responsibility of citizens to consciously seek to mend, rather than further rend, this tapestry."[19] In this framework, social and political engagement are necessary to overcome the ills of "triumphant materialism."[20] Lisa, however, is willing and spiritually called to feed the needy one sandwich at a time. Either way, the sin of poverty does not wait for God's judgment.

Like Lisa, Carol and Hank Schuberth have never felt "at home" in a world of social inequality. They have lived in the Ashburn neighborhood of Chicago for nearly fifty years and that is just a few less than they have been married. In that time they raised eight kids on Carol's grit and dedication to family, and on Hank's job as a telephone installer in the city. Both believe that God protected and strengthened their marriage to withstand the demands of raising children and living faithful Christian lives. Brought up in "good Catholic" households, Carol and Hank believed that living as Jesus taught in the Gospels meant having children, loving your spouse, worshiping regularly (at St. Denis), keeping God's commandments, and doing what the Son of God did. "We have to fight the injustice" is how Carol explained her and Hank's involvement in social justice issues. Hank added simply "that is what His [Jesus'] life was all about." While nearly all of the working-class Christians I spoke with held the same understanding of Jesus' life, few had actually stood up to abusive power the way that the Schuberths had.

Carol and Hank were not strangers to social activism. When in 1966 Martin Luther King Jr. took his Poor People's Campaign to Chicago, the Schuberths were there marching in Marquette Park when the civil rights leader was stoned by racists. But these were not all anonymous race haters. Many came from the same neighborhood of working-class bungalows with statues of the Virgin Mary sitting in the middle of small, green front yards where the Schuberths lived. Good Catholics actually, like Carol and

Hank, who threatened to kill Carol and Hank for fighting racism. Jesus knew the cost of his social criticism and was undeterred. The Schuberths, too, were courageous disciples.

> HANK: [Jesus] did not think it was beneath Him to sit down and have a meal with someone that others look down upon. He told the story of working with the Samaritans and about the man that was beaten along the side of the road. The priest came along and looked at the beaten man but then continued on his way. It was the Samaritan who took the beaten man to an inn and paid the inn keeper to bring the man to health. That is a powerful story.
>
> CAROL: [Jesus] was always for the outcasts of society. He always tried to approach them and help them. He tried to point that out to others as well that this is what they should be doing.
>
> *Who would be the outcast today?*
>
> HANK: I think you would have to think of the homeless to begin with.
>
> CAROL: The outcasts were those of a different race. Those of a different color. A different language. Anybody who does not fit into the "normal" society of people.
>
> HANK: Bigotry—that is probably the biggest problem [in the world].

Along with being good Catholics, Carol and Hank were also children of good union people. They had union electricians and pipe fitters in their families, and being religious was perfectly consistent with owning a union card. When I asked Hank whether he could be true to his faith and be antiunion, he answered, "That would be very difficult." Carol added that "the union was definitely aligned with social justice." The Schuberths once again lived out their faith when Hank and 699,000 other telephone workers went on strike for twenty-two days against AT&T in 1983. It was an experience that permitted them both to better understand Jesus' ministry among the underclass.

> CAROL: It was very difficult. We were put in the position of having to support the strike and marching and it was something that we had to do because with our marching and striking, it was letting the public know what was happening with the company.

HANK: I carried my son Bob on my shoulders because he had a broken foot at the time. We took all of the children down to where they were walking around the telephone building with picket signs.

CAROL: We did not feel that we were getting decent wages and that we had to work too many hours for it. [Jesus] taught us to look out for the poor. For those who do not make a decent wage or have benefits.

HANK: I cannot imagine how His message [i.e., sermon] on the Mount rang through the hearts and souls of the people listening. That must have been so uplifting to the people who lived in His shadow.

The Schuberths' willingness to take their faith into the streets does not represent the practice of a majority of parishioners at St. Denis (or of any congregation in this study), but it certainly did reflect the way an active group of religious white, black, and Hispanic-Latino folks reacted to injustice. Fighting racism in Marquette Park and refusing to cross union picket lines is also perfectly consistent with the gospel message and political activism of the parish's onetime pastor Father Larry Dowling.[21] Recognized by civic, labor, and religious advocates alike as the "social justice priest," Dowling preaches and practices a liturgy of collective salvation. He hears God's message of community building clearly in the textual terms of the Communion prayer. "The Eucharistic prayer states that *we* are the body of Christ, may *we bring one another* to life eternal" (emphasis in original). Pastor Larry, as many of his parishioners refer to him, placed the emphasis on the word "we" as the "body of Christ" and on "we" as bringing about "life eternal." In Dowling's Catholicism there was no individual path to God.

The pastor's call to his parishioners to "preserve the human dignity of others" by opposing injustice was robustly turned into action during the intense debate that occurred throughout the spring of 2006 over a Republican Party congressional proposal to criminalize illegal immigrants and anyone who brings them comfort. Appalled by what he viewed as a mean-spirited and evil response to the scriptural "stranger," Dowling joined a contingent of priests in holding a rally outside the Illinois office of Republican Congressman and House Majority Leader Dennis Hastert. Disappointed by Hastert's refusal to meet with the clerics, they decided that they would fast until a meeting was scheduled. Coincidentally, the unplanned fast would take place during the Jewish Passover and Christian Holy Week. Dowling became the group's spokesperson. "It's partly coincidental that we are fasting during Holy Week, but I feel like it's also providence." St. Denis's "worker priest" did not fail to see the opportunity to unite the suffering and crucifixion of Christ with the treatment of immigrant workers. "It gives a sense of being in solidarity with those who carry the cross and also thinking about carrying the cross of Christ."[22]

St. Bruno parishioners Jim and Susan Stewart also feel the weight of Christ's cross. Jim is an affable man in his late thirties who most recently had done some work as an insurance agent, but was unemployed when we spoke. Susan, who is a few years younger, was working as a client service agent for a credit reporting firm. Both siblings were eager to talk about injustice, evil, and sin. Jim agreed that "lining your own pockets" and "companies shutting down and merging and doing stuff just for a buck" is sinful. Corporate heads "are making a profit, but we are laying thousands of people off or folding [businesses] or merging so that they [i.e., CEOs and stockholders] have an even higher lifestyle." Speaking also for his sister, Jim went on to recite a familiar story of greed. "We look at it this way: if your profit one year was $60 million and then the following year it went down to $40 million, these people [CEOs] will actually lay off people. [But] they are still turning a profit . . . they are wrong." In addition to greed generating economic inequality, there are other dire behavioral challenges to God's message. Jim stresses that he is terribly offended by "the legalization and outright acceptance of homosexuality," and Susan caps his remark by insisting "that [homosexuality] degrades the morals of our country." Both St. Bruno working-class Catholics are equally troubled by the "acceptance in a nation that greed is wonderful" and where "abortion and having a child out of wedlock are no big deal." Jim and Susan are genuinely outraged by a multidimensional ring of sinful behavior. I asked them what their faith compelled them to do to oppose these twin injustices. "Pray. Pray on it," Jim quickly answered, and then he added, "[D]o your best to make sure that you get out and vote to elect the proper official." The Stewarts and I acknowledged—a bit cynically—that prayer seemed to offer the more coherent, consistent, and accessible option.

In the presence of injustice, Mennonite Denise Wilson also turns to prayer. Her work in a hospital has exposed her to terribly difficult working conditions that sometimes leave her in impossible moral positions.

> For example, if I gave the wrong medication to a patient we are told [by management] that you will have to worry about getting your own [malpractice] insurance, separately from the hospital. The hospital has their own lawyers but yet they do not make it as clear as to say that if you follow policy that sometimes mistakes happen. Okay, we're human and mistakes happen. But I have seen that they will turn the tables

> and pretty much push it all on the nurses to get the hospital out of any liability. Even though they are not looking at the fact that I was given four patients and I should have had one patient. Okay, I cannot refuse to treat a patent or I will lose my job. Then a mistake happens but they kicked me out there to the wolves. I have seen them do that.

It was not hard for Denise to label the above example of poor patient care and the scapegoating of a worker as a sin. But when Denise also informed me of how the employer reduced the staffing levels at the hospital, thereby dangerously increasing the patient-nurse ratios, her declaration of sin was surprisingly missing. I asked her bluntly, "If not sin, then what?" Denise's reply was repeated often by congregants. "That is just cost effective. They are trying to make money or preserve money." The employer's decision to place profits over quality medical care and fair treatment of workers seemed to violate Jesus' warning against misplaced objects of desire. "No one can serve two masters; for either he will hate the one and love the other, or he will be devoted to the one and despise the other. You cannot serve God and mammon" (Matthew 6:24). Nonetheless, firing an overworked intensive-care nurse for accidentally giving a patient the wrong medication is sinful, but firing nurses who have committed no infractions in order to shore up the hospital's bottom line, thereby creating the opportunities for sin, is just business. Either way, Denise's response to being pushed hard at work is to "pray a little bit harder." "I ask God to help me to be a little bit more focused. In my line of work, I have to work fast but efficiently. So it helps me to key in a little bit better and I am a little sharper." Denise's patients are lucky to have her prayers at their bedside.

Sylvia Wald is a Jewish woman who works as an inventory control clerk at a North Chicago supermarket. She spends most of her scheduled work shift assisting thirty or thirty-five drivers to unload products at the back of the store. She is a member of United Food and Commercial Workers Union (UFCW) Local 1546 and feels blessed to make a decent income. But it is only decent. She sometimes wonders about those whose wealth is indecent. "We [store employees] are gainfully employed, but you have to wonder. Look at those who just went to United Airlines and what did the CEO [Glen Tilton] get when it came out of bankruptcy? Sixteen million dollars!"[23] In mock exasperation Sylvia raises a rhetorical question, "Will I earn sixteen million dollars in my entire lifetime?" But would the CEO's financial windfall be a sin? "It is definitely a sin. I don't think that anybody who went through that [bankruptcy] could honestly take the sixteen million dollars knowing that somebody else further down on the totem pole who is actually working [gets nothing]."

Taking the wealth earned by others is theft. Cheating a worker out of the value of their labor is a sin. While it is a simple ethical precept for Sylvia to understand, she has her doubts that corporate leaders are influenced by matters of sin. "Do I think that anyone in big business thinks that the little peons that are employed have any sense of it [of being wronged]? No, I do not." Despite her condemnation of sinful business practices, Sylvia is not advocating any corrective action. In her view, bad as some employers can be, the best option a person has is to either quit her job or just put up with the hurt. But that does not mean that justice is forsaken. Sylvia is willing to tolerate a highly unequal distribution of wealth in American society because "God has a sense of it." Sylvia is not a Torah reader, but if she were, the following verse in Exodus may have, with a little adaptation, summed up her disapproval of corporate greed: "If you take your neighbor's cloak [the employees' labor] as a security for a loan [bank refinancing], you must return it before sunset [when work resumes]. This coat [workers' jobs, incomes, pensions] may be the only blanket [economic security] your neighbor has. How can a person sleep [survive or retire] without it?" (Exodus 22:26–27). Will God punish those responsible for not returning the wealth to those who have earned it? Sylvia is uncertain how to answer the question: "If it is part of the master plan, yes." But I worried about what happens to the corporate sinful if eternal damnation is not their fate. "In that case," Sylvia shrugged, "it is the way it is supposed to be." How fortunate that would be for Tilton.

"I have witnessed it," Our Lord and Savior of Jesus Christ congregant Cheryl Lawrence confidently answered when asked "Is God a God of justice?" In Cheryl's case God's intervention avoided a sin of commission. "There are some people who have really done wrong to me. I asked God to handle this for me because I wanted to strike out against them." Instead of attempting to even a score by committing an un-Christian act of revenge, Cheryl remained still. "He then removed things from them [the wrongdoers] and did things in a way that now they look back and tell me that they are sorry. He has made people come back to me and ask how I am doing and ask if they can help me. They have come back to help me knowing that they have wronged me." According to Cheryl, her faith in God allowed God's justice to transform the hearts of her antagonists. But how long should a person wait for justice to be done? "Everything happens in God's time."

The Church of Our Lord and Savior Jesus Christ pastor Reginald McCracken was not hesitant in his depiction of God's judgment: "Vengeance is mine, saith the Lord." Pastor McCracken is a preacher gifted in Bible verse and street vernacular. While McCracken is not a seminary-trained man of the cloth, his experience defending workers in a unionized workplace has given him a unique view of what scripture teaches.[24] As he sees it, "what so ever a man soweth, that he shall also reap," or put another way, "when you do these acts what goes around comes around." McCracken is not waiting for God to do justice on some unknown Judgment Day. He clarifies for me that "[w]hat you reap of the spirit, you shall deal with in the spirit," but "of what you shall reap of the flesh, you shall deal with in the flesh." In the "spirit" alludes to a predicted religious time when all people are shorn of their bodies and come before God as pure souls. In the "flesh," however, means while our bones and muscles are firmly attached. This is not a view of a God who waits for our death to punish the evildoers and to reward the righteous. Injustice happens in our neighborhoods, schools, workplaces, voting booths, and halls of government. What does God want the faithful to do about such earthly wrongdoing?

Florence Joseph, Cheryl Lawrence, and Angela Blunt are all Church of Our Lord and Jesus Christ congregants. Their comments on witnessing injustice are illustrative of a cognitive split between a robust belief in the nature of sin, but a caution as to what Christians should actually do about *someone else's* unchristian behavior. Florence, for instance, is not quick to judge or to act. She contends that in the company of sinful behavior her faith leads her to "close her mouth and control her tongue." Her patience to act, however, does not grow out of an uncertainly about sin. Sin, according to Florence, is as common as holding a "bad thought against someone." Cheryl prefers "to stand still and wait to see what happens" when someone does wrong. She confesses to being prone to "always want to put [her] hands in the pot and fix it first." Angela, on the other hand, cautions that "what we need is patience . . . that most of God's children do not have patience." The consensus approach from these three women appears to be that their faith foremost compels them, as Cheryl put it, to "let God work it out."

Each believer attests to a relatively passive version of her obligation as Christian witness to injustice. No doubt the women are in part restrained by the knowledge that it is dangerous to act out of anger and before thinking through the situation. It is also certainly helpful to take in wise counsel before acting. But while each believer was adamant about confessing her own sins and condemning those of others, she did not express a corresponding Christian charge to fight injustice. More succinctly, there was no obligation to fight all injustice. The workplace proved to be a fascinating and common location in which a difference played out. For example, letting someone in authority know that another employee had stolen the employer's property (a definite sin) was the "Christian thing to do." But when these working-class people of faith self-defined the withdrawal of health benefits by a profitable employer or the refusal to provide affordable insurance coverage (i.e., Wal-Mart) as a sin, they also hesitated to commit to any action. As will be discussed later in this chapter, with few exceptions, congregants of all faith traditions responded to employer injustice more like bystanders than followers of Christ, Allah, or Hessham.

Caroline Garcia, however, has little patience for passivity in the face of injustice. Garcia attends Immaculate Conception Catholic Church on Chicago's south side. She is a Latina parishioner, but in the 1880s a growing number of Polish immigrants churned into Chicago's South Side steel mill district seeking a mutual aide association that would support the worldly needs of working-class immigrants and a way to sustain their deeply Catholic loyalties. Talk of organizing a neighborhood parish found enthusiastic local supporters and one week before Christmas in 1881, the Catholic bishop of Chicago contracted with the Calumet and Chicago Central and Dock Company District to purchase a piece of land. The next year Immaculate Conception Church of the Blessed Virgin Mary was founded.[25]

The original eastern European "[f]ounders of the parish of Immaculate Conception B.V.M. came to south Chicago to work in what some day would become one of America's major industries, steel."[26] But during the1950s and 1960s, a shifting ethnic mix of South side residents reconfigured the church's racial, language, and cultural identity. While Poles s till represented the largest single contingent of congregants, Mexican and, to a smaller extent, black believers were assuming a growing presence in the church. Sadly, the 1950s also saw the death of the church's beloved pastor, Reverend F. M. Wojtalewicz. After his death, the *Chicago Daily News* wrote how Wojtalewicz had "helped thousands of workers as emigrants to adjust themselves to American life and had been their mediator in industrial disputes." The *New World* went even further in citing the pastor's pro-worker credentials by declaring that Wojtalewicz was "the unofficial working delegate of the workingman before the union became strong."[27]

In the early 1980s, Immaculate Conception was a church of 1,500 families, with Spanish-speaking families having replaced Polish attendees as the church's dominant group.[28] The trend toward a largely minority congregation continued unabated throughout the rest of the century. The church also saw a change in the class composition of its congregants. Working-class congregants still fill the pews at Sunday mass, but the loss of union manufacturing jobs has also increased the numbers of attendees dependent on public assistance. On my visits in the winter of 2005, worship services at Immaculate Conception were conspicuously devoid of men in suits and ties, and women in heels and furs. Jeans, sweatshirts, sweatpants, leather vests, union logo and American eagle VFW–emblazoned jackets, and keys dangling from the belt buckles of men and women alike were the garments of the liturgical season.

Caroline Garcia has worked the past two years as a loan processing clerk in a bank. She has an intense grasp of the burdens of her faith. "I'm telling you, you have to have a very strong faith to stand up for what you believe in." Caroline's faith is not a wilting or easily forgiving Christianity. She sees it as a Christian obligation "to not let an injustice go by you or look the other way." Society has too many problems, too many people hurting other people, to tolerate a "turn the other cheek" attitude. How, she asks, can you justify a national minimum wage that at the time of our discussion was only $5.15? It was also at a fifty-year low when adjusted for inflation and before a 2007 increase, the first in ten years.[29] Caroline does not intend to leave the matter of human suffering to God. "Let God" is not a principle she finds appropriate when someone is in need. In her theology, tolerating the evil done by others is an accommodation with sin, and if indifference becomes widespread, "how is this world going to survive?" Worse yet, using your religious beliefs to justify not confronting societal wrongs can only have a terrible consequence: "[W]e will have another Hitler in our society."

Avoiding responsibility for tolerating the existence or solicitation of a great evil was also a compelling religious commandment for Sudanese-born Muslim cabbie Muhammad Abdallah. "It is very important that we do the right thing[s] and do them honestly and God will not punish us." God's retribution was promised to Abdallah and loomed large in his consideration of his own behavior. "There are true believers of Allah but people make mistakes. If, however, you are not a good follower of the book [Qur'an], you will be punished by God." Evading the temptation to act sinfully was also accompanied by an equal duty to perform acts of kindness. "It is a commitment to whatever faith tells me to do—help the animals, help the environment, to do good deeds and not to forget Allah at any time."

Abdallah stressed that the prophet Muhammad had taught him to be attentive to the needs of others. "Some of the ways in which we do good is by sharing whatever we have." He cites an example of generosity that many cab fares would not expect. "Some of the passengers that we carry do not have money and we let them ride. Many times this happens." I inquired why taxi drivers didn't just call dispatch and try to collect the fare? "It is the thing, what goes around, comes around. One day maybe you will be in a situation." Religious scholar Karen Armstrong cites the Qur'an as issuing a "clear social command: men and women must look after the disadvantaged people in their tribe."[30] Abdallah must then learn to do as Allah did: "Did He not find thee an orphan, and shelter thee? Did He not find thee erring, and guide thee? Did He not find thee needy, and suffice thee?"[31]

Acting to perpetuate at most a just society or at least a less corrosive one also justified a cabdriver demanding greater pay for his work. Abdallah saw no religious conflict between demanding fair treatment of his employer and being faithful to Allah. "In terms of being fired or any forms of injustice, you have a duty to resist. You cannot compromise with injustice." And risking firing was not too high a price to pay for resisting. Abdallah did make certain that I understood that resisting should not be done in hatred or with a mean spirit. "You must do it with kindness." But if after jumping through "the hoops . . . there is anything wrong, whether it is a crime or the pay, you have a duty to correct it." Abdallah's duty was grounded in a Muslim commitment to create a just society that reflected God's will. To turn away from the wrongs you have witnessed was not just an abrogation of personal duty, but a further sin against God's plan for the world. Karen Armstrong points out that Islam has been considered by scholars a "religion of social justice."[32] It appears that within the confines of a four-wheeled sedan, Abdallah is trying to earn a living in the most righteous manner possible.

Pakistan-born Azmat Ali was also adamant that Islam required all Muslims to work for a better society. Ignoring the pain of others, he mused, must certainly be a sin. Armstrong has declared that treating the vulnerable decently is the "bedrock of the Qur'anic message." While Muhammad did not condemn wealth and possessions as Jesus did, Armstrong points out that the resource rich "must be generous with their wealth and give a regular proportion of their income to the poor."[33] Ali explains that almsgiving (*zakat*) became one of the five essential pillars (*rulen*) of Islam because Allah demanded a social code of honor. To ignore the needs of others was to tempt God's wrath: "woe to the idolaters who pay not the alms, and disbelieve in the world to come."[34] On the other hand, Ali understood the blessings of contributing to a just order: "Surely those who believe, and do righteous deeds shall have a wage unfailing."[35]

While grocery store butcher Sherwin Epstein knows little of any Jewish ethical codes, he does believe that God wants him to act justly. Most of the time that means just being respectful to others, but sometimes more is needed. Take work, for example. There have been times at work when Sherwin felt that people were not being treated right and to stay silent would have allowed evil to be done. "They [managers] do not look at individuals, they just give you a number and they say that this is what we have to have done and it will be done." Bossing is taken a bit too far when it becomes lording over a worker. "Some people just go and totally disrespect the employee and try to browbeat you to get those numbers [corporate performance goals]." In situations of worker abuse in the name of sales, what does Sherwin Epstein's faith ask of him? "I used to go off semi-physically, verbally," but now at a more mature age in his life Sherwin just goes "through the union and let[s] them handle the situations."

Sherwin's reliance on the union is consistent with Talmudic teachings on the employer-employee relationship. While Jewish law warns that "whoever disregards the instructions of his employer is called a robber," the employer has the responsibility of fairly directing the employees. And not paying workers what they have rightly earned is "condemned as a heinous sin and rebuked unsparingly." Rabbinical teachers noted that failure to compensate in a timely fashion actually "transgresses five commandments of the Torah."[36] In order to correct the abuse, Sherwin's union acts to balance the obligations and rights of employers and employees. "The union, in looking out for the individual worker, is controlling the evil" that appears as a mad rush to satisfy store production quotas. Even good supervisors are corrupted by market pressures. In situations like these, then, Sherwin sees a faith-based role for the union. "Yeah, I believe that God would look upon the union and be happy with them." Sherwin then adds an important added endorsement. While acknowledging that going to synagogue is probably the best way "to do God's work," Sherwin stresses that when it comes to correcting wrongs in the workplace, "the union is doing its fair share."

Barry Blaustein sees the evil seduction of wealth and knows injustice is in the world. He supervises a kosher kitchen for a major grocery chain store and understands the large consumer market for correctly prepared foods. As a *masgiach* (i.e., Orthodox kosher supervisor), Barry recognizes the moneymaking potential of catering to people with religious, ethnic, or cultural dietary requirements. "These people [company executives and owners] are multi-multimillionaires, and even if it is a small profit, they are doing huge figures. With the kosher market in the store, they said in a meeting the other day amongst the workers that we were number three in all the stores in total sales." Barry is proud of his contribution to the company's bottom line, but working hard has not earned him his just due. "I don't feel the system [is fair]; see in one way corporate America utilizes you and milks you for everything and then they say that they compensate you, but they really do not compensate you in the way that you should be compensated." How would Barry like to be compensated? "I am not talking a communistic or socialistic sense, but you have the CEO of the company who makes millions of dollars a year. Okay, I can dig it if he makes a million, but also he gets benefits and bonuses based on that! Two years ago he made thirty million and now he is trying to get fifty million. There is too much disparity from these guys in management positions to the guy who's really in the trenches and doing the business of work. Look at the social stratus today . . . the middle class is going down and the upper class is getting richer and richer. I feel that we should be making almost double what we make because I cannot live off what they pay us."

The symbolism could not be starker: management guys safely ensconced in cushy positions way above the proletarian grunts toiling away in trenches, producing the world's wealth. Perhaps not in the "communistic or socialistic sense," but Barry sure sounded like a Marxist critic of American capitalism. I was certain that Barry must have believed that gross wealth disparity was a sin. Surprisingly, he said, "No, it's not a sin." As a "man of the book" with seven formal years of rabbinical study, Barry was well aware of Jewish laws governing the proper treatment of workers. According to David S. Ariel, rabbinical prohibitions against unfair economic advantage were "likened to encroaching upon a neighbor's property."[37] What, according to Barry, could possibly remove the stain of sin from appropriating the wealth created by others? "You have to be cold. It is not that you are not a good person or that, don't think these guys are bad people, they're just businessmen." No one to Barry's knowledge has broken any laws. People are working and making decent wages. The store is unionized and workers have their rights protected. Most important to Barry, the company is selling a good and needed product with important religious meaning to Jewish consumers. The fact that a CEO pockets millions and millions more than a *masgiach* is nothing more than the spoils of hard-nosed for-profit business practices. True, workers are taken advantage of, but there is apparently no sin in making someone else wealthy.

Evil impulses, on the other hand, do exist, but Barry's faith demands that he maintain a respectful distance. "If I really felt that corporate America was dealing me a bad hand . . . [well,] a person has the choice to do what he wants. But Jewish communities are not made up of missionaries." Orthodox Judaism has inspired Barry to respond to injustice by acting as an honest, dignified man, "as a role model for customers and my family." It is important to Barry that he be respected by his fellow men. But within his faith there does not appear to be any obligation to resist injustice. Instead, "do no harm" prevails uppermost as a guiding behavioral principle. Barry acknowledges that the Talmud makes clear that a "wrong done to a fellow man was an offense against God . . . more serious than the breach of a precept which affected only the relationship between man and his Maker."[38] So Barry avoids doing wrong and trusts that God's judgment will avenge the harmed.

Renee and Jim Pletsch of St. Denis Parish want to do more with their lives than avoid sin. They desire to actively resist injustice, but admit to feeling individually powerless. Renee works as a receptionist and was furious at the way her employer forced a more expensive health-care plan on the employees. She has also taken note of how employees who complained about conditions at work are treated.

> There are people who have gotten fired. [Management] takes them out of the room and they take them out the back door and I see them leaving. They are being escorted out by security guards. Some of these people have been there a long time. They will have a security guard waiting for someone to have an outburst. They do not want that. They do not want us stirring up anything or any problems. They did not want any kind of reaction. They work at getting the troublemakers out of there quickly. They will tell us the reason for the person leaving was because of this or that, but we know.

Renee is faith inspired to speak out, but understandably explains "that as individuals we can't do that."

"It is really hard," adds her husband, Jim, "because if you step forward, you are not just affecting yourself; you are affecting your children and your wife." As a truck driver, Jim is hopeful that his Teamster union local will provide him with the best opportunity to correct workplace injustices. He would like to see the union "take a more Christian or a more moral righteous standpoint in their negotiations when they are dealing with these companies." Jim expresses a common religious dilemma: "I still want to protect my own family and yet be able to help myself and my co-workers. That is really the hard past." And, unlike Jesus, he admits that "I am not courageous enough to risk everything." Renee points out that "[Jesus] stood up to injustice [and] I think that we are here to get out and stand up for one another and to support one another. That is the message that He gives to me." Jim and Renee believe that as Christians they should help create the just society that Jesus gave his life for. But finding the way to share in carrying the cross without falling under its weight is the challenge.

Defending workers against the sin of abusive employer behavior is best mitigated by the presence of an effective union. But workplace injustices can also be tempered by a foreman or low-level supervisor with a strong sense of ethics. Mennonite Community Church member Chuck Kozlowsky worked for a while as a maintenance supervisor at O'Hare Airport. His job required him to oversee the work of a number of janitors and, according to his wife, Gwen, there were a lot of times when he had to "stick up for the man who was being abused." Chuck was not apologetic about admitting that he "was very much for the workers' rights." There was one particular occasion where his "Christ-like" behavior nearly got him fired.

> This one custodian we had would always be taking a break for a cigarette or something, and my manager would always walk by and see he wasn't working. He kept on about it and I kept saying "I'll take care of it. The man's getting his work done." And he was. And [my manager] came in one day ranting and raving about the custodian and I said, "I have more important things to talk about than foolishness and if you don't like it I'm going home." So I stayed home for two weeks.

Chuck may have been the extraordinary supervisor who was willing to risk his own economic status to defend a lowly worker. But in his mind there is nothing uncommon about his Christian principles. Speaking of his wife's and his own faith, he said, "You'd have to have action to back up your belief and I hope that's what we are doing, we are backing up our belief."

Barbara Lee has endured twenty-seven years as a food service worker for United Airlines. In her career she has seen a lot of unfortunate and painful changes to the workplace. Most of her experiences have been good, but in the last ten years the workplace has become more unjust. "I was only troubled by [the company] hiring people and giving them less money because the people didn't feel good about the job, that they were working beside me and we were doing the same work but they weren't getting paid as much." Barbara worships at the Community Mennonite Church in Markham and easily recognizes the divine throughout her day. But she has come to doubt that God is present at United. "I thought He was absent because after a while you're just a number, you know, just people coming in and it got so it was a fast turnover." Barbara's response to United's coarsening labor relations was to basically "keep to myself because a lot of times, I felt if you would blow up and speak out it might not be [in] your best interest." But was not speaking out, even though she had the protection of a union, consistent with her faith? Barbara had never really thought about it before, but offered that God would assure that people "got their due." In the meantime, Barbara would "pray and mostly be quiet about it."

St. Denis parishioner Laura Dawson prefers a God of mercy to a God of justice. Why? "Because justice is what we deserve and I do not think I deserve a whole lot of goodness. But mercy is unmerited and I think that most of us could say there are a lot of things that we do that requires God's mercy." Laura feels undeserving because she believes that the Bible declares that everyone is a "sinner and has fallen short of the glory and the grace of God." But Laura acknowledges that it is also the Bible that educates her as to what is a just or unjust action. So what does her faith require of her when she experiences injustice? "Sometimes I pray." Sometimes she does not. "I must be honest, though, sometimes I'm so overloaded I ignore it." Laura is frank to admit that "if it involves a telephone call, I will do something about it," but sadly, there are "so many different things that need to be done everyday." Laura's faith is the basis upon which she determines right from wrong and good from bad, but always acting in a righteous way to "comfort the afflicted" is more complicated. "So many things are wrong and I could get overwhelmed and I have to pick and choose and it's not always which one is bigger or better, but which one you have the time to take care of right now or which one speaks the most closely to you."

On the other hand, Laura has found that acting against injustice can be as simple as personal witnessing. "If you felt someone sinned against you, as a believer you should go to the person privately and talk to them about the sin." By her accounting, a sin is a form of injustice and Laura saw some obligation to address the sinner. So what was Laura's definition of a sin? Surprisingly, Laura had a hard time answering and never really clearly defined it, but her musings suggest a definition that went beyond personal behavior. "I know there are societal sins like racism which is embedded in our society, corporate sin maybe when they are putting their own profits above the welfare of the people, so that could be a sin." And if there are "societal" and "corporate" sins, are they to be condemned in the same way that the Ten Commandments proscribe human transgressions?[39] Laura believed so but was not always sure how to proceed. For example, she had recently witnessed a clerk at a retail store make some "very racist comments about Arab American people and it really" bothered her. This incident seemed to Laura to be a case of "bearing false witness against your neighbor" (Exodus 20:16). "So, I went home and the next day called the store manager. I didn't want this woman [employee] to be fired but just wanted the manager to know."

A phone call was something Laura could do about a personal act of prejudice. But what should a Christian do about "white-collar" corporate sins, such as firing workers who want to join a union or like Enron, stealing retirement income from employees?[40] Office assistant Bernice Feltz, who attends St. Bruno Catholic Church, was quick to condemn the Enrons of the world. "You have a company like Enron where these people were so greedy that they were falsifying their documents. Is it a sin when the company falls apart and these people lose their job? Yes, that is a sin. Can you put Enron in hell? No, but you can put the people [in hell] who were up there and did this for greed." In this instance, Bernice believed that God would severely punish "these creeps," but exactly what she should do as a *Catholic* about corporate abuse was unclear. Laura Dawson also believed that corporate actions violated the commandments given to Moses, but nonetheless, "I do not do the simple things, like signing a petition when I feel strongly about it." She shyly notes that in the Catholic Church "there are sins of omission and I have a lot of these."

Pat Glatz also believes in a merciful and forgiving God. To her, a God of justice "sounds too much like punishment and retribution." Still, her faith is the primary guide to distinguish evil from all things holy. Her faith has inspired Pat to be active in various neighborhood organizations and she has done advocacy work around homelessness and community safety. Having an ethical and moral guidepost, however, does not guarantee a doable course of action. Pat knows when wrong has been committed, but her faith does not proscribe a particular response. "I don't do marches or picketing, I don't do that kind of stuff." Pat's religious catechism was something she fondly recalled as she chuckled over how the idea of sin was first conveyed to her. "Sin for me is still wrapped up in those milk bottle pictures. Mortal sin [very bad; the worst kind] was the milk bottle that was colored black and a venial sin [bad, but not real bad] is a spotty grayish kind of thing." The pictures of bottled sin help Pat to discern two degrees of ungodly behavior. But no matter the level of sin, faith mostly compelled Pat to live as a good example to others. She believes that she should be kind and act justly. However, while her God loudly pleads to feed the poor, God's directive on how to keep people in a land of plenty from ever becoming hungry is unthinkable. Pat noted that when Jesus was asked what "good deed must I do to have eternal life," he answered that to be perfectly fit for God's kingdom a person needed to "sell what you possess and give to the poor" (Matthew 19:16–22). According to Pat, God is not saying that wealth or material possessions are bad, but "that if you have these things, frequently people tend to get caught up on them, in their own world." Instead, Jesus taught that people should be "using their status or wealth for good things." But what happens when wealth or status are the product of greed or doing abusive things to the environment, or to other people? What should a working-class Christian like Pat do? The answer depends on whether or not wealth is a consequence of sin.

Sin, in turn, depends on the motives of the person or people or employer responsible for the wealth-accumulating action. If, for instance, a business had to lay off workers or cut their pay in order to remain profitable, then that would be a sound business decision and not a sin. But if employers cut worker benefits "so that they can get a raise themselves" or like the Ford Motor Company enjoy a $250 million tax break in 2004 despite cutting 10,000 jobs, then that would be sinful. The distinction workers drew between honestly earned benefits and ill-gotten gains was reflected in the following Proverb: "Better is a little with righteousness than great revenues with injustice" (16:8).[41] Rudy Ramirez attends Immaculate Conception Catholic Church and pointed out that underpaying a worker was also sinful behavior. Ramirez worked as a food service aide in a hospital. He was not certain of the biblical passage, but believed that "the wording says that we are to be justly paid." Perhaps it was the following one from Genesis:

> So Jacob sent word to Rachel and Leah to come out to the fields where his flocks were. He said to them, "I see that your father's attitude toward me is not what it was before, but the God of my father has been with me. You know that I've worked for your father with all my strength, yet your father has cheated me by changing my wages ten times. However, God has not allowed him to harm me." (Genesis 31:4–7)

Sin to Pat Glatz was "doing what you know in your heart is wrong." Still left unresolved, however, is what Pat or any good Christian should do about sins of the heart that cause thousands of workers to lose their health care, pensions, and jobs. It turns out that Pat did know of one suitable defense against the lust for Mammon. As a unionized Chicago public school teacher, Pat had been out on strike more than once in her career. Was striking an appropriate Christian response to her workplace grievances? "It did not bother me because teachers need to stand up for what they feel." Pat went further and proudly noted that she was "not a scab that was crossing picket lines." Pat may not walk picket lines, but she honors them as if they were sacred. She is not one to thunder against injustice, but believes that sin requires a response. To many working-class believers the "uneven ground" need not wait for God's second coming to become "level" (Isaiah 40:4).

Park Lane Christian Reform congregant Andy Schutt drove a cement truck for nearly forty years and the road experience cleared up any doubt about the possibility of a sinful employer. Andy was a lifelong Teamster member and recalls a number of strikes in the late 1960s and early 1970s.

One particular work stoppage lasted nine weeks. I asked him whether on this occasion there was anything inconsistent with acting Christ-like and going on strike? "No, no, no!" Andy was adamant about his response because he believed that there were times when the company's behavior was sinful. "So often they [the employer] forget that the working man or the man on the bottom is really the strength and the health of the company." Forgetting that simple truth was, according to Andy, the biggest reason why employers sinned against their workers. "I feel that if you are working for an organization, then you are part of the organization and you have to be fair and do your job right to the best of your ability and then you should be treated fairly." Simply put, Andy stood up as a Christian worker against moments of employer injustice and "when the strike was over we did have better working conditions; along came a pension and health plans, too." Sin is an affront to God and God expects that "what was done wrong has to be righted." It's a gospel that Andy has practiced.

Katie Jordan has spread the "Good News" of Christ's salvific resurrection in workplaces all over Chicago. She has been a minister for righteousness without portfolio. And most of her godly work has come not in the form of preaching the good word, but in being an instrument to do the right thing. Katie's workplace experiences have showed her the evil that men are capable of doing. In her life, garment shops were the places where men most often sinned against God. It was in the relationship between an immigrant woman working at a sewing machine and the employer's compulsion to "sweat" her laborers that God's promise of salvation was made real. Katie knew a God of justice that "cared no more for one than the other." Despite the shameful gap between the earnings of the company boss and the needle trades worker, Katie explained that "He himself had not chosen any particular person to have it all." A just God demands equity. "Why does this one have all the money? It is not because God wished that one person have more . . . God wants me to do well as much [as] he wants anyone else." But in manufacturing and tailoring garments, principles of profit took precedent over the egalitarianism that flows from creation "in the image of God" (Genesis 1:27).

If it was in the process of making textile goods that caused men to sin, then by God's will it was in that process when they would be forced to repent. As a union leader Katie negotiated labor agreements. "In my shop when we would start talking about negotiations and what it is that we wanted to ask for, I would tell the women to go home and pray about it and God will give you some insight." Once at work, calling on God for help continued. "We used to have some group Bible sessions at noontime. We would read passages and see what it was saying to us pertaining to our work." Katie added the word of God to her formal labor education and directed the women she worked with to be as Old Testament prophets. "I would say to them that the mind is speaking to us through someone else and there may be something in this scripture that is meant for me and you might be the one that finds it." Once finding the inspiration that God provided, the union would go, like the prophet Daniel, into the employer's lion's den. "There were times when it was so bad that all the employers were asking the union locals to give something back in the negotiations . . . but we never gave back anything that we negotiated for our people and who makes a way for that?" As Katie explained it: "God sent his angel and shut the lions' mouths."[42]

To Katie, God's will is unyielding. But God's plan must find a willing carrier; an agent to act justly. In Katie's description of God she underlines the source of her capacity to act against injustice. "I describe God as being a power within myself; a spirit within me." Here is a willful, forceful God, a Spirit that inspires action and calls out for justice. "He said that we are made in his image and that God does all of His work through me—not just me alone—but through people." But the work of God requires an initiative that not everyone has. "We ourselves can stifle the power of God, because when we sit and He prompts us we don't always hear. When we don't respond, the power of Him in us is not reflected." Katie's commitment to social justice advocacy is her response to God's concern for those oppressed in their daily labors.

According to biblical text, God first speaks to Moses about the abuse of the Israelites at the hands of their work foremen: "So they made the people of Israel serve with rigor, and made their lives bitter with hard service, in mortar and brick and in all kinds of work in the field" (Exodus 2:13–14). But God assured Moses that "I have seen the affliction of my people who are in Egypt, and have heard their cry on account of their taskmasters" (Exodus 3:7–8). Darren Cushman Wood interprets the Exodus that follows as the "first successful labor-organizing campaign in history and the inspiration for numerous struggles for political and economic freedom throughout human history."[43] Just as God used Moses to end the Egyptian system of labor exploitation, Katie acted as a faithful servant to help bring an end to sweatshop conditions in Chicago's textile shops.[44] In a lifetime of service to workers, Katie had grown certain that "[w]e are not going to stop any of God's work—it will be done one way or the other. When it is Him that is guiding us we always get an affirmation."

Painter Todd Macdonald does not claim any certainty when it comes to understanding sin. But at a minimum, he figures that a "sin is doing something bad in the eyes of the Lord. It is also making someone feel bad." Todd adds as an afterthought that "doing something willfully wrong, I guess it would be a sin." If sin is doing something willfully wrong, then Todd has never been out of a work because he has sinned. He has, however, been unemployed because he refused to do something which he found to be willfully wrong. So, is being laid off when you refuse to do something wrong a sin? What about cutting a few corners in order to save the employer a few bucks? These situations are harder for Todd to say.

> TODD: When I get laid off sometimes it's 'cause I am a little slower. I get into it [the paint job] more, but the boss does not make money—he gets paid by the job and the sooner I get done, the more money he makes. But I still want to give a good job to somebody. Maybe when you're painting the baseboard, you are just going too quickly and the job isn't nice . . . I get down into it and paint it all the way.
>
> *So that squeezes the profit margin?*
>
> TODD: Yeah.
>
> *Why is it important for you to go right to the end of that baseboard?*
>
> TODD: Because I feel like if I don't, then the customers will not be happy and will see it.
>
> *Even though your boss would be perfectly fine with the job?*
>
> TODD: Yeah, my boss would be okay. He tells me time and again that it does not matter.
>
> *That bothers you to hear that?*
>
> TODD: In a way, yes. I am a professional and I want to show that I am a professional. I want to do it right and the best that I can.
>
> *Would God be pleased with you "going to the baseboard"?'*
>
> TODD: I feel that if I didn't I would be unfaithful to the customer . . . maybe it's like a spiritual thing because I don't want to have someone after I leave [the job] say, "This guy did not do a good job, he was just trying to get in and out."

Would cheating the customer be a sin?

TODD: Some customers just want it done and don't care how perfect it is.

How about in a situation where the customer expects the job to be done perfectly?

TODD: I don't know if that would be a sin. I don't know.

An act is sinful if it's murder, stealing, taking the Lord's name in vain, or infidelity. But shaving expenses off a painting contract to increase the profit margin may or may not be a sin.

Todd is not a moral relativist. He refuses to do shoddy workmanship. Yet he understands the economics of commercial and home painting and acknowledges that sometimes neither the contactor nor the customer seems too bothered by a slightly unfinished baseboard. Using a little less paint than is warranted does amount to stealing from the customer, but it just does not register the same degree of offense that, say, a burglar breaking into your home and swiping your plasma television would do. At what point would business practices be a sin in "the eyes of God"? Would terminating worker health-care or retirement plans be a sin? "That is hard to say," Todd equivocates, "in a way yes, but depending on the circumstances." And there's the difficulty. Circumstances may get the employer off the hook. Like Todd, most of the people interviewed had a hard time conceiving business behavior as sinful. Rebecca Danforth, for instance, was asked if it would be a sin for her telecommunication employer to reduce her pay so that the company's stockholders could get a larger dividend check. Her answer cast a cloak of infallibility over the firm's actions. "No, it would not because they know their budget. They know what they need to survive."

Park Lane Reform Church congregant Sandra Aardsma has been a nurse for three decades and she has lived through a lot of hospital cost cutting. But was any of it sinful? Her answer expressed the confusion that many working-class people of faith felt when talking about nonpersonal sin: "An injustice and I guess injustices are sins, but I don't know. I think there are different things that you could call it, but it would not be right, it would not be fair, it would not be appropriate." Somehow devout believers like Sandra could readily describe a corporate act as unjust, not right, and not fair or appropriate, but still not sinful. They were not, however, so ambivalent about their own personal behavior.

Michael Morman also refused to condemn business practices as sinful. He did have plenty of critical comments about the employment practices of the Chicago Transit Authority (CTA), but even after he pointed out the un-Christ-like behavior of authority executives, he insisted on providing them with a get-out-of-hell card.

MICHAEL: I would consider the CTA one-sided.

But not sinful?

MICHAEL: I think they are doing it [shifting from full-time to part-time workers] to save money.

Would Jesus have laid off workers and downsized?

MICHAEL: No, he definitely would not have done that.

How come it is not a sin, then?

MICHAEL: It is not sinful.

Why not?

MICHAEL: They [CTA] need to survive.

Except for violations of the law, most corporate practices were not considered sinful. Low wages, downsizing, dangerous jobs, outsourcing, and meager health and retirement benefits were all managerial prerogatives. They may be bad things, but because they were done in the name of supply and demand, the employer was not guilty of any commandment violations. Business, after all, is business. Refusing to give care to an injured person at your door would be a definite sin, but a company like Wal-Mart that makes health insurance nearly impossible for its employees to purchase is just being competitive in the marketplace.

Without a finding of sinfulness or injustice, the faithful have no compulsion to act. But even when an injustice is manifold, some believers take pause before acting. Rebecca Danforth "always prays for knowledge or a clear understanding of what" she should do. She has seen a few strikes in her working days and while "most people would tell you to strike, . . . if they don't know your situation then how can they help you?" Rebecca believes her spirituality directs her to do something about injustice but not before consulting with God. But Michael Morman knows precisely when his faith compels him to act. "In my job [bus driver] I see what the managers do and how unfair they are. I know that some people in the same situations do not get treated the same. So when a person makes an honest mistake and the manager overreacts to it . . . then I go to my union representative and say that I think he really needs to take over this situation." Rebecca and Michael believe that God administers justice in this world by using "human beings to act on it." Michael imagines God's justice as being like the fortunes of a baseball player who, after going a long time hitting line drives but never getting on base, suddenly starts getting on base by blooping balls in front of outfielders. "I think God does have a way of evening things out to wrongdoers. I think that once people start to do wrong, it sets them on a path where nothing is going to go right. I think God has a way of making adjustments and leveling the playing field."

But Michael sees no inconsistency in being a good Christian and defending his work turf. Michael's union, the Amalgamated Transit Union, Local 241, had just completed a difficult contract negotiation with the CTA. According to Michael, the city's demands for contract concessions were not justified and would have imposed further hardship on bus drivers. CTA's actions may not have been a sin, but Michael believed they were unfair to the workers and needed to be challenged. "We have to fight back. I recently read the *Art of War* and the author said that when your enemies are many and you are few, you pick the battleground. We needed to pick the battleground that favors us. If we did everything the way we are supposed to [follow all the city's operational rules for driving a bus], I swear no bus would be on time. There are other ways that you can attack a problem." Michael would have preferred to be thought of as a "turn-the-other-cheek Christian," but his faith relied on a more Old Testament sense of justice. Perhaps it was the influence of Michael's favorite Bible passage that inspired his Christian sense of right and wrong behavior: "The Beatitudes. I read it in religion class once." Apparently once was enough. In unison with his fellow bus drivers, Michael confronted injustice and helped bring about the promised kingdom of God "on earth as it is in heaven."

It is also true that unlike Michael's experience, some believers hear God's guiding voice as a call to ignore the plight of other workers. During a long and bruising 1990s struggle between Caterpillar Incorporated, the nation's largest earth-moving equipment manufacturer, and the United Auto Workers (UAW), workers living in central Illinois were confronted with the difficult choice of either honoring a union picket line or crossing one. In 1994 the company offered to hire people to fill the jobs left vacant by striking UAW members if they would be willing to work for less health care coverage than the current union workers were receiving. Despite the allure of a relatively good hourly paying job, thousands of striking workers intially chose to endure the daily sacrifices of forsaking the company's determined job offer. But as the strike wore on, thousands of union and non-union workers also accepted the deal. The reasons workers gave for holding out or giving in ranged from economic to ethical. However, the *Chicago Tribune* reported on one non-union member who was certain that God had showed him the way: "But a Bible-quoting 39-year-old truck driver who said he earns $9 an hour declared he had no qualms crossing a union picket line, or taking work from someone on strike. 'If God opens the door, that is where I am at,' he said. 'In times like these, people ought to be thankful they have a job.'"[45]

Arthur Reliford has been a teacher for many years and he is bothered by the serious inequities in educational funding. "You can go into the poorer communities around Chicago and see the result of it [insufficient school funding]." When some children have to function with antiquated basic learning tools while others have an excess in modern teaching devices, it creates an unjust situation. Arthur knows that God would be displeased with the vast inequalities existing in America. Conspicuous riches exist in abundance, but God's "fruits" are not fairly distributed. "I think that is sinful that we do not share and the way we separate ourselves [by race and income]." What then does his faith compel Arthur to do about poverty and inequality? "For the majority of my life, my role has been to roll up my sleeves and fight injustice." Arthur is aware that Jesus did not just administer to people's souls. God also provided sufficient material resources to allow for the satisfaction of everyone's needs. Unfortunately, in our market-driven economy people live by a set of values that turns food into a commodity and housing into an investment. However, at Holy Angels Parish, Arthur has had a special opportunity to do something about the sin of homelessness.

In 1996 the parish began to address the lack of affordable housing in the city's Grand Boulevard area. It formed, along with three other African American churches, a faith-based community housing development corporation under the connotative name Genesis. The primary purpose of Genesis was to build and occupy homes in the largely poor and working-class black community. Through the development corporation, parishioners could "re-neighbor the community" and combat the evil of homelessness. Arthur Reliford sat on Genesis's original board of directors. His work, along with the efforts of many others, including the corporation's executive director, Donnie Brown, housing service director, June

Sargent, and then chairman, Reverend Robert Miller, has resulted in the construction of one hundred low-cost homes.[46] In addition to building a refuge for people, Genesis has sponsored over a hundred educational seminars designed to support home ownership and financial planning, and it administers a federal grant to provide young people with job training and placement in the construction trades. Here is a religious community that is dedicated to "empowering the community" as well as saving souls.[47]

Holy Angels parishioner June Sargent speaks of Genesis as "a safe place organization." Her primary nine-to-five job is helping neighborhood residents find affordable housing, but very often she is talking mortgage rates at Sunday mass. The job can be tough because there is so much need and so little income. "I haven't been able to help everybody and a couple of people get upset." June knows the scriptural call to house the homeless, but real homes cost real money. "I mentioned to one lady that even if she was Jesus Christ and wanted one of these houses, you have to be preapproved." Ironically, while June helps others to find a house, she does not have one. "I am still trying to get myself together and I am still renting." June believes in God's justice, but does not expect it to come without human intervention. "We as disciples, we need to create that justice." But what is *that justice?* "I am from the old school. Right is right and wrong is wrong. Everybody should be able to have jobs. Everybody should have a house or someplace to stay. Everybody should have food." But not everybody does. In 2005 at least 45 million people did not have health care, another 800,000 lacked permanent housing, poverty rates were at a shameful 12.7 percent, and nearly 7 million citizens were out of work.[48] Under these horrible social conditions, June does not know whether God is being just, but admits "that we don't know the whole picture." What she does know is that her faith imposes an obligation to do something.

"I am only supposed to be doing housing, but I am running across people who need jobs or need food or need other things." June could just stay focused on her job. But being called to be a Good Samaritan requires helping unconditionally. "Instead of me staying in this box, and I used to be angry because I thought I was supposed to be doing this nine-to-five job, but people still come up to me for different things telling me they need a job or house, so what do I do? I prayed on it and decided that I was going to help people in whatever they need. I am not going to be in the box." The "box" June speaks of is a metaphor for a limited, single-issue response to injustice. Doing her job as Genesis housing director would be godly work, but it would not be sufficient. "If you need something or if I am on the bus and somebody needs carfare, and I just might have $5, I will give them carfare. I feel like I have to be obedient and do whatever

God wants me to do; I have to do it." Just like the Samaritan who came across an injured Jew walking from Jerusalem to Jericho and "when he saw him, he had compassion, and went to him and bound up his wounds, pouring on oil and wine; then he sent him on his own beast and brought him to an inn, and took care of him" (Luke 10:29–37). June is walking her own road to Jericho and along the way "you can't be in the box; you have to help people whatever." Arthur Reliford and June Sargent have been moved by their faith to follow Jesus' example to multiply the loaves and fishes, and find some way to feed "the 5,000."[49] In their efforts, God's justice is being channeled through the commitment of believers to aide the "jobless, homeless, freedomless" or those people "just plain sick and tired of being sick and tired."[50]

Rosemary Sykes, who also attends Holy Angels Church, works for an insurance company. There have been some unfortunate changes at work and she has responded by trusting in the Lord. "Like right in my area just like other areas you have people losing their jobs. They are going through downsizing. I have a particular co-worker who I knew years ago and she sort of worked her way up. She is a wonderful person and she has two kids. She's in this position where if she is not able to find another job within the company by the end of the month she is out. This is very disturbing to me." Neither Rosemary nor her friend is in a unionized position. She is upset over her friend's pending layoff but not sure if the company is acting sinfully. "I become very angry because I see that our company is spending money on stuff and we've got people here who were in management and retired, then they hired them back as consultants. I don't understand this because they have got more than enough money and here you have a secretary and the sole support of her family with two kids . . . I just don't understand that." Rosemary sees the firm's behavior as harmful to some workers, but no matter how bad things appear she is confident that God is in control of the situation. "I know that He has something for her, that He needs her to do or her to get another job . . . because He is in control and because He is all good." Then does Rosemary's faith inspire her to do anything to help her co-worker? "We talked about it and she had an interview and she came in that day afterwards and she looked really super that day. I knew something was going on and we talked about the interviews. I tried to lift her spirits and I told her that we may not know what's going on now, so we just have to pray and at some point in time God will let you know what the purpose is. He always opens doors." Rosemary was acting like a good friend, offering a supportive ear and encouraging words. Her preferred method for helping to right what she perceived to be a wrong was to pray. Rosemary figures that "to be competitive to fight this economic system" people need to ask for God's mercy. While organized forms of opposition to downsizing might be available, "running around shouting about it is not going to help." It is God who "opens doors," but first you must "knock and it will be opened to you" (Matthew 7:7–9). Rosemary's knocks are usually quiet, but she believes that God is always listening.

Eileen Foggie is an active member of Holy Angels Parish and she feels blessed to have worked the past six years with the State of Illinois unemployment office. She once had a very good-paying job and owned all the trappings of success. Recalling what seemed like another lifetime, Eileen spoke of "money, material items, positions, everything." But the good fortune did not last and her life drastically changed. Eileen lost her job and suddenly found herself shopping at thrift stores. "I started working those thrift shops and I had a complete wardrobe that I would never [have] been able to afford." Slowly her life condition improved and she ended up with a public sector post. What was it that she did that restored a measure of prosperity to her life? She prayed more and read the Bible. "The closer I got to Him, the more I had and the more I benefited." Eileen's life renewal now guides her on how to assist the unfortunate victims of economic struggle. "When I see someone lose their job, I know that they might feel the fleshy loss for the moment, but God can bring you up." Her job loss and the wreckage caused to the lives of others by a forced unemployment is indeed a cause for suffering, but Eileen believes that it would be judgmental on her part to call unemployment, as Darren Wood Cushman would, an "individual" or "institutional sin."

Cushman is the senior minister of Speedway United Methodist Church in Indianapolis, Indiana, and he refers to company downsizing as a sin brought forth from a "sinful context." In a capitalist economy the "desire to create wealth and accumulate capital is sacred . . . and the needs of people are secondary." In a mad pursuit to please Wall Street speculators, companies shed loyal workers and in doing so, Cushman argues, "[t]he image of God as collective human action marked by creativity and compassion is replaced with a product of human design."[51] While the idea of an "institutional sin" or "sinful context" was alien to most of the working-class believers that I spoke to, Holy Angel's Sandra Houst believed that some wrongs required more than peaceful contemplation. When she was nineteen, she traveled to Mississippi to march with Martin Luther King Jr. and in her thirties she lobbied at the Illinois state capitol for child care. At fifty-seven, Sandra is less inclined to street activity, but that does not mean that she easily turns the other cheek. She praises God's will, but is not ready to be victimized by injustice. "Even though our own God heals, I don't think He should step on us." Sandra's faith not only inspires her to take up a shield against injustice, but it also allows her to be critical of God.

There are times in her life when Sandra is not certain what God would have her do. But she is comforted by knowing that God is with her. "He speaks to me in my mind when I have to make a decision and I don't know which way to go." In cases where Sandra feels harmed by another or witnesses wrongdoing, she is not easily forgiving. "I have a problem with forgiveness. I have to work very hard at that. When somebody has done something that hurts me, I can say that I forgive them, but I don't know that I do because I want to move away from them." It is a character trait that Sandra believes God has tried to rein in. "He [God] spoke to me again and again and said that this is concerning such and such and that I need to make peace. I heard that and I felt that, but I didn't do it." Sandra confesses that not listening to God's advice can be a painful lesson. "I think you suffer the consequences when you are not obedient." Yet, Sandra acknowledges that some people suffer devastating consequences from evils that are clearly not the work of God. Sandra has been a circuit board designer for the telephone industry for more than thirty-five years. In 2000 the company closed the office in which she was working. They did so without warning on a Friday, one week before Christmas. Sandra tearfully recounts what happened to some of her colleagues.

> One of the girls went into the hospital that Sunday. She was a happy-go-lucky person in appearance and she got stressed out and nobody knew it. She had an aneurism and passed away. [One pregnant young woman] was so stressed that her baby was born early and was a preemie and had to stay in the hospital for a long time. Then one of the other guys threw a brain clot. We lost about ten or twelve people right in a row after.

Sandra came to church often during that time and asked the congregation for prayers of healing. But she was also supportive of her union's (Communication Workers of America) efforts to force the company to pay medical and severance benefits to eligible laid-off workers.

This "Friday Massacre" was one of those instances when Sandra was not willing to make peace with the wrongdoer. "They have no loyalty for us and they want you to just forget." Sandra managed to keep her job with the firm, but while she feels blessed to have been spared the pink slip, she feels some guilt about her fortune. "It was such a mixed feeling when you have a job. Okay, I would ask how could I be upset because I did not lose my job . . . I am still here. But then there is anguish over the fact that I am still here, but look [at] everybody that is not. I wonder why I am still here and why I have the job." Sandra has been taught to love her enemies and to forgive those who hurt her, but she no longer fully trusts her employer. She does not call the company's actions sinful.

Sandra understands that the company made a business decision, but she describes it as "unfair and hurtful." According to Sandra, and so many other working-class Christian, Jews, and Muslims, acts of injustice are clearly sins except when unjust acts are committed by employers. The double standard is odd considering the Gospel accounts of Jesus condemning the Roman and Jewish elites for their indifference and exploitation of the poor. The obligations of the powerful to act justly are resonant throughout the Bible, Torah, and Qur'an. Nonetheless, the best critique Sandra could muster was to speak out against a bad, if not sinful, business decision.

Sandra also needed her job. Approaching the job after colleagues were fired required Sandra to rely on her faith to get through the day. While she admits to harboring anger at the company, she also remains faithful to it. "I have to do my best job because no matter how it appears to me, God is looking." Sandra is a still a dedicated employee, but her motivation for showing up to work is now influenced by the employer's betrayal. "It's my faith that makes me give them 100 percent, but I don't want to give 100 percent, I don't want to give them anything. I don't want to do the work." To help her cope with the reality of working for a hostile business, Sandra has written a daily prayer that puts her soul and mind at peace. In the middle stanza she calls on God to lift her up: "Lord, when I am confused, guide me. When I am weary, energize me. When I am burned out, infuse me with the light of the Holy Spirit." Sometimes the best a person can do in the face of injustice is to ask her God for the will to carry on.

Ed Carrile regularly attends St. Denis Church, but he is reluctant to use his faith as a moral compass to judge right from wrong behavior. He is a Christian and a skilled carpenter who acknowledges having a nonreligious ethical sense of good and bad. While there are certainly times when life is pretty grim, Ed refuses to "fall into the trap of being a fundamentalist." Faith too often is used as a weapon to do evil. "I see all of these people who do not believe in abortion to the point where it is okay for them to kill a doctor . . . it can be crazy." Ed has little patience for people who think that being a good Christian is all about adopting a narrow set of beliefs. Too many folks have a kind of faith by the numbers: "with these people, it is all about the Bible." It's not that Ed has not read the Bible, but he does not depend on it for moral clarity. To do so seems rather oppressive—not enough free choice. "I have met people who the first thing they ask me is if I am saved." To answer yes is to be credited with a holy seal of approval. To answer no is to be damned. Ed is too humble a person to make such absolute affirmations. He accepts that sin happens, but denies that any person can always know whether a particular act is sinful.

So, what is a sin? Ed's simple reply reflected his calm demeanor: "Anything that keeps you away from God." His definition was deeply personal. "Something that makes you feel bad about yourself or makes you feel guilty." Sin here is not formulaic, but subjectively felt. No one else can claim the sin. The sinner must be self-identified. "God put you here to be who you are down on earth and it is our life's job to find out what it is." When a person acts consistently with being the person God had intended him to be, then sin is not present. But since people have different life plans, it's possible that a sin for me is not necessarily a sin for someone else. "I truly believe if a woman is really good at stripping and she strips very well and she has a talent for that to make money for her family . . . is that a sin? No, I don't think so." Ed's subjective approach to sin makes it hard for him to claim that social problems (i.e., poverty, homelessness) are products of sinful human behavior. "There will always be poor people. You cannot help everybody."

But does faith inspire any attempt to ameliorate bad conditions? Ed's reply is not a clarion call to act against injustice. "I think we live in a me, me, me world. Yet if I was homeless, I guess I would be looking at it from the perspective of why is God doing this . . . I would be wondering if I was supposed to learn something from this." It appears that random misfortune or exploitation at the hands of others is an opportunity for self-reflection and not a reason for resistance to evil. Ed is critical of all the "me-me-me" in the world, but using his faith as a basis for actually doing something about it would jeopardize God's plans. "I like to think of it as God giving us what we need today. Maybe it's something that we need. Something that will challenge us." Injustice and sin are part of the human condition and in the midst of harshness Ed yearns for the feelings expressed in the book of Psalms. "They are so uplifting. They are joyful, bright sunshine; I guess they express God's love in words." Instead of a faith-based response to injustice, Ed takes great comfort in knowing that the "eye of the Lord is on those who fear him, on those who hope in his steadfast love, that he may deliver their soul from death, and keep them alive in famine" (Psalm 33:18–19).

Perhaps the reliance on divine intervention to eradicate evil originates in what many of the working-class faithful expressed as a religious endorsement of authority. If nothing else united the religious views of every believer, it was that personal righteousness required obedience to laws sacred as well as secular. Lamont Harrison is a twenty-one-year-old attendee of the Church of Our Lord and Savior Jesus Christ working in an entry-level position in the marketing department of a fashion designer. When asked about the nature of sin, he answered that "one big thing" is not being respectful to people who make decisions for us. Not respecting your parents was certainly an offense to God, but so was acting disobedient toward teachers, law enforcement officers, the elderly, and your boss. Lamont gravely noted that "[i]f we abandon authority that is set in front of you to lead you and guide you," then chaos will ensue and a sinful world will reign.

Among these working-class Christians it appeared that the biblical advice to "Render to Caesar the things that are Caesar's" was interpreted as a judicious call to be very mindful of authority—even an authority that made profits at the expense of denying workers their wages. The other half of that passage was also understood by Christian believers as a command not to take justice into your own hands. To Caesar should be given his due ". . . and to God the things that are God's" (Mark 12:17), like the responsibility for punishing the wicked. Echoing the words he heard spoken in church service that day, Lamont was insistent that "to obey is better than sacrifice." He meant of course obeying God, but Lamont and all other working-class believers have at least one other boss who they must take direction from and are careful not to displease. As I listened to these hardworking people of faith speak boldly of the existence of evil and strongly against sin, but yet muddle through distinctions between individual theft and corporate fraud, and what if anything can be done to right the world's wrongs, I wondered if the reality of economic dependence made it easier to embrace a religion of commands than one of resistance.

Certainly it is difficult and very often dangerous to confront an abusive employer. The most effective means of doing so—the right to organize a union—is badly undermined by the very same legal and administrative machinery set up in this country to enforce workers' rights. In addition, agencies commissioned to investigate civil rights violations in the workplace are overtaxed and understaffed. And few working-class people have the personal wealth necessary to bring tortuous action against an employer in a court of law. In the end, many workers calculate that eliminating job abuse is not worth risking job loss. When in the face of workplace evil, a person could, as some interviewees suggested, "quit your job and go find another." But even if the exit option provided personal relief, it would do nothing to alleviate the evil that continues to exist. Most workers said that they would first speak to their employer about something they were unhappy about. But none had a plan B if talking proved futile. Pastors like

Darren Cushman and the many religious leaders supporting the efforts of the national Interfaith Committee for Worker Justice would undoubtedly encourage workers to nonviolently and collectively stand up for themselves. They would do this because, like famous labor organizer Eugene Debs, Cushman and other "labor-priests" did not "believe Christ was meek and lowly but a real living, vital agitator who went into the temple with a lash and whipped the oppressor of the poor. . . ."[52]

But what about race, gender and sexual discrimination, poverty, homelessness, unemployment, inadequately funded schools, shockingly high incarceration rates, lack of medical care, and billions of dollars invested in military outlays? What does a committed Christian, Jew, or Muslim do about these things? They could, among other activities, join a union, sign a petition, write letters of complaint, march in protest, contact government officials, file lawsuits, or even ask their religious leader to get involved. Sharon Aftab, a charismatic unionized customer care representative for an airline and member of St. Bruno Catholic Parish, is unapologetic about her willingness to fight injustice inside and outside of the workplace. "I would have a point of attack first. I would start off with a letter-writing campaign. I'd cc them to the world. If that doesn't work, then, if you have to strike, then you have to strike." Sharon felt that "big business is really hurting the proletariat," and believed that President George W. Bush was an "impression of evil" in the world. As a Catholic, she felt a duty to stand up to corporate and political abuse of power. "Look, you have to be willing to wage war against [injustice] and you have to protect those who are not necessarily capable of protecting themselves."

But for the majority of workers I interviewed, actual collective or even personal acts of resistance to injustice of any kind were nonexistent. More important, the decision to remain a bystander was further justified by the belief that it was not inconsistent with being a faithful Christian, Jew, or Muslim. It was as if the religious laws only commanded that individuals respect God's word and avoid doing harm to others; not that individuals do anything to affirmatively eradicate the evil done to others.

There were, however, some intriguing exceptions. Kim Vargas felt strongly enough about the lack of seat belts on school buses to write a potent "Letter to the Editor." She posed the reasonable question "How did the school bus industry get exempt from the law that applies to the rest of us?" In her letter, she also responded to a published claim by Illinois Senator Dick Durbin that the school buses "are some of the safest vehicles around" as just "dumb luck." After all, she reminded the readers, "It was also not required that the *Titanic* have life boats to accommodate all on board."[53] Along with her husband, Gerry, Kim attends Family in

Faith Lutheran Church. When we spoke, the Vargases had three children under the age of eleven and Kim had opted to not work outside the home. Gerry was employed as a shipping and receiving clerk working at a nearby hospital. They admitted that money was tight and that the economic policies of President George W. Bush were not good for working people. But nothing the president did, including increasing American job loss through "free trade agreements," was a "sin." While they would like to see more middle-class paying jobs created in America, Kim and Gerry could see no justification for protesting against the country's economic policies. In fact, they acknowledged that in voting for George W. Bush they were in fact voting against their economic well-being. But both felt Bush was a faithful man and, more important, that on economic issues it was necessary "to surrender to God's will." Gerry was confident that the "Lord would provide" and that "faith required acceptance."

Still, Kim was adamant that there were good reasons to speak out against evil. The school bus letter was not her first foray into First Amendment territory. Kim was deeply disturbed by what she believed was an intention "to represent the occult" in the well-known OUIJA board game. Her concern motivated her to write a letter to the Hasbro Toys Consumer Affairs Department. The company response assured Kim that "OUIJA is simply a board game and has never been promoted by us as anything else."[54] Kim and Gerry also have been part of a community coalition opposing the building of a waste transfer site in their neighborhood. They even walked the community collecting signatures on a petition to force a referendum election on the issue. As Kim proudly displayed the bus and game letters, and a copy of the petition, the vibrant look in her green-brown eyes made it clear to me that she understood that faith should be used to fight evil. It's just a matter of picking your evil.

CHAPTER 4

A Repertoire of Worship

FUNDAMENTAL to religious adherence is some degree of devotional behavior. People who believe in God usually spend some time in prayer, attend worship services, read holy books, listen to spiritual tapes or faith-based radio stations, or participate in congregational behavior. My father occasionally made it to church, but the Bible in our home never exhibited his fingerprints. Mom, on the other hand, said she read the "good book" off and on. I know she prayed a lot. Neither of my parents thought very highly of religious television and radio broadcasters who were more often derided than praised. Mom and Dad, however, never failed to leave an envelope in the weekly collection plate and volunteered their time at Friday night Bingo parties and spring festivals. Most important, both insisted that I believe in God as they did. My parents' "repertoire of worship" was not unlike the ways that the working-class believers I talked with expressed devotion to God.[1]

Worship services were important to most working-class people of faith and everybody prayed. None, however, kept as exact an accounting of their prayers as St. Bruno parishioner Jim Stewart. "I spend approximately five hours a week in prayer. That includes once a week going to mass and then doing the Rosary daily and then a couple of other prayers as well." Some people knew their way around a holy book but most left spiritual readings to the weekly worship service. They had deep respect for their congregational leader and believed it was important that the congregation prosper. But few thought that attending worship services was essential to their faith. While an inventory of their worshiping revealed nothing exotic or unexpected, it was illuminating to hear what they prayed for and what sermons or holy book readings left an impression. If, as Mark Chaves contends, a repertoire of worship activities can reveal cultural dimensions to religious practice, then perhaps by being attentive to the devotional behavior of working people will the beginnings of a working-class cultural picture emerge.

As noted, all the workers I interviewed spent time praying. They did so in the morning before going to work and in the evening after making it home safely from work. Some talked privately to God during work; others shared their prayers in the company of other workers. In most cases the words spoken were not recitations of formal scripted prayers. Usually people just quietly conversed with an attentive God. Very often the conversations were about finding a job or being blessed with a better one. Changing jobs was also the occasion for serious petition. Marilyn Vanden Bout, a congregant at Park Lane Christian Reform Church, spent long hours in tortuous prayer deciding to leave one job for the next. She had previously worked as a church secretary (not Park Lane), but the job offered no health benefits. When her husband's job security and its accompanying family medical coverage were threatened, she began to ask God for another employment opportunity. Marilyn's answer came by way of her sister-in-law, who recommended that Marilyn apply for a secretarial post at a hospital. She got the job and gave thanks to God for the intervention. But the experience has forever taught Marilyn a different approach to prayer.

> My sister-in-law told me about this position and that I would be a wonderful fit for it [the job lies within the hospital's prenatal department for high-risk pregnancies], but it is a killer job. It's very difficult and I'm working three twelve-hour shifts a week. We are open from eight until four. I get there an hour early and I will get there earlier if I know that it is going to be a really horrible day so that I can get a jump on all of the paperwork that has to be done before the first patient walks in. Then I'm there until at least 6 or 6:30. Usually even 7. There are times that I am there until 7:30 or 8 if it is really an impossible day. That is just too much.

Despite having prayed for an employment change, Marilyn planned to quit the job, but her supervisor pleaded with her to reconsider. After once again taking the problem to God, Marilyn surprisingly agreed to stay at the hospital. But why tolerate a job that appeared to be killing you one shift at a time? Marilyn's answer expressed a powerful faith in God's judgment and a realization of her own humble limitations. "I am old enough to have prayed for a lot of things and gotten some things that I prayed for . . . now I know better. When I pray for things now, I am far more willing to say that I would rather have God's will than mine. I have gotten my own way a lot of times but maybe I shouldn't have. Now I ask for God's will rather than mine. The job opened up and it was offered and it was given to me." In Marilyn's mind, God knew where she belonged; maybe not forever, but at least for now. "It isn't an easy job and I knew that when I made up my mind to stay. I am working at a tough job for a tough boss." Marilyn accepts that an answered prayer brought her to the hospital and that an answered prayer now keeps her at work, twelve hours a day, three shifts a week.

Ed Carrile also firmly believes that prayer can change the world, but only if God answers the prayer. "I just lost a friend about a month ago to cancer. He was a good guy. He beat cancer and he was fine, but then he had a melanoma and he thought it was a mole. So the doctor did a grafting and got it all out—they thought—but it had gone to his liver, his prostate, his bladder . . . God could have healed that guy." When God did not heal his friend, Ed simply accepted "that it was his time to go." While a prayer for mercy did not spare his friend's life, it did reinforce the mystery of God's will. "I don't know what God's will is . . . you just have to be thankful for whatever you get out of life, whatever relationships you are in, whatever that person is that day, you should be thankful for it because that person may not be there tomorrow. We don't get to know why, I guess. I wish I did know." Ed does not expect prayer to help him better understand the power of God. But it can serve as a wake-up call to life's impermanence. When Ed prays he begins to think about the simple wonders of life. Prayer "gets me into realizing that time on earth is blessed." His prayers are not usually requests for help. They are more like thank-you cards. "Just simple things really, like you wake up in the morning and thank the Lord for letting me wake up. I have both eyes, I can breathe, and I don't have pain."

Sometimes, though, praying takes on a more urgent quality. "Lately I have been praying for wisdom so that I know the right thing to do." Ed is a carpenter who often finds himself in dangerous work situations. He fears being seriously injured. Do you pray at work? "All the time. If I'm up on the top floors I am always praying that I do not fall." In fact, work is where Ed probably does most of his talking to God. At his workplace he keeps a devotional book. "I'll pick it up and read it every single day." Ed prefers to start his work shift with a formal silent prayer "to get going." Praying for safety at work is one of the rare times Ed offers personal petitions to God.

"I always pray for other people. I cannot see people praying for themselves. I'm uncomfortable with that." Prayer, according to Ed, should be about asking God to intervene for others and for giving thanks. To pray to God for your own well-being is not to accept that God has already provided for you. It seems selfish; not Christ-like. But prayers of intercession are more powerful and more likely to be answered.[2] When you pray for family, friend, and stranger, you impress upon God the love you have for others. Ed believes that God is pleased by such devotion.

Ed also prays in church. He attends every Sunday where he offers his voice and guitar-picking skills to the music ministry. The need to worship with others is important to Ed. "I'm just one part of it [the faith community] and I want to take part in the celebration." Worship is a time to celebrate God's graces. With the mass Ed plays his guitar and can "really be intimate with God." Both the church service and the music close the gap between Ed and God. The service is an opportunity to establish a faith-based communal relationship, something the workplace does not do. Music is a special talent performed only as an offering to God. When he plays in church, Ed contributes to the faith community, as well as helps to give it form. Congregants sing along and in collective voice become a singular presence. Ed feels it. When he "gets to sing, it is more of a spirit thing." Spoken language is inadequate. "Can't put it into words, but our spirits can . . . I guess I am just being in the spirit and that rejuvenates me." Church and song energize Ed and awaken the Holy Spirit. It is in worship where Ed feels closest to his working-class neighbors. His favorite part of the service is when the choir sings the Lord's Prayer. "One guy's arm goes up when we say 'for the Kingdom and the power and the glory' and when you feel the warmth of another human being," that is transforming.

Jim Stewart and his sister Susan are devotedly committed to following the Ten Commandments and the sacraments offered at St. Bruno Church. They both believe that it is incumbent on a person to try and live in a constant "state of grace." A "state of grace" exists, according to Susan, "when you are under [God's] protection." The Lord's cover is weaved from a regular effort to stay in the Holy Word, through prayer, Bible readings, and worship services. Evil, the Stewarts urge, exists in the world. "There are forces that are dark that are moving against people of faith," Susan warns, and without the power of God "you can lose your faith." But the cumulative effect of never wandering too far from church practice is an increased likelihood that a person will live faithfully. Susan notes that "if you are in a state of grace and you go to church and you believe in your religion, then whatever troubles you happen to manifest or whatever road you choose, if you are getting the grace, then you can get through it."

Brother James adds, "[I]f you are silent and listen to the silence inside of you, you are not going to hear an audible voice of God telling you something, but you are going to be more apt to allow Him to work within you and you will be able to make the right decisions." Prayer and worship are two indelible exercises that enable the Stewarts to do more than keep a religious obligation; they inoculate them from evil temptations.

Holy Angels' parishioner Sandra Houston keeps a Christmas ornament on her desk at work. The piece is a little cross with the word "Hope" in the center of it. "I sit in a cubicle, so I have the walls all around. I have the little 'Hope' directly in front of me," available at all times. "When I'm stressful or I'm discouraged, I look at that." Sandra has needed "Hope" ever since her employer began to ruthlessly cut the workforce. She kept her job, but still feels persecuted. Sandra knows her work relations are hostile and needs a higher hand to cope with and contest the injustice. "You have to feel closer to the struggle, so that I am not just struggling by myself." I questioned how a religious icon at work helped her. "Because I know that God died on the cross. When I see the 'Hope,' then I know that this is what it's all about. This is not more than I can handle." "Hope" is Sandra's sustenance. It is her promise from God that she is not alone and that she can endure the agonies of Pharaoh all over again.

On occasion prayer at work also takes on a communal quality. Sandra and perhaps eight or nine other female workers join in a regular circle of religious conversation. Their work space is situated in a way that permits each woman to easily converse with one another. "We have work stations but what they did was that they took down the shelves. We used to not be able to see each other. We still have partitions, but we can look over them. So we talk about religion all the time." Mostly, though, faith arises as a topic of conversation when times get hard. "I think when we have difficulties, God comes to us. That is always my position; we can't solve problems by ourselves." To Sandra, prayer in moments of strife is less like a petition to God than a call from God. Sandra keeps a written prayer in her purse that she recites before beginning work each day. It is a prayer that I have seen posted in a number of office workplaces. The opening stanza is an answer to the spirit of God: "My heavenly father, as I enter this workplace, I bring your presence with me. I speak your peace, your grace, your mercy, and your perfect order into this office. I acknowledge your power over all that will be spoken, thought, decided, and done within these walls."[3]

Sandra's workplace strife has sensitized her to the importance of prayer in bringing help to others. During a meeting of a church book club she met three women who were desperately looking for work. Sandra was not a fan of the book they were reading, so when she learned of the women's economic situation she suggested that they stop talking about the text and pray. "But they did not pray and then when it was time to go," suddenly one of the women suggested that they should end the meeting with a prayer. Sandra quickly agreed and offered up a prayer of employment. Next week when the group met again, Sandra found the three women transformed. "They were jumping up and down because two had interviews for jobs and one had already gotten a job." Was this God's answer to the previous week's prayers? "I am sure that God already had it in the works . . . but when we came back they associated it [the jobs] with the prayers."

Without exception every believer interviewed was adamant that God does not just grant requests for help. The petitioners must also take action to help themselves or others. If you need a job you must look for one. If you want to stop being sick you have to quit smoking. If you want the poor to eat you have to feed them. If you want workers to be paid fairly you have to demand that the employer share the wealth. God expects people to use their talents and to be good stewards of their bodies, one another, and the environment. Praying for world peace while nations thrive as major arms producers and sellers is more likely to bring about Armageddon than paradise. But if a person makes an honest effort to help himself or others, and if it is in God's will, then prayers for help may be answered. Unanswered prayers, however, are a mystery. According to working-class believers, though, they do not mean that a person was lazy or undeserving or ignored or not faithful enough. Why God saves some and not others is unknowable. But when a person's prayers are not answered, it may only be apparently so. Nearly all of the interviewees agreed that what people experience after heartfelt prayer is either what God determined they needed or what God willed. The emphasis was repeatedly on God giving us what we need and not necessarily what we want.

June Sargent believes it is critical that a person always "remain prayerful." No matter the endeavor or the fortune, a person must never forget the need to ask God for guidance and understanding. In June's work as housing director for Genesis, Holy Angel's nonprofit corporation, there are numerous difficulties and disappointments. By being prayerful June is staying focused on the objective: to help the homeless become homeowners. Prayer becomes one of the tools she uses to do her job. June turns to prayer to conjure up the strength to overcome the problems that beset the poor. Her intelligence and hard work are supported by a prayerful state of mind that never relinquishes hold of God's grace. Prayer here is a necessary job skill. It also occasionally works that way for Donna Schiavone. As a massage therapist Donna's job involves laying hands on people in pain. While she admits that she is "not always in tune with praying and working at the same time," she does pray over her clients "about 40 percent of the time." Typically the prayer comes "before the therapy" and it involves Donna simply asking God that "it go well and ask for the person to have relief of pain or if they needed to be able to move their arm, that they have greater range of movement." The prayer is part of a healing process that is very focused on the source of pain.

Donna's husband, John, prays at work, too, but for a different reason. "Praying comes down to praying for myself, that nothing is going wrong and that I am not going to have major problems or get in trouble or anything like that." John's prayer is not a formal one, but a short request for help. It is like the prayers of many other working-class people of faith which serve as a kind of insurance against bad spirits let loose in the workplace. I came to think of these prayers as a form of spiritual capitalism; a purchase on expected protection. Besides John's personal moment with God, he has also participated in a scheduled once-a-week prayer group at work. His experience with a workplace ministry was not common among the people I interviewed. Some folks, like Katie Jordan and Sandra Houston, did occasionally pray with their colleagues in the workplace. Usually this occurred when someone at work was in need of support. In Katie's case it was usually during contract negotiation time. Union garment workers prayed for the strength to confront a reluctant employer. But praying together in the workplace was mostly episodic. Some folks talked about faith but most never brought the subject up.

However, Rosemary Sykes feels so strongly about the work-related power of prayer that while processing insurance claims she keeps a prayer book out on the desk, right next to her daily planner. "It is like you want to pray to sort of put it out there and sometimes it strikes up a conversation with people. What a calming effect it can have . . . people will come to you and it is like it is your day to help them get through whatever it is." Doing the job can also overwhelm Rosemary. "I pray to be shown or told how I can get all of this stuff done. It helps me to stay in the right mind so that when I come in and when I sit down, I feel like I have made progress." Rosemary's prayers feed her mental capacity and bring help to her side. Virginia Coleman also attends Holy Angels Church and she works as a clerk for the City of Chicago. A Bible rests on her work desk all day long and she believes more now than ever that she needs to "feel His presence."

Financial cutbacks in the city's budget forced a painful "early retirement" on many city workers. "There is so much turmoil going on now at our jobs. So people are so stressed." But Virginia is not worried. "I tell my co-workers that I am blessed and I am doing well and I tell them that I cannot complain." Is her job more secure than others? Turns out she has only five years of seniority. Virginia's calm comes from another sense of protection. "I look and I know where the Lord has brought me from situations in my life, not property-wise, but through sickness and death in my family. So I feel his presence and I am just thankful for it." Here a prayer book takes on a kind of talisman quality. It magically draws people away from their stress toward a receptive spirit. Once in the company of Rosemary, a work colleague can find a degree of solace or an opportunity to help.

Rosemary's public placement of a prayer book was unlike most of the interviewees who had no visible religious icons at work. Most went to work without a Bible, devotional book, rosary, or cross. Eileen Foggie, however, kept written prayers and religious texts in her desk at work in the state unemployment office just "in case." "I go through Bible readings in the morning and I even have stuff at work that I can fall back on in case I don't get this done before I leave home." Eileen makes a point of noting how projects come up at work without much time to prepare. "But then as you are going along, you say, 'Lord, would you please help me?'" Prayer in this case serves as a lifeline, an emergency measure. Eileen keeps her prayers close by "because if you don't and things don't work out . . ." The implications were obvious; you will have only yourself to blame for not staying in the word of God.

Believers talked to God informally throughout the workday and each Muslim worker kept to the Islamic requirement of praying five times a day. Muslim workers admitted, however, that there are times when they are working and it's impossible to simply stop what they are doing and pray. Each Muslim worker drove a Chicago cab for a living. They were typically on the road for no less than ten hours a day. Sitting behind the wheel of a sedan with your foot moving off and on the accelerator is not conducive to timely prayer. Drivers, like Somalian-born Mohammad Hareed, admitted that they had to sometimes wait until their cabs were empty before they could formally pray. "After you drop the fare off, then you pray." But Hareed insisted, "You have to find the time. You have to pray as you can but on your own time." The required prayers are not forsaken just because a person has to earn an honest dollar. While time for prayers must be found, the work schedule is not exactly spirit-free. Hareed pointed out that "during the time we [Muslims] are praying, that time is only for Allah, but the hours that I am working, I have to think of Allah too." Thinking of Allah is much more omnipresent than reciting a formal prayer. Prayers have specific beginnings and definite endings and happen during an uninterrupted period of spiritual reflection. But consciously considering Allah's will is a twenty-four-hour commitment and Hareed is certain that work time is not exempt: "I have to think of Allah and if this is a good way to work or a bad way to work."

But for Muslim cabbies sometimes keeping the faith can cost them their daily bread. According to the Chicago Professional Taxicab Drivers Association, in September 2007, just one week after the start of Ramadan, more than five hundred cabs were ticketed for parking in designated access lanes leading to O'Hare Airport terminals. Airport police ticketed Muslim drivers because they parked their cars and then proceeded to kneel and pray on the concrete pathways. As reported in the *Chicago Sun Times*, despite being provided with a space to "practice their faith," the city "punishes them when they park and pray."[4]

It struck me that a Muslim who keeps the daily prayer requirement and is also thoughtful of the Islamic prescripts about performing work duties might pray about work. But according to Ali Hussein, this is never so for him. "Prayers are from my heart, and during this time you don't think about anything around you or what you did or what you are going to do; this time is the time to talk to Allah." The Kenyan-born Hussein has been driving a taxi for two years and his prayers "ask blessings for everything." He gives thanks for his fortunes, but does not speak to Allah about the vagaries of the time he spends chauffeuring people around the city. Surprisingly, none of the Muslim drivers I interviewed admitted to ever praying about or engaging in an overt religious practice that focused on their occupation. This surprised me because the work these believers do is filled with hazards. The Council of Islamic Organizations of Greater Chicago has reported that more than fifty cabdrivers have been murdered in Chicago in the last ten years.[5] Pocket brochures outlining the rights of drivers to be free of abuse are produced by the council and made available to the drivers. The council notes that "cab driving has become a hazardous business that requires an extraordinary amount of time, energy, humiliation, and abuse in exchange for a paltry salary."[6]

At the Kabob Restaurant at Jackson and Halsted, where my interviews with each Muslim cabbie took place, brochures announcing that "We Move the City and We Deserve Better" were stacked near serving trays and utensils. The restaurant caters to a Middle Eastern cuisine and has become a favorite west loop congregating spot for Islamic drivers. At the Kabob, Muslims can pray in a separate downstairs room and enjoy a meal in the dining area. They can also talk about the need for a fair hike to offset the rising cost of gas, travelers who refuse to pay the fare, harassment from the city police, and the hideous death of cabbies like Haroon Paryani. At about half past midnight on February 4, 2005, Paryani picked up a rider in the prosperous Lakeview neighborhood. Shortly thereafter, Paryani argued with the passenger who claimed to be unable to pay the fare. According to eyewitnesses, the passenger then battered the Pakistani-born Paryani, threw him from his car, and then hijacked the cab and "ran over him several times, rolling over the father of four's head and neck."[7] The assault mobilized two thousand Chicago cabdrivers (60 percent of whom are Muslim) to sign a petition asking that the passenger not be freed on bail while awaiting trial.[8] But despite the tribulations and high safety risk involved in cabbing for a living, none of the Muslim drivers saw fit to make work a subject of prayer. In their minds it was not a suitable subject to address when giving thanks to Allah.

Jeffrey Goldberg does not usually pray about his work either. His work as an electrician for the city's transit agency typically places him in a commuter train station that is having mechanical problems. Work can be befuddling and his presence at the station usually elicits groans and dirty looks from impatient commuters. "I work with trouble shooting to plum wires and to check voltages. . . . I deal with the public, so I find myself dealing with a certain amount of tolerance." Jeff's work would certainly warrant a plea for assistance from a God whom Jews as well as Christians refer to as the "Light of the World." Still, he does not bring his prayers to the jobsite. But that does not mean he is not observant. Jeff was raised in the Jewish faith and along with his wife, Sarah, who converted to Judaism, takes seriously being religious. He admits to occasional lapses, but tries honestly to honor the Jewish *Shabbat* by making it to temple every Friday evening. Saturday observance is admittedly more difficult owing to work and family obligations that he is reluctant to ignore.[9]

While Jeff sounds almost apologetic about his level of religious observance, his wife takes pride in the family's attention to Jewish customs. "We hold sabot the best way that we can. We always make sure that if there is a religious ceremony coming up and if we cannot actually get to the formal services, that we at least acknowledge it in the household." Sarah's point about participating in a private moment of Jewish faith raised a question about her own work life. She works at a Wal-Mart and very often finds herself in the store right up to closing. "Last night, for instance, I worked and had to close up the store. So of course, being the only Jew in the store, I am not going to hold sabot service myself. So I thought about it [the meaning of the Sabbath] and I said the blessing before I ate and then I called my husband. Even though I was still working, that was my little break time." Sarah's private work sabot was strikingly like the Muslim cabdrivers who could not always make evening prayers but could pause between fares to give praise to Allah.

But does their degree of worship and observance satisfy God? Sarah and Jeff were both adamant that "not kissing a Mezuzah does not make us any less Jewish."[10] Sarah made it clear that "we don't have to always go to temple to be Jewish or to have God look at you as being a good Jew. I think it is what you hold in your heart." "Sarah is right," Jeff exclaimed. "Going to temple does not constitute that you're doing exactly what God wants you to do and that is what is making you a good Jew." Jeff can account for a more mundane, physical way of being faithful. "If I go to work and I am compassionate to somebody who needs it" (Sarah interrupts to proudly point out that her husband daily gives money to a homeless man who sleeps near the station), "if I go to work and I skip my lunch because I know that the extra thirty minutes will get this job done which will or could have a domino effect. This could give me power within the station which would make it easier for passengers to get on the train. If I am willing to just basically do the best to my ability. If I'm willing to give forth the effort that God wants me to. I honestly believe [this] is symptomatic of being a better Jew." Jeff has apparently found something sacred in his labors. Helping strangers to travel along an electronic byway is the way he praises God every day. Sarah does it in retail sales. The Goldbergs have firmly planted their faith in the world of laboring bodies and yet still yearn for more time in the temple. Sarah's and Jeff's struggle to be "religious" may not have been exactly how the Talmudic rabbis drew it up, but it was certainly a respectful compromise for two working-class Jews needing to stay employed and wanting to be faithful.

Barry Blaustein has lived 90 percent of his life within a forty-mile radius in North Chicago and the synagogue has been central to his existence. For an Orthodox Jew, going to temple on Friday evenings and strictly abiding by the codes of *Shabbat* (i.e., honoring the Sabbath) are essential rules for living. While his job as a kosher supervisor at a large grocery store can sometimes conflict with his need to fully participate in the Sabbath, Barry is nonetheless a traditionally observant Jew. "Saturday is a day of rest and day in which we do not do transactions. We do not handle money. We do not drive cars. We don't do any kind of work. Even flipping a light switch, we would not do that." Barry maintains a Jewish ambiance in his two-storied home and speaks proudly of raising Jewish children who are guided by the fundamentals of Judaism. He reads the Torah, is president of his congregation (Sherith Yisroel), and has been certified by the Jewish Orthodox Union as someone who can attest to the legitimacy of kosher food preparation. He is by Orthodox standards a "religious Jew in good standing." For Barry, the words of the ancient rabbis are moral guides: "However high He be above His world, let a man but enter a Synagogue, stand behind a pillar and pray in a whisper, and the Holy One, blessed be He, hearkens to his prayer. Can there be a God nearer than this?"[11]

Barry's standing, however, goes well beyond the time he spends in temple or respecting the Jewish holidays. Like no other worker I interviewed, Barry defined his work as a direct act of faith. The synagogue, daily prayer, and reading the Torah were at the core of his Jewishness, but there was more. "To be a religious Jew and to uphold the traditions meant doing what God expects of me," and working as a *mashgiach* gave him the opportunity to allow other Jews to practice their faith. Barry humbly acknowledges that he is not a rabbi, but explains that his work extends the teachings of the rabbis and therefore helps to not only keep holy the Lord's commandments but also to provide for the religious community.[12] The synagogue is by definition a central place of worship where Barry regularly reignites a powerful sense of belonging to a community of faith. But in Barry's line of work, that community never really disbands. It simply goes shopping on Thursdays and Fridays before sunset. In the kitchens of a grocery store's kosher market, Barry Blaustein reaffirms what author David Ariel has claimed for the synagogue: "[I]t is the place where we [Jews] affirm our values within a social context."

Laura Dawson hears the voice of God in St. Denis Church every weekend. Going to worship is not an obligation. She goes because it fills a vacuum. "I need to be reminded of God's goodness and I need to take that time apart to be with other believers. To be with other people and draw strength from them." Congregational worship is one of the common ways that Laura and most believers consciously practice their faith. Mark Chaves has studied congregational life and concluded that its core activity is "expressing and transmitting religious meaning through ritual and religious education."[13] Believers join and go to a church because they expect the experience will enlighten them and embed them in a loving, supportive community. Laura is a faithful person who prays privately, but she needs to worship with others. She needs to make a public declaration of her faith and to offer communal "praise to God." In doing so, she is practicing the relational ethic of Jesus. Religious scholars have elucidated how Jesus shared meals and discussions with people no matter what their human flaws or social condition and was a man of unconditional fellowship who practiced an "open commensality."[14] All were welcome to his company. All deserved to eat and to be loved. It is not surprising, then, that Laura's favorite part of the Catholic mass is the congregational response recited in preparation for receiving communion. "Lord I am not worthy to receive you, but only say the word and I shall be healed."

Homilies, however, rarely stick in Laura's mind. Except for an occasional Christmas message, the pastor's words do not appear to have any real resonance. Laura is similar to most of the other members of faith communities who were unable to recall the message of a specific homily or sermon. With very few exceptions most could not even conjure up a preferred topic. Not that worship services didn't offer up memorable prayers, sermons, recitations, or declarations. Pastor Reginald McCracken at the Church of Our Lord and Savior Jesus Christ pours his spirit into straightforward, uncomplicated, universal, and reassuring preaching. He favors repeating to his congregants that "Faith tells God,"

> I depend on you, even for the things I cannot see
> For my salvation
> For my deliverance
> For my healing
> Faith tells God, my business is in your hands
> My children
> My home
> My husband
> My wife
> My finance
> Faith tells God, I trust you
> What ever happens to me in this life
> My job
> My health
> My past
> My present
> My future
> I am in your hands.[15]

Pastor McCracken and his congregants find strength and comfort in the belief that the "righteous shall live by His faith," and not necessarily recalling where they heard the message (Habakkuk 2:4) Donna Schiavone did recall a sermon or two. "A few that he [the pastor] did on worship and what it is and why do people worship. Another one was one on tithing." It would come as no surprise to minister-turned carpenter and author Armand Larive that Donna retained a memory of these sermons. Larive contends that focusing on institutional church needs is one of the primary purposes of "professional preaching and instruction at the congregational level."[16] Congregants understand the need for their congregational leaders to ask for financial support and for people to come to worship. Without member tithing or Sunday offerings, worship would have to take place in public spaces or private homes, and be led by volunteers.

The inability to recollect particular worship messages is not related to any of the workers' feelings about the religious leader addressing them. Pastors, rabbis, and imams were deeply respected and considered good speakers. But while their words and message may have had an immediate impression when first heard, they did not linger in the consciousness of believers. It was actually more common for worship attendees to cite sermon topics or themes that they disliked. Craig Rutz, for example, attends worship at Family in Faith Lutheran Church because he grew very unhappy with the pastor's sermonizing at his previous church. His remarks expressed a tension that many working-class Christians acknowledged between being good people of faith living in a secular world and having to comply with religious dogma.

> What I don't like is when a pastor comes around and speaks dogma to you. I will probably get hell for saying this, but our pastor one, two, three times a year would give a sermon about abortion and how evil it is. Now I am not saying that abortion is a good thing, but there has to be people sitting in the congregation who have had abortions and nobody knows about it and they are saying, "He is talking about me. I'm a sinner because I did that." But they were not sinners when they did that, they were people looking for an answer and if they made the wrong choice, they did not make it out of a lack of respect for human life.

What Craig opposed hearing was something a lot of people found objectionable. "When a pastor tells you that the only way for anything is 'this way,' it bothers me. Nobody knows that for sure."

Nearly all Christian and Jewish congregants preferred a worship approach that invited attendees to speak out. Craig Rutz applauded his present pastor for asking "people in the congregation to speak" because "you can get a lot out of their stories." In the majority of the worship services the congregation was invited to speak out. Where the option was available and encouraged, individuals repeatedly described how meaningful it was to have their fellow believers publicly witness in church. Craig was always surprised by what he heard. "Things that I would have never guessed about the people who have gone up to talk . . . can be very valuable and I learned a lot of lessons from that." Telling stories of struggle and redemption was the way that participants in a faith community educated one another and built the bonds of unity. Listening to someone like you speak of a crisis in faith or a moment of God's grace was effectively relating theology to real life. It made religion more practical, more useable, and more valuable. Sharing personal narratives from fellow travelers was better than hearing formulaic sermons from a well-meaning pastor. In fact, faith community members were most enthusiastic about the pastors' worship skills when they were relating faith to the world. And in most cases that did not require extensive biblical references. Almost no one could account for a single holy book reading during worship and they were even more forgettable than homilies. It was as if the Bible were little more than a program filler or a way to transition from one point to the next.

All the interviewees did admit to being interested in the sermon or homily, but few cited listening to the pastor's message or readings as the principal reason they attended service. Todd Macdonald was one of the exceptions. He came to worship at Family in Faith for the sermon "because the sermon is where you learn." The theme of a formal religious education was mentioned by surprisingly few other congregants as a reason for attending worship. Instead, besides listening to others share their personal accounts, everyone loved the music ministry and miscellaneous artistic performances of the worship ceremony. Worship was more an opportunity to be in celebration with one another than a chance to become more religiously informed. My interviewees' worship experience appeared to be strongly shaped by the same forces influencing attendees throughout the nation. Mark Chaves's review of the National Congregations Study found that congregational singing was nearly universal and "large majorities also experience choir singing (72 percent) and performances on musical instruments (91 percent)." He further points out that music makes up 25 percent of the average worship experience. The worship services I attended in each of the congregations I studied easily and regularly met that one-quarter threshold. Chaves also reveals that 70 percent of worship attendees "are in congregations in which a skit or play was performed at worship during the past year," and 29 percent have seen dance performed at worship service over the past twelve months.[17]

Worship at every Christian service was a wonderful opportunity for working people to be in God's spirit through singing, dancing, playing musical instruments, and dramatic performance. Extending an open fellowship table to the community at the Community Mennonite Church included two intimate Sunday worship services that take place in a comfortable modest room where wooden pews are arranged in theater style to allow the congregants to see one another and the pastors. There are no structural dividers separating pastors from congregants; no two-tiered or elevated sanctuary. Everyone's feet touch the same surface. Except for a single stenciled banner written in Spanish, there are no religious icons decorating the walls. The worship space feels like the family's living room. Pastor and assistant pastors Chuck and Bonnie Nuefeld are particularly adept at constructing a warm, engaging, and participatory liturgy service. The Nuefelds both play assorted instruments and everybody at service sings. Everybody also reads from scripture and shared personal testimonials of suffering, healing, promise, and praise. On my visits people came early and left late. It was easy to see why.

Singing was a staple of every worship ceremony I witnessed, but none was as emotionally uplifting as the collective voices heard at Holy Angels Church. While some parishioners prefer the early morning or the late afternoon service, most come for the two-hour or more spirit-filled Gospel mass. Music, singing, praise, and call-and-response preaching lift the Gospel mass beyond any Catholic worship I have ever seen. Part Baptist, part African spiritual, and part Catholic liturgy, the service is an energizing, exhausting, and cleansing experience. As if the worship were not inspiring enough, parishioners receive the Spirit of God before a large mural painted by the late Cameroon Jesuit priest Engelbert Mveng. Hanging above the sanctuary, the multicolored mural depicts the roles and interventions that angels have played throughout the history of the world. From St. Michael the Archangel to the Virgin Mary appearing as a common Nigerian woman to a likeness of the apostle Peter closely resembling South Africa's Nelson Mandela, the iconic images adorning the masses at Holy Angels provide an evocative setting for the spiritual expression of racial pride, social justice, and the Catholic gospels.

But when the music ends, the question remains: is a church homily or sermon important to the worship experience? Laura Dawson thinks so and has an explanation. "Sometimes I think homilies are like a lot of other things that we do—reading books—going to classes—you do not always remember a lot specifically, but I think it somehow shapes you and helps you as a person as you move along." The homilies and, in Laura's case, the Gospel readings seem to be like so much other educational material: hard to remember but good for your growth. Believers went to worship for spiritual nourishment and a feeling of communality. Once there they listened to a lot of God's words, but they were most impressed by the ones that they heard sung.

Nonetheless, the written word was something Laura clung to. She is an avid reader of the Bible. "I see the Bible as a story of God's love affair with people and how an understanding of God changed and the way that people relate to God." Her favorite part of the book is the Sermon on the Mount. Laura prefers it because she thinks that it points to a powerful truth about Jesus' public ministry. "I think God has a special place in his heart for the poor. There are a lot of rich people who are spiritually empty." Bible readings have opened Laura to the reality that Jesus' public ministry championed the material as well as the spiritual cause of the poor and working classes. The rich and powerful were typically chastised for their greed and abuse of the lower economic classes. Laura recalls two of the Beatitudes in Luke's Gospel that influence the shape of her life: "Blessed are you poor, for yours is the kingdom of God," and "But woe to you that are rich, for you have received your consolation" (Luke 6:20, 24).

Rudy Ramirez also referred to a Bible story that he interpreted as favorably judging believers of meager means and possessions. Rudy has worked as a food service aide in a Chicago public hospital for a quarter of a century. He has been a member of Immaculate Conception Parish for a little longer. "One of the stories in the Bible about this king or rich man that gave so much to the church, like thousands and thousands of dollars, which was good in its own right, but the poor woman had very few dollars and she put a smaller amount, but it was much more than the other man." Rudy retells this story because he wants to stress that a person like himself with a modest income can actually be more faithful to God than the CEO of the hospital. Embedded in Rudy's preference for this parable is a belief that people of great earthly means and power are less satisfying to God.

Working-class Christians agreed that anyone who believed could get into heaven, but they also admitted that people of simple means and deep faith were the "salt of the earth," and it was how the powerful people treated the powerless that determined whether they lived right by God.[18] Exposure to Bible readings introduced Laura Dawson and others to the difficulty believers would have in living in accordance with God while acquiring more and more material riches. John Schiavone reads the Bible every day and has reread the Gospel of John many times. The reading has convinced John that under particular circumstances there can be a conflict with money and God. "If you let the material and the wealth get in the way of praising God and get in the way of just how you live your life, then it is a conflict. It is a conflict if you let material wealth run your life in the way that you chase it." Wealth did not automatically disqualify a person from God's love, but it was important how a person earned his riches and how those riches were used. To have fairly earned great wealth and to share it broadly with people in need was to live without spiritual contradiction. But to be a profiteer from exploitation (i.e., child labor, immigrant labor, low-wage labor) or immoral behavior (i.e., drug sales), or to be indifferent to the needs of others (i.e., denying medical care or housing assistance) was to be spiritually condemned.

Pat Glatz believes that God has a definite opinion about wealth. Biblical stories like the rich man and the eye of the needle speak volumes to her. Pat and I read the following passage together from the Gospel of Mark: "And Jesus looked around and said to his disciples, 'How hard it will be for those who have riches to enter the kingdom of God . . . it is easier for a camel to go through the eye of a needle than for a rich man to enter the kingdom of God" (Mark 10:23–26). Was God warning the rich and powerful? "I don't think that God is saying that those [wealth] are wrong things. I think He is saying that if you have these things, frequently people tend to get caught up in them, in their own world. The world of social stuff, the world of wealth rather than using that status of wealth for good things." Pat's judicious concern about conspicuous consumption reflects the prophet Isaiah's stern condemnation of the people who fetishize their own creations: "All who make idols are nothing, and the things they treasure are worthless. Those who would speak up for them are blind; they are ignorant, to their own shame . . . he bows down to it and worships. He prays to it and says, 'Save me; you are my God'" (Isaiah 44:9–17). On the other hand, people with fewer material possessions can be in a more right relationship with God because "when you are meek, poor, disenfranchised, and jobless you have nothing but your faith." Having less makes it easier to be with God.

Now this does not justify poverty. None of the workers in this study thought being poor was a good thing. They all recognized the extreme differences in living standards between the "haves and have-nots" and none preferred being part of the latter. Social indices of economic disparity were hard to miss. The distribution of America's wealth has become more unequal than at any time since World War II. By the late 1990s, 50 percent of the nation's wealth (property, cash, savings, stock value, and insurance policies—minus mortgage payments, credit card debt, and other debts) was owned by a paltry 5 percent of the population.[19] A miniscule 1 percent owned a gaudy 38 percent. Distribution of income and capital investments was similarly concentrated. It is not a blessing to be poor or a prerequisite to salvation. But just as a modest means allows for more attention to the Spirit, a life of conspicuous wealth blurs the presence of God. In part, that's why Michael Morman goes to Sunday worship. He claims he needs the worship service to be "renewed." Michael reaches for spiritual renewal no matter his status in life. "I have been to mass and my house has been in total chaos, when my family was not going right." Here in the midst of harder times Michael feels the pull of communal worship.

He is not distant from God when life is cruel, but because of life's barrenness, God looms larger in his life. Michael is not a committed Bible reader. But yet he has a favorite passage: "I think it would be the Beatitudes." No passage was more often cited by working-class Christians than the Sermon on the Mount. Time and again this collection of Jesus' instructions to converted Christians seems to place God squarely on one side of an economic class divide. It's not important whether these working-class people of faith are theologically correct in how they are interpreting the passage. What is important is that they have infused the message with a meaning that they believe inches them closer to God than the top 5 percent of Americans who own half the nation's wealth. "Woe to you that are full now, for you shall hunger" and "Blessed are you that hunger now, for you shall be satisfied" (Luke 6:25).

Bible readings that communicated a message of hope, strength, and redemption were occasionally mentioned most often by working-class Christians. Holy Angels parishioner Vincent Washington was quick to point out that Psalm 30 was his favorite. The passage is a thanksgiving for healing and Vincent was a man who needed healing. He was recently hired by the Chicago public school system after a prolonged period of unemployment. "I was down in the pits and He would not let me go any further. He lifted me up and brought me out of that pit. I was way off the right track and I am only in an instant in my spirituality, but I am now a miracle walking." It is the psalm's second verse and last line that best expresses Vincent's admiration: "O Lord my God, I cried to thee for help, and thou hast helped me," and "O Lord my God, I will give thanks to thee for ever" (Psalm 30:1–12). Fellow Bronzeville neighborhood resident and Holy Angels parishioner Virginia Coleman has her own special reading. "I keep saying Second Corinthians, chapter 4, verse 13 over and over every day." The part that she finds easiest to recall is "we too believe, and so we speak" (2 Corinthians 4:13). Virginia clings to these words "because we are weak and there is so much [trouble] out there. Sometimes we are tested to the max." Believing in the face of struggle requires constant affirmation. Virginia finds strength in the few words of one of Paul's letters. Ellen Kilmurry of St. Denis Parish discovered a total life transformation within one ancient working woman's story.

Ellen is a certified public accountant by education and trade, but for the past few years has worked for Chicago's Port Ministries doing outreach for the poor and homeless. "The woman at the well is my favorite story." As told in the Gospel of John, a Samaritan woman encountered a tired Jesus sitting beside a well. Jesus asked the woman for a drink from her water jar. Her first response was to question why Jesus, a Jew, would be talking to a Samaritan, "for Jews have no dealings with Samaritans." Jesus eventually reveals to the woman that he is the Messiah "who is called Christ." The woman then "went away into the city, and said to the people, 'Come, see a man who told me all that I ever did'" (John 4:1–42). Ellen explained that she was greatly inspired by this story. "This woman was not only just a nobody, she was an outcast. I mean, if you are in such bad shape that you have to go to the well at noon [the text says it was about the sixth hour], so that means you are really hated by even the town's women. Then she became not only a disciple but an evangelist. So she went from being nothing to being very powerful." In not only believing in Jesus, but more important, because "many Samaritans from the city believed in him because of the woman's testimony," she had attained the power of discipleship.

"I love her energy and her attitude." The experience of the unsuspecting woman at the well has taught Ellen compelling lessons about Jesus' open and radical fellowship. "I work on her story all the time. I am working on how tight you would have to hold your hands to be able to bring up that water from the [very deep] well. If you are so tightly holding on to what is, then you never open your hands and let what will be happen. So I'm working on opening my hands to see where I am called next. I have a statue of a kneeling woman with open hands. It is a total life transformation in a very common place. At a well Jesus will ask you, you do not have to be a pious little thing running after Jesus and grabbing his coattail, Jesus will ask you." To be "nobody" and called by God in a "very common place," to drink the "water welling up to eternal life," has empowered Ellen Kilmurry to work in a ministry for the poor.[20] She, too, is a working woman who chose to be like the woman at the well and heed Jesus' call to labor for what Michael Harrington called the "other America."[21]

In truth, prayer and church worship are far more common means of conventional religious expression than Bible readings. Workers in this study were a lot like Arthur Reliford, who prayed at least twice a day. Arthur particularly liked to pray a certain way during worship. "I like when we gather around the altar and pray." At Holy Angels Church the priest calls the congregation forward to stand before the altar. There, in a circle of outstretched clasped hands, they offer prayers for people in need and give thanks for the gifts of grace awarded to the church family. It is a series of brief and passionate prayers of the faithful, presented in a staccato call-and-response Baptist format. At the prayer's conclusion the congregation participates in a collective embrace and spends the next few minutes roaming about the church joyously greeting one another. The exercise adds considerably to the worship time, but no one seems to mind. Prayer done in such a kinetic participatory way ensures that the worship fulfills the need for a communal faith experience. And as a communal event, the worship moment most cited as spiritually uplifting is the Eucharist. Arthur put it in simple, but contemplative terms: "I like the fact that people can share a meal. Really, it is like everyone sitting around like the Last Supper and they are about to nourish themselves."

Anthropologists and sociologists have found that breaking bread together is the most fundamental communal activity. Table fellowship is a "map of economic discrimination, social hierarchy, and political differentiation."[22] Jesus used meals as an opportunity to establish open and equal rules of association and socialization. Arthur Reliford feels that Jesus' "open commensality" taught everyone an important lesson and he was reminded of it each time he received the Eucharist. "Help the poor. His constant unwavering devotion to those less fortunate: when someone came to him for help he would not refuse." Craig Rutz of Faith in Family Church also connects with the biblical message of taking care of others. Having wealth and being close to God can create a contradiction. "If I only had twenty bucks in my pocket and I ran into someone who needed twenty dollars and I didn't give it to them, that would be a conflict." During worship Craig has the opportunity to symbolically reaffirm the value of a shared meal. "I feel that communion is a really critical thing. [I] can share my faith (i.e., nourishment) with other people at the same time at the rail." Caring for others, feeding one another, and welcoming strangers are all captured during the communion ceremony. For the working-class Christians in this study, communion is the high point of worship because it is when they are most spiritually and temporally one people.

The sense of "wholeness" or "oneness" is a major transformation of the worship service in primarily working-class congregations. Tex Sample noted that within working-class religious expression there is a strong "communal orientation and relationship."[23] To working folks, the churches which minister to them are not mere associations or secondary relationships. Instead, the church becomes what many of the Christians in this study have described: a community. In sociological terms a "primary group" is where individuals with disparate identities come together to form a "we." Sample contrasts this bonding form of worship with middle- and upper-income churches where the "membership is primarily an audience."[24] These churchgoers come together primarily to worship and have few close personal ties with one another. Conversely, in all but one of the working-class churches featured in this study, parishioners had multilayered relationships with an assortment of their fellow members. It was not uncommon, when asked about the frequency in which individuals came into contact with members of their congregation outside of church, that interviewees answered with elaborate explanations of fellowship. Church attendees saw many people only in worship, but nearly all of them socialized or interacted with a dozen or more of their peers in nonworship settings.

For Muslim believers these contacts were also particularly well developed. Each worked in Chicago as a cabdriver. While they worked for different cab companies, they all regularly congregated at the Kabob Corner Restaurant for prayers before and after work shifts. The restaurant also provided each driver with a place to get a good meal, a bit of playful relaxation, and, of course, extensive fellowship. On the evenings that I went to the restaurant to interview drivers, it was very clear that the drivers knew one another by more than name. Their experience was of course much different than any other group of believers interviewed. First, each Muslim shared the same occupation. As taxi drivers they worked a similar terrain, performed the same job tasks, held similar job skills, earned similar occupational rewards, and assumed common work hazards. Second, while each attended mosques, it was the Kabob Corner where they combined prayer with work associations. Prayers occurred in a separate room where Allah was dutifully thanked. In a larger dining area, cabbies ate, talked, and laughed. They also passed out pamphlets that addressed the need for the drivers to stand united on issues of safety. This setting is, of course, not comparable to a Christian or Jewish worship service, but here were Muslims praying and discussing workplace-related issues in the same personal time and space. Except for St. Denis Church, this conjunction of corporate spiritual activity and overt workplace discussion did not occur at other congregations.

Among the congregations I visited, St. Denis was unique in its attention to a social justice, working-class ministry. Nestled in the Ashburn section on the far south west-side of Chicago, St. Denis Church was built in 1964. During its first two decades of existence the church ministered to a predominantly white, ethnic working-class community. But the results of a civil rights campaign against segregated housing produced a regrettable white flight that changed the area's demographics. The parish today is part of a large majority Hispanic-Latino and African American working-class neighborhood. But surprisingly, despite the racial transformation of the nearby residents, the church's 750 registered families retain a significant number of its older Caucasian members. The contrast of a predominately white, blue-collar membership worshiping within a largely minority community has challenged the parish to be attentive to what is happening outside of its beautiful stained glass windows. In the neighborhoods surrounding St. Denis Parish, issues of race and class have largely defined the community's identity and well-being. Where before, plentiful decent-paying jobs and homes were once the norm, a less than stable working-class milieu is now seeking the American Dream. It is a calling that Pastor Larry Dowling deeply embraces.

Father Dowling is a soft-spoken man of middle height with a neatly trimmed white beard. His voice and demeanor are disarming and welcoming. But the pastor's mild mannerisms obscure a passionate commitment to social and economic justice for working people. Father Dowling was sent to St. Denis in 1996 by then cardinal Joseph Bernardin to help the parish deal with the area's changed racial and economic dynamic caused by racially motivated white flight. The church had always had a social justice tradition, but Dowling's activism regarding homeless issues while a seminary student and his involvement with the Chicago-based religious-labor coalition "United Power for Action and Justice" convinced Bernardin that Dowling could best ensure that St. Denis remained a socially viable faith community.[25] What Bernardin likely understood was that Dowling took seriously the radical teachings of Jesus to act as a public prophetic witness for social equality and dignity. At age thirty-three Dowling quit a good-paying job as an actuary to enter the priesthood. Ever since, he has been spiritually driven to take Jesus' command "to love our neighbor as we love ourselves" and redefine it as a call to collectively "make sure that people don't go hungry."[26] While Dowling acknowledges the importance of all believers having a personal relationship with God, he holds to a philosophy of stewardship that places equal weight on the "tithing of time outside the parish."[27] His favorite scriptural passage is Matthew 25:31–40 ("For I was hungry and you fed me. . . . For I was thirsty and you gave me drink. . . . For I was a stranger and you welcomed me. . . . For I was naked and you clothed me. . . . For I was ill and you comforted me. . . . For I was in prison and you came to visit me"). According to Dowling, "it is the only judgment scene in scripture" and it is not, as too often described, "about personal salvation."[28]

Matthew, Dowling argues, is really about a collective human effort to ensure that everyone not only gets to heaven after death, but lives in God's kingdom on earth. Giving someone sitting in tattered clothes on a street curb a dollar is an example of the Christian being "good at the basic care stuff," but what about "hearing the call to collective action"?[29] How do you keep God's people from being poor in the first place? Dowling has answered that question by making a conscious choice not only to preach, but to act upon Catholic social teachings, particularly on the rights of workers.[30] He has, for instance, participated in union demonstrations against worker abuse, advocated for church-inspired strategies to prevent racism, and spent much of his clerical life organizing on behalf of the homeless. He has done this and more as an outspoken Catholic religious leader. At the time of our interview, Dowling was the only priest on a thirty-member committee formed by the Chicago Archdiocese to address racism in a predominantly white clerical culture. Perhaps that is why some of his colleagues refer to him as the "leader of the priest's union." It is an informal title he deserves and carries honorably.

One of St. Denis's annual events is its Labor Day mass. In truth, if it were just a mass, it would not be distinguishable from what some Catholic and Christian churches do over the end-of-summer, holiday weekend. However, the worship that takes place at St. Denis to acknowledge the one day authorized by Congress in 1896 to honor working men and women is not an ordinary service. Beginning in 2003, Pastor Dowling authorized a special "Mass for Workers." Organized principally by the parish's pastoral associate, Adrian Dominican sister Noreen Burns, and lay ministry team member Ellen Kilmurry, the service has become a mix of an old-fashioned street rally and a somber religious observance. Church and community members are invited to a celebration for everyone who is "employed, unemployed, self-employed, retired, a homemaker, public employees, union and nonunion workers." Even "management" employees are welcomed. The day begins unlike any typical Sunday. Instead of an opening prayer recited from the pulpit, a procession of unions parades the large block around the church. Union flags and signs are waved behind the colors and symbols of St. Denis Parish. Along the march, two classic labor ballads that have inspired and animated the workers' movement for generations are sung. The lyrics to Ralph Chaplin's "Solidarity Forever" and the nineteenth-century coal miners' anthem "The Eight Hour Day" are provided to marchers.[31] While not everyone belts the tunes out, most sing the songs' choruses. The labor singing, however, is only a warm-up act. The processional ends its spirited walk back at the church entrance accompanied by rousing renditions of "This Little Light of Mine" and "We Shall Overcome." And only after the last verse of Daniel Schutte's "City of God" is harmonized do the attendees enter church for a religious worship.

Once people have found their places in the wooden pews, St. Denis's "Mass for Workers/Misa Para Los Trabajadores" begins. Instead of reading from conventional mass bulletins, congregants participate in the service by consulting a specially and simply prepared black-and-white paper booklet detailing the worship. The booklet is distinct by its complete lack of any recognizable religious symbols. Instead, the cover features graphics of a hammer, screwdriver, pliers, ruler, and three nails. On most days these items would be symbols of workers' tools, but on this occasion they are workers' tools and religious icons. During the service actual hand tools are presented by congregants as offerings of praise to God and the gifts are arrayed along the altar. In this situation the sanctuary and the workplace are united as a place of worship. Here again, it is the "communio" (i.e., "united as one") moment that unifies the working-class congregation. As Dowling prepares the Eucharistic celebration he publicly recites a prayer that he first says privately: "We are the body and blood of Christ, may we bring one another eternal life." At this point the pastor is reminding the parishioners that the symbolic conversion and consumption of Jesus' body and blood is an act that transforms them into people who can give sustenance, relief, support, and protection to others. Christian believers can now do as Jesus did and "speak truth to power and uplift those in need."[32] On this Labor Day, communion at St. Denis is not merely spiritual nourishment and a sign that Jesus has been accepted as Lord and savior, but an act of social empowerment.

Dowling's homage to work and the working class was strongly reminiscent of the way that the martyred archbishop of El Salvador, Oscar Romeo, spoke of the toilers of the world. Romero, like Dowling, recognized a unity between the sacred and secular, the divine and the mundane. In one of his more poignant public prayers Romero expressed his own belief that the work of God was also the work of people.

> How beautiful will be the day when all the baptized understand that their work, their job is a priestly task. That just as I celebrate Mass at this altar, so each carpenter celebrates Mass at his workbench, and each metal worker, each professional, each doctor with a scalpel, a market woman at her stand is performing priestly office! Cab-drivers, listen to this message: You are a priest at the wheel, my friend, if you work with honesty, consecrating that taxi of yours to God, bearing a message of peace and love to the passengers who ride with you.[33]

The worship is also filled with hymns that have a clear work- and social justice-oriented theme. Steven Warner's "Christ Has No Body Now But Yours," which opens the service, has the following refrain: "Christ has no body now but yours, no hands but yours. Here on this earth yours is the work, to serve with the joy of compassion." Verses call on the church participants to use their hands, eyes, and feet to "heal the wounded," "journey with the poor," and "give back to those in need."[34] The worship's final hymn draws even more strongly from the idea that work and the body are tools for glorifying God. In the song, Jesus' "lowly human birth" is proof that he came "to join all workers" who are "burden bearers of the earth." As the "Son of Joseph," Jesus is hailed as a "gifted worker" who spends days much the same way that working people do who have only their own physical labor to offer to the marketplace: "toiling for your daily food."

Between the opening and closing hymns the congregation listens to a homily the like of which is rarely heard in Catholic or Christian masses. Pastor Dowling's words on this Sunday are all about discipleship, on following the example of Jesus of Nazareth. Discipleship is a common theme of Christian homilies and sermons, but most, according to Dowling, "are about personal salvation and not collectively getting one another into heaven." Dowling, however, has something more radical, more transformative, and more Christ-like in mind. Below is an extended excerpt from his 2004 Labor Day homily:

> As we gather this morning, in this Labor Day weekend, we reflect on the gift of work, work that is meant to utilize our God-given skills, reward us with fair wages and benefits for that work, enable us to care for ourselves and our families and if possible, for those who cannot work or do not have the opportunities to work. There is a movement going on in some states led by a corporate lawyer whose name is Robert Hinckley. The movement is to change the basic tenet of corporate law which says, "The duty of directors is to make money for shareholders." That is basically what companies are required by law to do.
>
> Hinckley suggests that the basic tenet of corporate law instead be changed to read: "The duty of directors henceforth shall be to make money for shareholders, but not at the expense of the environment, human rights, public health and safety, dignity of employees and the welfare of communities in which the company operates." What Hinckley is reflecting is something at the heart of Jesus' call to discipleship and regard for all human beings and for all God's creation. What he is reflecting is the heart of our Catholic social teaching which declares the right of people to decent and productive work. To fair wages, private property, economic initiative, and freedom to organize. What he is reflecting and challenging all of us to do is to work to realize the basic teachings of our Catholic Christian faith, the teaching of Jesus to regard all people with the dignity due to a son or daughter of God. Jesus tells us that "Whoever does not carry his own cross and come after him cannot call themselves his disciple." Oftentimes we take that challenge as just reflecting on Jesus' cross and death and resurrection. He's not talking about doing that exact same thing. But keep in mind that all Jesus knew at the time was

> that those who were crucified were of two types: those who were actual criminals and those who stood up to voice and to right an injustice. The cross was the destiny of anyone who sought to speak the truth to authority and hold them accountable. So the cross Jesus is asking us to carry is not just the personal crosses of our jealousies, addictions, illnesses, losses, and other personal problems. If we are to follow him, we must be willing to carry the cross that demands all people be treated fairly, that all people be given the opportunity to use their God-given gifts and potential, that all people from conception to natural death have an opportunity to know the basic dignity that God created them to enjoy. And we must be willing to face the cross of being labeled as troublemakers, or as radicals or as difficult employees or even as un-American. The cross that Jesus is asking us to embrace as disciples is one that requires of disciples the courage and strength to stand for the dignity of all God's people. . . . If we are to claim discipleship, we must be willing to take risks necessary to learn and speak the truth to our employers, to our politicians, to our church leaders, and to one another. And we must be willing to join other disciples to learn together and then to speak with one voice, a voice which reflects the purity of truth and the compassionate strength of our teacher, Jesus Christ.

Dowling's homily equates discipleship with social action. The liturgy becomes an opportunity to literally stress the "work of the people."[35] His parishioners are challenged to be bold, defiant protectors of the oppressed.[36] To stress the suffering and rejection inherent in what Dietrich Bonhoeffer called the "cost of discipleship," Dowling uses the essential Christian literary and iconographic reference of "carrying the cross."[37] He does not mean it precisely as Jesus did on the road to Calvary, but as public citizens obligated to challenge abusive employers, even if it means being called "un-American." The revolutionary nature and transformational power of the "cross" was revisited in the spring of 2005 as St. Denis worshiped on the day of Jesus' death, "Good Friday." Christian tradition acknowledges Jesus' crucifixion with a somber reenactment of Christ's fateful walk up the hill to Calvary. The walk is made more burdensome by having Jesus carry the large wooden cross that will eventually serve as an execution spectacle. During the Catholic worship service I attended as a child, I recall the congregation collectively reciting readings or "stations of the cross." The entire simulated service was done in the comfortable and removed quarters of the church. But St. Denis's "stations" were real and in the community.

Parishioners were led by Pastor Larry on a walk through the Ashburn neighborhood. At fifteen locations, including a park, an alderman's office, a day-care center, an empty storefront, a gas station, a house for sale, and a school, the parishioners stopped and prayed together. As people moved from one station to the next, a wooden cross was carried by a different person. Each site along the walk was chosen to represent the faith that the church has in finding ways to improve the living conditions of the community. At every stop another chapter in Jesus' grueling walk is retold, along with a corresponding prayer. The entire program is detailed in a printed St. Denis *Stations of the Cross* worship booklet. I have included below three sample paragraphs taken from one page of the booklet. The first passage is a story narrative read aloud by Pastor Dowling. After a brief silent reflection, a decidedly temporal prayer concerning the dynamics of a residential area's changing racial makeup is collectively recited. The station visit concludes with a final passage explaining the significance of the physical site selected. The entire process is a powerful testament of how the church embeds a religious story of sacrifice into a material critique of actual lived experiences and continues to make "carrying the cross" relevant.

> *Seventh Station: Jesus Falls the Second Time (House for Sale 3212 W. 83rd St.)*
>
> The sun beats across the cobblestone path traversed by Jesus, its heat blistering his feet. The taunts and tirades of the soldiers and crown weigh all the behavior upon his heart. The memories of loved ones bolster his resolve, yet for a moment their abandonment saps his inner strength. And he falls a second time. As he lies on the stone street, he seeks to draw strength from within. He remembers his love for the Father, and his need to love in return. He looks up to see the face of a soldier, a young man, trying to do his duty, yet unsure of this particular assignment, and he cannot help but care for him. The soldier helps him to his feet, issues an order to keep walking, and Jesus proceeds on to his destiny at Calvary. How many times have we felt abandoned by others and failed to try to understand their motivations? How many times have we abandoned others, let them fail, because we chose not to understand?
>
> *Prayer:* Ever-faithful Lord, you constantly urge us to continue the battle to build good hearts, loving families, and strong neighbors. Lord, help us in the midst of change in our area to welcome those who are new and to graciously let go of those who leave for reasons that sometimes violate our own desire for true community. Assist us in strengthening our resolve to fight for fair housing for all and to work together in eradicating the elements of crime and gangs that we may build a neighborhood that is unified in peace and care for one another. We ask this through Christ, our Lord AMEN.

> *This House for Sale sign is not an unfamiliar yard marker in our community. It can often stand for some as a sign of abandonment by neighbors, but it also stands as a sign which is erected by fear and hatred. Our challenge is to overcome that fear by building bridges among old and new neighbors, as well as to not judge harshly those who seek to move. It also challenges us to stand against realtors who may prey on the fears and insecurities of our friends and neighbors.*

Dowling's worship homily and the recreation of the walk to Calvary through the Ashburn neighborhood underscore St. Denis's belief that Jesus' call to love one another is not limited by national boundaries, racial composition, gender or sexual orientation, political ideology, or economic status. If you claim discipleship then you must "know Jesus, the human being, Jesus the man."[38] It is a radical project to inspire the faith community to collectively overturn the modern moneychangers and revitalize the life of working-class neighborhoods. Father Dowling passionately believes that the "story at the heart of scripture, is the basic defense of human rights and dignity" and therefore, "the story of labor struggles has to be raised up."[39] There is no confusion here. The heart of Catholic social teaching and what "we are called as a Christian community to do" is to take the side of the oppressed, the abused workers, and the labor organizations that act morally in the defense of workers.[40] Dowling underscores the need for labor organizations to be ethically driven and democratic in their operations. He is intolerant of unions that act as modern Pharisees who exploit the people they are supposed to protect. But the pastor is not ambiguous about what Christian discipleship demands: "As a church, we are supporting labor unions that are an instrument for social justice."[41]

Raising the awareness of union and worker struggles was what Dowling had in mind when St. Denis hosted a religious-labor forum on employee health care and health-care workers. Taking seriously the Old Testament scriptural call for a Jubilee period of debt forgiveness for the poor, St. Denis opened its sanctuary to discussions on the state of health care in America. Speakers, including myself, took to the pulpit to point out the shameful fact that millions of American citizens lack affordable quality health care. Combining references from the Gospels to "heal the sick" with contemporary statistics of increasing numbers of workers assuming the burden of shifting health-care costs, presenters challenged the congregated to put their "faith in action." The most moving voices, however, were not those of the experts or Larry Dowling. From the modest platform dwarfed by the large wooden figure of Christ's crucifixion hanging directly behind the altar table, health-care workers from the large multidenominationally owned Advocate Hospital chain in Chicago spoke out about their oppression.[42]

Advocate employees startled the congregants by pointing out that many health-care workers in Chicago and America cannot afford the kind of health care they provide to their patients. Workers such as patient-care assistants who earn approximately $10 an hour and do not have employer-provided health-care insurance have qualified for public and charity assistance to stave off homelessness. Desperate for help, Advocate workers turned to the city's and nation's largest health-care union, the Service Employees International Union (SEIU). The union responded by commencing a national Hospital Accountability Project to hold non-profit hospitals (e.g., Advocate) "to their mission of placing the needs of patients, communities, and workers before financial objectives."[43] Union research revealed that the hospital was charging uninsured patients 139 percent more than approved insurance company payments and had only rebated half of its $70 million in annual tax breaks to low-income communities in the form of free care.[44]

In addition, while Advocate was a hospital employer with over $123 million in profits and $1.4 billion in unrestricted cash, it aggressively opposed its workers' right to be unionized.[45] Advocate's willful resistance to unionization and its bad corporate citizenship prompted St. Denis to join with the union to demand a "hospital Jubilee" for patients and workers. Relief was not just a matter of social values, but part of a Hebraic understanding that all wealth is vested in God and consequently, laws should prevent man's economic exploitation of man. Dowling believed that Advocate should do more to forgive the medical debts of low-income patients and recognize its employees' right to join a union. He relied on scripture to make the point: "And you shall hallow the fiftieth year, and proclaim liberty throughout the land to all its inhabitants; it shall be a jubilee for you. . . ."[46]

In Father Dowling's hands scripture often became the source of more than a personal ideational or behavioral map to salvation. God's words were a prescription to creating a just and equitable society on earth. When working-class people pray, read the Bible, listen to religious tapes, and come to worship, they should expect to have their consciousness raised about how as "disciples of Christ" they can confront the problems of a society mired in racial, sexual, and class exploitation. Dowling is trying to move his congregation to a higher level of civic engagement characterized by religious sociologist Robert Wuthnow as beyond "common symbols, common leaders, and perhaps common ideals," but to and toward "one another."[47] To help the faithful begin to think more about the "call to action," Dowling believes it is necessary to correct unfortunate and limited understandings of many scriptural passages. He is most insistent that Matthew 25 get its proper due. As Dowling sees it, Matthew's "great judgment" is too often interpreted as an individual command to offer care to needy family, friends, and the occasional stranger. In other words, it is a call for individual charity. But Dowling thinks that interpretation is incorrect at worst and minimalist at best. Individuals bringing soup cans to a food pantry is good, but it could hardly be all that Jesus expected from his followers. Dowling is certain that Jesus' public ministry and teachings taught people to "take up the cross in opposition to the forces that will take advantage of others." And if the meaning of Matthew 25 was properly understood, the church's cry for social justice would be unmistakable.

Dowling has attempted to free Matthew 25 from its literal straitjacket. At a seminar on Catholic social teachings, he offered a reworking of Matthew's seminal passage that he believes accurately reflects Jesus' call to discipleship. Beginning with the first verse, Dowling has added text which explains what is required in order to fully satisfy the demands of social justice. Matthew's original writings and a sample of Dowling's additions, printed in italics, appear below:

> For I was hungry and you fed me, *then you worked with others to transform national and international policy so that one day soon no one would need to go hungry; you worked to guarantee the rights of workers to be able to provide sustenance for themselves and their families;* For I was thirsty and you gave me drink, *then you worked with others to help build wells, and hold governments and corporations accountable for removing pollutants from all water supplies;* For I was a stranger and you welcomed me, *then you worked with others to welcome immigrants searching for a home, helped change the laws so they could have a realistic path toward becoming citizens, then worked with others to make sure the homeless of your own city would be trained for jobs and given the opportunity for decent and affordable housing;* For I was naked and you clothed me, *then you worked with others to make sure everyone, no matter what race or ethnicity or economic class, had a chance to move beyond the nakedness of ignorance to realize their potential and offer their God-given gifts to society through quality education and job-training;* For I was ill and you comforted me, *then you worked with others to create a health system for everyone which paid for preventive care and guaranteed respectful and thorough healthcare for everyone;* For I was in prison and you came to visit me, *then you worked with others to organize prison reform so that those in prison might be rehabilitated, and you worked to set up a system to reintegrate nonviolent ex-offenders back into society and you worked within schools to create an atmosphere where nonviolent resolution of conflict is the norm.*

Expressions of faith, whether through prayer, readings from holy books, worship services, or study groups, are primarily transmitters of religious meaning. In the case of St. Denis Catholic Church and Father Dowling, the life of Jesus educates His followers to be not only devotionally faithful, but public advocates for a just society. Worship or showing love for God is to be expressed in the deeds we do on behalf of our brothers and sisters "through the actual circumstances of each day."[48]

CHAPTER 5

Luther's Wall

THOMAS CARLYLE may have been one of a kind or at least the last of his kind. In a collection of essays written in 1843 titled *Past and Present,* the English philosopher put forward a view of work that elevates it to an exalted status unequaled by any philosopher, economist, union organizer, religious leader, or prophet. He saw more to human labor than mere economic production or material sustenance. He also conceived of a person's labors as fostering more than his or her self-satisfaction, cognitive skills, and moral values. For Carlyle, as Miroslav Volf states, "work took on explicitly religious overtones."[1] Unlike the preaching of any religious leader I have ever heard or the religious teachings familiar to most working-class Christians, Muslims, or Jews, Carlyle puts work forward as a secular means to salvation. Carlyle wrote that work is "the latest Gospel in this world," because it has the potential for elevating people "from the low places of this Earth, very literally, into divine Heavens."[2]

Imagine if the work you do could get you into heaven or, at the very least, God's good graces. Miroslov Volf writes that "[with] Carlyle mundane work replaced prayer to God," and, therefore, the work of the believers should be treated as divine.[3] But according to conventional religious orthodoxy it is not by the sweat of their brows that sinners are redeemed. As Armand Larive explains, "only faith . . . faith quite apart from any vocation, being something entirely free, unassociated with work," can get you into heaven.[4] He identified the revolutionary teachings of Martin Luther on *salvation by grace alone* as the reason for a misguided Christian underappreciation of human labors. However, Luther did make an important declaration: according to him, work could now serve God if it served humanity, and the work of a pig farmer was no less valuable to God than that of an esteemed cleric. In fact, the farmer may very well be doing more for humanity than the pious priest. Luther expressed a Protestant reverence for all kinds of work by preaching to his congregation that "the carpenter at his bench, the shoemaker at his last, the housemaid at her cow—all of them were to find in the humble tasks of daily duty an authentic vocation from God himself."[5] Nonetheless, as far as the kingdom of heaven goes, work could not be an entry ticket. Larive referred to Luther's discourse as "putting up a firewall" between work and salvation.[6] For many of the working-class faithful interviewed, Luther's wall was never dismantled, but it was very often significantly breached. Unfortunately, formal religious observance has badly neglected the world of work and, as a result, most believers assume that "ministry happens only within the bounds of the congregation."[7] But if work is sacred, then when Christian, Jewish, and Islamic believers are asked "What do you do?" the answer should reflect more than their moral character.

Americans work a great deal and their hours are getting longer. Juliet Schor documented that in the late 1980s the average employed person was working 163 hours more than in 1969.[8] Even the famed—if destructive—Japanese worker obsession "karoshi," or "death by overwork," is no longer more lethal than Americans' "work-at-all-cost" mentality. In their annual *The State of Working America*, Larry Mishel, Jared Bernstein, and Sylvia Allegreto have extensively reported how American workers are intensely laboring into an early grave.[9] By every standard of social analysis, work is the most prominent activity in the lives of most adults and, to be honest, far too many teenagers. It is also through the work we do, according to James Bernard Murphy, that "most people derive their sense of personal identity and their sense of social status."[10] Al Gini declares that work "is our signature on the world . . . to work is to *be* and not to work is *not to be*"(emphasis in original).[11] In many cases the workplace is where we prefer to be, over home, community, and, I suspect, even religious places of worship.[12]

Work and the workplace consume most of our waking hours. To Christians, Jews, and Muslims alike, what happens during work cannot be carved out of a spiritual life. While prayer, worship, and Bible study can happen more or less in a person's life, if people work for a living, their formal religious observance will, by necessity, be at best a secondary human activity. Believers may claim a privileged place for God and religious practice in their lives, but even a cursory check of where they spend their time and what they do with it will expose a tension between truth and self-perception. Pointing out that disconnection is not meant as a criticism. In fact, I cannot imagine how in our modern capitalistic society people can be more religious than they already claim to be. Unless of course we redefine what it means to be religious.

It seems to me that the workplace and the work people do present believers with the most fruitful opportunity to expand their spiritual identity. But in conceiving work as a domain of religious expression I am not endorsing the unfortunate management trend of using "religious ministries" at work as a means to sweat additional labor out of their underpaid, underappreciated employees. Nothing could be more contrary to recognizing the divine quality of a person's talents then equating laboring with production quotas or a for-profit company brand. The divine nature of work expressed here is one that finds an inherent spiritual value in secular jobs. It is the profound possibility that cleaning hotel rooms is for the Christian, Jewish, or Muslim cleaner a religious activity deserving of the utmost respect and human dignity. If by nature, economic necessity, or moral choice, work becomes the activity that most defines the passing of human life, then Christians, Jews, and Muslims should have thoughts about the role that it plays in their faithfulness. In other words, as Armand Larive provocatively asks (and which by extension applies to all faith traditions), "Because people's occupations often center life's meaning so powerfully, does that mean they are bending the knee in de facto obeisance to secular gods, Kingdoms and morals of a workaday world, saving only Sundays for Christian activity?"[13]

Virginia Coleman of Holy Angels Parish insists that she is no "Sunday Christian." She has worked for five years as a processing clerk for the City of Chicago and she knows why she has this job. "It's where the Lord wants me to be." Virginia views her job as a "calling," meaning that God had chosen her to work in a particular field.[14] She believes that her work praises God as surely as her church singing does. "I am the liaison between the building department and the title search companies. I do title searches and I figure that my work praises the Lord because we [her department] are throwing these strong landlords into court. We are getting them in as fast as possible. I figure that what I do praises the Lord because it helps people that are in no position to help themselves. They are at the landlords' mercy. The main thing is to put them into court so that they can be fined." It is evident from Virginia's sense of purpose at work that she views her labor as a device to bring justice to those who have been wronged by more powerful people. As a Christian, Virginia explains, her work has become a way to bring the world into the right order that God intends.

Virginia's work is inspired by the words of the Old Testament prophet Amos, who offered hope to the world that human beings could act justly. In the much-cited passage listed below, Amos confirms that God wants justice to reign on earth. I suspect that God wants it even more than Virginia's singing and worship rituals.

> I hate, I despise your feasts, and I take no delight in your solemn assemblies. Even though you offer me your burnt offerings and cereal offerings, I will not accept them, and the peace offerings of your fatted beasts I will not look upon. Take away from me the noise of your songs: the melody of your harps I will not listen. But let justice roll down like waters, and righteousness like an ever-flowing stream. (Amos 5:21–24)

Work in effect becomes the primary vehicle that Virginia uses to express her commitment to live as God commands. The time Virginia spends at work, then, feels more like a pilgrimage than an obligation or a necessity. It is certainly more than a pecuniary exchange. "You know to be able to let people know that I am there for them, and lots of times people come to me and say that they know they can trust me. It is such a blessing to be able to have that kind of relationship with people." Virginia is not just well satisfied with the work she has to do, but she believes she is doing what she is called to do. "People can tell at work that I am a person on a mission." Her mission goes well beyond efficiently producing property titles or holding building owners accountable. It is also about teaching others to be better employees. "I guess that is my ministry to be able to mentor to people." Notice the religious terminology: Virginia sees her work as a ministry to others. She uses her God-given talents to help other "children of God" employ their own talents more effectively. And once again it is through her work that she serves God and God's people.

The workplace, in Virginia's case, is a crowded space characterized by computer keyboards and four-foot-high cushioned cubicles. It hardly sounds like a holy place. To be sure, Virginia distinguishes between her beautiful ornate church of vibrant African iconography and a functional city office. But the Holy Spirit is not kept within the walls of the church. "My cubicle is surrounded by scenery and spiritual words—my daily words." Virginia's favorite religious posting is "Let go and let God." These invocations are an integral part of Virginia's workday. "I start off my morning at work by reading my daily words." And as the day goes on, Virginia keeps God close. "I usually keep my Bible on my desk all day long. I just feel His presence." The Bible is both a reminder to Virginia of her "calling" and an important tool for surviving the workday. "There is so much turmoil going on at our jobs." Shortly before we spoke, Virginia's office went through an imposed workforce reduction. "So many people took the early retirement, so people are stressed and they cannot understand why I am so at peace. I tell my co-workers that I am blessed and I am doing well and that I cannot complain." When the workday becomes particularly hard, Virginia simply opens the Bible and turns to the word of God. Virginia's belief that her job is divinely inspired also fortifies her against fears of job loss or being so badly overworked that she would consider quitting the job. "I look and I know that the Lord has brought me from situations in my life, so I feel His presence here [at work] and I am just thankful for it."

The blessing of working where you believe you are meant to work is a rewarding feeling some working-class believers have. Satisfaction at work is no small accomplishment. Work is rarely confused with play; by most comprehensive sociological reports, earning our daily bread more often alienates than gratifies people. For instance, the seminal 1973 government study *Work in America* depicted a whole lot of "blue-collar blues" among manufacturing employees.[15] The substantial absence of job satisfaction was also prevalent among all types of workers throughout the 1980s and 1990s.[16] Villanova University's Eugene McCarraher laments that American workers "work longer hours, are more harried, tired and distracted and dislike their jobs and bosses more."[17] Fortunately, Mertis Odom of Community Mennonite Church is one of those workers who have always felt "deeply satisfied" while on the job.

She worked a lifetime as a rehabilitation counselor for the physically challenged on Chicago's southwest side. The work could have worn her down. "One of the things that I asked God to do is to keep me healthy mentally, physically, and spiritually so that I may serve people other than my family." Mertis feels driven to serve people because she takes seriously her Christianity. "I know that is the way that He would want me to be as a Christian." Mertis is a regular at Sunday service and on occasions has led the small congregation in prayer. But praying and working are a lot alike. "I want to be a servant. What I mean by servant, I don't just mean serving God, but I feel that you can serve as a compassionate person, you can listen to somebody, and you can talk with somebody; to just feed somebody, to give somebody a place to live."

Work for Mertis was a chance to deepen her Christian faith. It was a moment to be selfless and caring of others "I think that is what He wants us to do; to go beyond ourselves. Look, I am a Christian and I go to church every Sunday and I do my part." But there is something else. "A lot of people want to just go beyond that. The easy part is to routinely be the 'good Christian.'" By "good Christian" Mertis means doing what is easy, such as going to church and praying, and basically "not bothering anybody." The "hard stuff," however, is found in the duty or "calling" to act Christ-like. Mertis's strong commitment to "take Christianity to the workplace" is her way of fulfilling the scriptural promise Jesus made to his apostles: "Truly, truly, I say to you, he who believes in me will also do the works that I do."[18] So when Mertis worked, she did Christ-like things and along the way she "enjoyed the job very much."

Not everyone feels the way that Mertis does about her daily labor. Feeling good about work does not necessarily mean that you are exercising the talents that God intended you to use. "No, not really," was Don Burklow's response to my question about whether his work as a plumber was a way he honored God. "I had to go to school and I had to have an apprenticeship for [plumbing]." Plumbing was an honorable trade that Don took pride in doing, but he never considered it somehow sacred. He did, however, acknowledge that God had blessed him with some special talents. "I like to do art work. I draw portraits." It seemed that authoring portraits of friends and family was a talent bestowed by God, but performing a 45-degree offset on a piece of pipe was just work. "I think I had to find a job and that was it." The closest Don came to seeing a connection between his trade and God was the time he spent installing the plumbing for an addition to his own Community Mennonite Church in Markham.

While cutting pipe or roughing out a bathtub did not conjure up visions of divine purpose for Don, he did think that God was pleased with people who do their work well. Don boasted that he was always honest with people. "When I would go into some people's houses, they would give me the key and I would go in when they were on vacation and I would do what I had to do. Nothing would ever be missing from the house. Everyone who knew me knew that I was honest." Plumbing work may not have been God's work, but according to Don, it was labor that should be performed according to principles that a faithful tradesman adhered to. Not that any real earthly reward would come from doing work in a manner pleasing to God. "I think whatever you do here on earth is up to you. He is not going to step in and give you riches or stuff. I think it is kind of foolish to think that way." So, I wondered, would being the best plumber you can be help you get into heaven? Apparently plumbing work is not much help after death either. "If you are a true believer," Don explained, "then you will be doing the right thing." To Don, work "ain't nothing but a job," and eternal salvation requires unyielding faith.

Right belief has its limits, however. Craig Doornbos has been a truck driver for over three decades and God has been a road companion for each mile traveled. Craig drives a gasoline tanker for a large international oil company. His work mostly consists of transporting 9,000 gallons of gasoline for ten hours a day from oil terminals to gas stations around the state. The dangers of the job conjure up frightening scenarios of devastating fires and explosions. I fully expected that Craig, a member of Park Lane Christian Reform Church, would have embroidered his truck cab with protective symbols of God. Surely he would have a cross or rosary dangling from the rearview mirror, a magnetized miniature statue of a saint sitting on the dashboard, a laminated devotional or a picture of Jesus clipped to the sun visor, or a yellow-stained copy of the Bible resting on the passenger seat. But Craig had nothing of the sort. The only obvious indication that God copiloted his cab was a prayer that he recited before shifting the gears into drive. "It would just be a sentence praying for God to 'watch me tonight that I do not hurt anyone.' Mostly I ask that He be there with me so that I don't make a mistake."

Craig used to think his job was a calling. "It started out as a calling because I really enjoyed the travel. I was all over the road and I got to see a lot of things and meet a lot of different people. But then the job left the area and in my next job [the present one], I was a local driver." The new company is unionized and provides great benefits, but Craig laments that "there's not a lot of personal involvement" among the employees and with drivers having to adhere to twenty pages of rules, the job now feels more like just a secure way to pay bills. So is driving a truck still something that God wants Craig to do? "Yeah, I think that it is where I am supposed to be because of the benefits." Despite the loss of emotional satisfaction, Craig has come to see God's hand in altering the path that he was traveling. "My son was tested earlier this year for depression and under the old insurance plan none of his expenses would have been covered. Now my medical coverage helps a lot with the bills."

Craig is deeply thankful for the work opportunities that God has provided, but he hastens to add that his praise is not only because of the job's rewards. "I don't think that when you are called to a job it is merely for the benefits, but what you can do at the job that makes the difference." Craig sees God's wisdom at work by placing him in a position to use his talents. "Everybody has a talent. I think that I am good at this. I have been driving tankers most of my life so it is not like it is anything new to me. I know that there is a talent driving." And when Craig drives in the glory of God, he uses his talents to serve others. "It's important how you do things. If you do work in a cutthroat way I think that is just being selfish because you are just looking out for yourself. But if you are looking out for the well-being of others, I think that is sacred." In Craig's theology, administering the Christian sacraments and downshifting a ten-ton oil can on wheels are equally sacred when done for the benefit of others. "We were built to serve and not come here and lie in the sand and drink piña coladas all day. We were meant to work in the service of God and to enjoy our work."

Craig says it plainly: "You do a good job, not because the boss says that you should do a good job, but you do it for God because you are working for God, not for the company." His words echo the mocking message from the profit Isaiah warning against the futility of working for selfish ego and making idols out of human labor:

> All who make idols are nothing, and the things they delight in do not profit. . . . Who fashions a god and casts an image that is profitable for nothing? The ironsmith fashions it and works with it over the coals; he shapes it with hammers, and forges it with his strong arm. . . . The carpenter stretches a line, he marks it out with a pencil; he fashions it with planes, and marks it with a compass; he shapes into the figure of a man, to dwell in a house. He cuts down cedars; or he chooses a holm tree or an oak and lets it grow strong among the trees of the forest; he plants a cedar and the rain nourishes it. . . . [H]e kindles a fire and bakes bread; also makes a god and worships it; he makes a graven image and falls down before it.[19]

Patty Brown also feels delivered into her work. She worked for six years at a fitness facility before being laid off. Without work she prayed most days. Months went by, then her prayers were answered. "I figured I needed to make at least $125 a week to make ends meet. The weird thing is that I just prayed on it and low and behold, two of my sisters called me." That phone call brought Patty a job and closer to God. "One asked me to take care of her son and she would pay me $75 a week. Nobody knows that I prayed for this. Then my other sister calls me and wants me to take care of her daughter and she would give me $50 per week. There was my $125 just magically appearing." Patty has been a state-licensed child-care worker for nine years and she has grown to believe that the job is more than an opportunity to pay the bills. "I think this has turned out to be my gift, I really do."

Most of the children that Patty cares for (eight kids under the age of twelve) are from families attending her Lutheran church, Family in Faith, in Glendale Heights. She is convinced that her ability to work as a caregiver for someone else's children is proof of God's satisfaction with her. "This must be what He wants me to do because I would never dream that this is what I would be doing today. I never asked to do this. I do not advertise and when I need to have more kids, they just appear. I think that if I did not do a good job my day care would not be full." Patty feels rewarded by God for answering a call to do something that was not of her own choosing. The interesting aspect of her understanding is that when she speaks of doing what "He wants," she points to the profound nature of a relationship with God. Patty attests to finding a higher meaning and significance in life by saying yes to the opportunity to care for her sisters' children. In answering the phone calls from her sisters, Patty believes that she strengthened the bond between herself and God. When asked when she feels closest to God, Patty responded, "When I am with the kids and I'm teaching them lessons of right and wrong." In other words, it is through her caregiving work that she answered God's call. But will the work she does with children contribute to Patty getting into heaven? "Sure, I think so. I spend twelve hours a day with these children. I try to do the right things for them and their families."

Ellen Kilmurry of St. Denis Parish has known the struggles of many families. She spends her numerous working hours trying to help the poor to find safe harbor. She earns very little money and feels that the job's modest compensation reflects on the nature of her labor. "It is a calling, absolutely. No one would choose, at my age, not to be able to pay all of her bills on time. Financially, it is very difficult to work in social service ministry. This is not strictly to pay the bills, I was called." In her case, called by a priest to leave a job Ellen had with an accounting firm. Ellen drew a real distinction between work that is divinely inspired and work that is just a job. "I feel that when I was an accountant that I was even working against godly things. I had to put up with a lot of people who kept telling me that they didn't want to pay taxes and wanted a loophole." What was ungodly about not wanting to pay taxes? Ellen's answer raised serious questions of class and social justice. As it turns out, paying taxes to Caesar was objectionable because filers did not want their money to go to "those people." Ellen understood "those people" to mean the poor, the homeless, the uneducated, welfare recipients, and anyone without a job.

To continue doing the job created an ethical dilemma for Ellen. "It always killed me because I am one of 'those people.' My father came from Ireland in July 1929 and never made a lot of money. He and my grandfather worked immigrant jobs building railroads and subways. But the accounting job was all about making people with money feel more secure about keeping their wealth and making sure that no poor people got hold of a penny of it." Work in this case had assumed the character of pure toil and Ellen saw a lot of evil in the job, so when "called" to serve the indigent she said yes. And now working fulfills what Ellen believes God meant for work to be. "It is a means of self-expression, and an educational thing. It is a self-actualizing experience. I think work is a gift. It is a way to learn your place in the world and to make the world a better place to be in." Ellen's "gift" is to reach out to the needy and offer help to the hungry, sick, and homeless through the PORT Ministries' many services.[20] When she does this she feels "like I'm acting as an instrument of God."

Ellen does her job for the same reason that prophets like Amos, Jeremiah, and Zechariah, and the disciple Paul did theirs. "I want to be a kingdom builder. Your work either is building the kingdom or isn't building the kingdom." Ellen chose to leave a more well-paying job for one that forces her to juggle payments of her monthly bills. But she made the conversion because she takes seriously her faith's denunciation of wealth that is accumulated at the expense of others. She would certainly find agreement with the prophet Jeremiah's warning: "Woe to him who builds his neighbors' house by unrighteousness and his upper rooms by injustice; who makes his neighbors serve him for nothing, and does not give him his wages" (Jeremiah 22:13). Ellen is also an active member of St. Denis's community outreach efforts and contributes considerable time to church matters. But it is primarily through Ellen's "after Sunday" worklife that she lives in accordance with the intentions of her God. It seems to me that as a *working being*—though not exclusively as such—Ellen is able to live most fully in the image of God.

Unholy work or labor that does not allow a person to be in the image of God is something that cabdriver Mustafa Ali agreed was an important element to faithful living. "I could not as a Muslim work at a liquor store." When asked about other examples of proscribed workplaces, Ali explained that he could not in good faith "work anywhere that can hurt a human being." By doing harm he meant places like gun factories and tobacco processing plants, which are designed to hurt or degrade the human body. For Ali the Qur'an was very clear about the type of work that must be avoided. It was also clear to Ali that if you drive a taxi for a living, you have to be willing to "drive where it is bad." Ali, for instance, could not in good conscience refuse to pick up a fare in an area of the city that had a high crime rate. Nor could he refuse to pick up a customer based on her or his skin color. Religion provided Ali with very practical guidelines as to what was acceptable secular work activity. But importantly, he stressed that his work was not a religious activity. "I am not mixing up my religion and my work. Driving a cab is what I do for money, but that work I do must be right."

Fellow Muslim cabbie Mohammed Hareed also had strong feelings about doing his job according to Islamic principles of fairness, but unlike

Ellen Kilmurry, did not adhere to the notion of a "calling." "No, it's not like that is what Allah wants for me. It's something more like what we would call luck. It's whatever you get. Allah does not say you do this and you do that job. He just said do the job rightly." In Ali's and Hareed's view there is no divine placement in a job that allows a person's God-given talents to be best utilized. Allah, of course, knows what work you are doing and harshly judges the way that work is done, but the relationship of occupation to person is merely random. Nevertheless, by doing a job "rightly" Hareed and the other Muslim drivers believed they were working in accordance with religious principles.

Omar Ali, a driver for over five years, knew the rules of the road. "When you drive a cab, you follow the rules of God. You have a covenant with God to obey the rules." Initially I thought Ali was referring to Islamic guidelines for doing work. But he then drew an equivalency between secular laws and religious obligations. "If you do not obey the traffic rules, you do not obey Allah." But how is it that obedience to the state is the same as living faithfully? "Because," Ali responds, "Allah cares not about what your work is, but how you do it. In Islam you should always do your best, whether you are driving a cab or not, you should do nothing less than your best." Doing work well is critical to each of the cabbies according to Ali because it is the "thing that keeps you going, the nourishment that sustains a human life." As Hareed explained, "If you do not work, you do not have the means to worship."

Work, then, is a means to a greater means, in that it provides a freedom from material want and thus ensures a greater end, i.e., God's grace. Through work we can live according to God's desire for a productive, just human community. But our labors are also instruments to make possible a life of prayer and praise. As a separate meditative activity disconnected from labor, Islamic prayer appears to be a primary means by which people of faith can act in accordance with their faith. Work may be a gift from Allah, but it is a lower-order good, secondary in importance to a life of worship. Yet, if done "rightly," work pays dividends in life and in death. Omar Ali again clarifies the point. "Whatever you do for your work now, you get your money now. It is money now—only money. But later on you will be rewarded for your good deeds." In Ali's theology, working rightly is one way to do "good deeds" or "good works" on earth. Each of the cabbies was certain that Allah looked favorably on a person who performed good deeds and that the riches of heaven are extended for one who believes and does good works. Verses in the Qur'an, like the following, even use the language of labor's pecuniary reward to foretell a greater spiritual bounty: "Whatever good you shall forward to your souls' account, you shall find it with God as better, and mightier a wage."[21]

In actuality, there are fewer earthly hourly wages that are better than those earned by union electricians. Jeff Goldberg is a well-trained member of International Brotherhood of Electrical Workers Local 134 and prides himself on his level of craftsmanship. Jeff is one of those nameless, faceless workers who make sure that the commuter trains are moving. Each day for the last eleven years he has been a part of a workforce that gives luster to the motto "Chicago is the city that works." While modest in talking about his own skills, Jeff becomes more animated when speaking about a deeper spiritual relationship that he has to his craft. "We are working as His soldiers. The work that we do is the work that needs to be done." Jeff explains that God needs human hands to get things done on earth. The city may employ him, but Jeff believes his labors contribute to God's kingdom on earth. Not only does he work with his union brothers and sisters, but he copartners with God to keep the power on. There is nothing mystical about Jeff's work relationship with God. He does not believe that he was chosen to be an electrician, but "the work that needs to be done" includes cleaning the streets, building cars, making beds, and wiring train stations. Jeff, it turns out, is pretty darn good at the latter. "He has given us everything to sustain our lives and to live a fruitful existence and a very abundant life. Everybody has to be accountable. This could be a partnership." One perhaps made in heaven and fulfilled in Chicago.

The role of work in Daniel Weinberg's religious life is much more than a random outcome of opportunity and individual choice. He is a sixth-grade science and social studies teacher who sees his students as an expression of God's plan for him. Tugging his Chicago Cubs ball cap down on his forehead, Daniel admits that "I think of [my job] as divine providence or whatever." Daniel believes that he is a good teacher and that his talents are "contributing to the repair of the world." "Everyday I go in [to school] and I hope that I am doing a good job . . . that all of this teaching is sort of happening for a reason. At least that is where I put my faith." Daniel also puts his faith in traditional religious observance. He diligently observes the Jewish Sabbath (e.g., no grading papers or planning school lessons from Friday sundown until Saturday sundown) and considers Jewish law to be a high priority in his life. He understands the sacred significance of "not working" and taking "one day to devote to prayers." The six days prior to the seventh (i.e., Sabbath) are necessary and yes, "holy things" can be done "within your work," but Daniel explains that the "ultimate goal is to bring the coming of the Messiah." And being a religious observant Jew is necessary but not sufficient to the task. Salvation to Daniel requires completing the material work that God began. "If you go with the idea that God did the first six days of work—that God created [the world] and it is our job to complete that—I think then that I am continuing as the molder or fashioner as a teacher." By teaching, Daniel is laboring in partnership with God to construct a world suitable for human beings. His hand holds the chalk that sketches the formula $E = mc^2$. His intellect conceptualizes the best way to explain the Bill of Rights. His voice lectures on responsibility, hard work, and values. But when his efforts "help raise [students] to their fullest potential," Daniel is confident that he is doing the work of God. "I am actually taking God's work quite literally and continuing to tend to the crops, so to speak." Theology professor David Jensen would support Daniel's co-creative spirit by noting that the "Bible assumes that God works" and that trades and crafts of all forms are central to biblical theism. "Prophetic literature suffuses with such imagery," Jensen writes.[22] While salvation may only come by the grace of the Savior, the six common days of toil that Daniel commits to his students appear to be crucial to his spirituality.

Teaching sixth graders not only makes the world a little healthier, but Daniel feels closer to God "because of the nature of my work." He speculates that certain jobs, like sitting at a desk, would make it harder for him to feel God's presence at work. "But that's probably why I don't do that." Teaching, on the other hand, is a sacred talent that God gave to Daniel in order to "repair the world." "[It's] not just knowledge, not just giving knowledge, but also certain understandings of the world and certain ways of teaching kids how to think and how to learn. How to look at the world—how to see things in a different light—how to investigate—how to just be aware. If I am successful in that, I would consider that very fulfilling." His ability to explain the works of the cosmos or where the sky begins is, in Daniel's words, "a gift of purpose." Daniel's teaching is a "blessing from God" with an expectation that the bearer will contribute positively to the world.

You could say that Sherwin Epstein lives to work. He not only regularly endures fifty-hour workweeks but welcomes them. Work defines Sherwin, and if Al Gini is correct that people "are what they do," then Sherwin is a 1,500-pounds-of-meat-a-day Jewish meat cutter.[23] He admits simply that "I like to work." Now a joyous commitment (or obsession) like his to hourly labor could be mistaken for a calling. Not so. "I'm a butcher, it's just a job." But it was once a job that was very fulfilling. "Years ago, yeah, but now there are different management styles." Work in a supermarket deli shop has become more standardized, less creative. "Today I don't feel fulfilled because today you are run like a computer. You cannot think. They [management] have boundaries set for you. You can't use your own head." Sherwin's been around long enough to fondly recall when butchers ground the meat and created their own specialty items on the premises.

"We use to be merchandisers and were able to use our own brains." But since the mid-1980s, corporate policy dictates what gets cut, how much, and where it rests behind glass. "You have so many spaces in the counter for pot roast, so many spaces for chuck steak or porterhouse or T-bone. You just cut to fill that spec . . . you don't use your own head."

While Sherwin claims to be a "non-religious Jew," he does have pretty strong feelings about what God intended for human toil. "I think God would want the workplace to be a pleasant place. Not as much pressure and tension and chaos that goes on. I don't think that He wants that for human beings." Working at a slave driver's pace with little or no control over the use of your skill demeans the meat-cutting craft and, in Sherwin's eyes, does violence to a person. "I don't think He wants people to suffer. God wants a nice place for everybody to work so that everybody could be happy. He would want everybody to be able to make a decent wage." Cutting meat, Sherwin nostalgically laments,"used to be an art." Now he does the job the best that he can and hopes that God is pleased. Sherwin does not expect any spiritually provided material rewards for doing his job well, but suspects that God "would not appreciate it" if he took his work lightly.

But why would God care how Sherwin cuts meat? "He cares because we as individuals all do His work. Just me working as a butcher, I am doing something that helps people eat. I am feeding the people. I help them get their food. That's something that God would want. It's just like the farmer raising food." The link of farmer to butcher describes a great chain of provisions that sustains creation. The connection is the work we do. Sherwin's humbly stated but profoundly claimed "I am feeding the people" evokes the dignity of labor that is upheld throughout the very same Talmudic literature he knows nothing of. Abraham Cohen cites from Genesis that "the Lord God took the man and put him into the Garden of Eden to till it and keep it" (Genesis 2:15) as rabbinical support for the idea that God gave human beings stewardship over the earth. And that stewardship meant that people would have to work to sustain life for themselves and others, even the yet unborn. Cohen retells a popular sage's story of the Roman emperor Hadrian who, while passing along the road, saw an old man breaking up the soil to plant trees. Hadrian stopped and asked the man how old he was. The man answered, a hundred. Upon hearing this Hadrian exclaimed, "You a hundred years old and you stand there breaking up the soil to plant trees! Do you expect to eat of their fruit?" The old man replied, "If I am worthy I shall eat; but if not, as my fathers labored for me, so I labor for my children."[24] It seemed to me that Sherwin Epstein cut meat to nourish the Garden. In doing so he was profoundly religious because he was doing what would please his God. "I am giving 100 percent every single day to the best of my ability."

The theme of "feeding one another" as a continuance of God's work on earth is more directly addressed by grocery store *mashgiach* Barry Blaustein. Through Barry's hands runs a direct hierarchical line of human labors that situates him in the chain of provisions. "We [kosher supervisors] do holy work. Our work that we do is on a holier level than, like say, running a nursing home or being a businessman. Even being a janitor is [holy], like a rabbi's work is the holiest." Barry contends that out of the 613 commandments in the collection of Jewish laws, "one of the most important is to earn a living." Everybody has meaningful work that they need to perform. Somebody somewhere is physically, psychologically, or materially dependent on a janitor's clean mop, a teacher's creative lesson, and a butcher's carving knife. Work is sacred, according to Barry, because it fulfills God's desire for a healthy human community, including time for worship. Work should also make a person happy. "There is a lot of fulfillment in what I do and I am faithful in what I do. It is very important, my job. I don't just reserve my faith for synagogue in the morning and evening. I feel that I am living my faith every minute of the day."

Barry also explains that working to fulfill the dietary laws of the Jewish faith achieves the dual purpose of not only providing for the Jewish community, but, more broadly, promoting the "mission of God" on earth. What mission is that? Barry answers with the brevity of a sage: "To help others." Our labors are God's hands sustaining, nurturing, and building life. Miroslav Volf contends that beyond gaining pecuniary gain or self-satisfaction, "work has not only personal utility, but also moral meaning."[25] In Barry's daily grind the architectonic of food preparation has become a path to holiness. And what of the "bagger" who bags the kosher food? Is her or his work also holy? By Barry's own account, "bagging" would not be the equivalent of the rabbi's Sabbath recitation from the Torah, but the work of a bagger still creates an opportunity to strengthen the divine image in the mundane. "First of all, I am making a living. But people trust me to make sure that the level of food is kept kosher. In a way, I have a tremendous feeling of having a noble profession. Like teaching, teaching is a very noble profession. Educating and teaching people—shaping their lives and their careers, can be deeply rewarding. Maybe not in the same way as being a rabbi, but being a supervisor in the kosher food business it is also deeply rewarding. Because of me, people are eating kosher. That means a lot to me as a person."

Labor, like prayer, worship, and cooking kosher, tightens the bond between rabbi, *masgiach,* bagger, cashier, butcher, truck driver, rancher, and farmer. The labors of many disconnected hands may unconsciously impact the lives of others, but in Barry's worldview the work is done cooperatively with the Almighty. Episcopal priest Matthew Fox points out that mystics like Meister Eckhart proposed the "preposterously wild idea that to work is to bring forth God."[26] The most pedestrian of views can accept that our labors mixed with nature produces a constructed world capable of sustaining human materiality, but Barry and the mystics are aware of an additional bounty. "The fruit of our work," Fox reveals, "is the bringing forth of Divinity."[27] God, it seems, *works in our work*. Barry firmly believes as much. More important, it is how God becomes "the all-encompassing presence who addresses humanity through the experience of living in the world."[28]

Barry does not feel, however, that all jobs are a service to others or God. While "there is no shame in any work that you do," some human labors bring nothing but heartache. "I have friends that are rich guys, but they have lousy personal lives [and] a lot of broken marriages. They have children that have so much to deal with. Sure, they have money, but what comes with it is a lot of problems. So I don't drive a Lexus, I drive a Buick; they all get me to the same place." Barry never described what his rich friends do for a living, but I had the sense that he saw their acquisition of wealth as a "soulless movement" for material fortune.[29] Barry earns a good living, and with union wages and benefits he owns a house and sends his children to college. He prays three times a day and twice a day rides joyfully to synagogue in his pale green Buick.

Time spent nursing in a pediatrics center and in a hospital oncology unit can evoke contradictory emotional responses to questions about God and work. Sandra Aarsdma fought back tears as she talked about being able "to make a difference in someone's life." Her cheeks were never dry as she spoke about working with children and people with cancer for thirty years as a nurse in clinics and hospitals. Nursing became a calling for Sandra, but not because she felt spiritually drawn to the work. In fact, the work was forcibly thrust upon her. "My dad said that he would pay for a wedding or school for me, but said 'I will pay for you only if you become a nurse.' My dad was not a believer [in God] and he was very controlling, but he had a high regard for nurses." Sandra accepted the limited offer and quickly grew thankful. "As I enrolled in nursing school, it was exactly where I fit. I loved what I did. It was confirmation of where my path lay. God works in mysterious ways." In this case, through a nonbelieving old-fashioned man who thought that women should either be married or nurses.

When we talked, Sandra's husband was the pastor at Park Lane Christian Reformed Church in Evergreen Park. She was intimately involved in church life, but her greatest joys came from occupational ministering to patients. "It was little things, like giving a back rub at night, settle them, and listen to them, these things really made a difference. I measured success by making a difference in a person's life even if it is only treating them momentarily." Her objective each day when she dressed in her nursing scrubs was an uncommon occupational purpose: "to give great love and to make life a little easier" for her patients. Many times Sandra's care was not enough to prevent a tragic shortening of a person's life, but healing happened enough to sustain her faith in a merciful God. Sometimes the healing was not of the body. "I had one gentleman who had a poor relationship with his son and it was a good time to talk about some of the things that he wanted to do before he passed on. He knew that this life was short. He wanted to get things right with his son. I encouraged that." Talk could also merge into prayer. Sandra was not hesitant to pray with a patient who was open to it: "Jesus is the great healer and we are His instruments."

God, in Sandra's eyes, blessed her with a talent for care, and when she used it she was doing good works for God. But was she special? Did she have something like a faith healer's power? Did her job bring her a bit closer to God than a person who works as a janitor in a commercial office building? "We should be glad to be a part of God's work in whatever field it is. It could be anywhere. It's not that my work is more spiritual than any other work. Whatever you do it is holy work. It's not only the stuff you do on Sundays that makes Sundays special. It's every day." Sandra's job may not have any greater value to God than the guy who picks up my garbage, but her familiarity with death and dying does give her a unique opportunity to draw on her Christianity. "As an oncology nurse you would like to see more people have more hope in their lives. Hope for a world yet to come. A hope that life continues even through the suffering to a better end." Work is more bearable and Sandra can do it more effectively because heaven is waiting for her and her patients. "You get close to people and sure you are hurt when they pass on, but many of them I will see in heaven again."

The one person Sandra most looks forward to seeing is someone she never nursed. "I went into oncology because my mom died when she was fifty-eight from stomach cancer." Sandra was at her mother's bedside when she died. "She was such a private person that when I looked away for one moment she chose to give up her life." Sandra does not pretend to understand why God permitted cancer to strike down her mother, but she is certain that a world which is infected with disease is also an opportunity to do God's work. "I believe that creation has brought us restoration that is good." Sandra's caregiving is now a tribute to her mom. But she continues to go to work because "God is still bringing about restoration."

While not all believers identified their work as a calling, they did recognize a morality of work or a workplace ethic which was acceptable to God.[30] In these cases, work itself was neither sacred nor sinful (unless illegal or proscribed by religious commandment). God entered the workplace principally through the way that people treated others on the job and the way that workers performed their duties. Occupational virtues, such as timeliness, dependability, honesty, and commitment to the job, were the typical paths by which working-class Christians, Jews, and Muslims traveled to godly work. Holy Angels' parishioner and Chicago Transit Authority bus driver Michael Morman was a good example of working righteously through customer relations. Every workday, Michael acknowledges with a mere head nod or smile hundreds of people as they get on and off the city bus. "I feel that sometimes when someone comes to me and says 'you're a nice bus driver' and wishes me a good day, it is acknowledging what I am doing." What Michael is doing is what God expects. "People can see that you are patient, that you are kind, that you are polite, and that you are going to treat them decently by your tone of voice. I think He sees that." Perhaps what God sees sitting behind the wheel of a Chicago bus is a Christian "modeling [his] spiritual values" as opposed to "evangelizing in the workplace."[31]

Sharon Aftab would be the last Christian alive to evangelize to her co-workers. She is a unionized customer care representative for an airline operating out of Midway Airport.[32] Now slightly beyond forty years of age, Sharon painfully recalls growing up in a severely austere Catholic environment. "I went to an Opus Dei high school which pretty much sent me as far as possible away from Catholicism."[33] The experience left Sharon deeply shaken about the existence of a loving God. "[One time] the priest told me to do the Rosary on jacks. I was maybe fifteen. I couldn't understand if he said jacks or glass at the time, so I decided to do jacks. It hurt." Feeling brutalized by what she considered a regimented, unforgiving, militaristic religious order, Sharon began skipping class and going out for coffee. Despite her struggles with the Opus Dei people "who were a little nutty," she never completely rejected her faith and even went on to earn a college degree in theology. But Sharon's "passion for religion" did not completely survive a "thrill-seeking lifestyle" and church attendance slipped from her schedule. Years later, after a nearly fatal accident, Sharon found herself in physical therapy and "talking more and more to God." "It was around that time that I started going back to church sporadically." Eventually she journeyed to St. Bruno Parish and the working-class bungalows, bakeries, and delis of the Archer Heights neighborhood. "My friend and I attended Holy Thursday services. It was packed . . . standing room only and we were in the foyer. We knelt down and I looked up at the crucifix and someone had cut out of construction paper the letters, 'Return to God.' I just felt it was a sign."

Getting to church is no easy task given Sharon's demanding airline work schedule. Even though it can be difficult to show up weekly, she usually attends the Saturday evening service. Interestingly, it may be more convenient for Sharon to put her faith to work during the long hours she sits in a cavernous airline hangar answering phones. The work environment is hectic, pressure-packed, and fast-paced. "We are troubleshooting and we are fixing things behind the scenes." Under constant stress to quickly respond to reservation and flight status questions, Sharon and her fellow workers often suffer from exhaustion and tension-related pains. In addition to using the union grievance procedure to secure relief, the workers also turn to one another in a less adversarial way. "We have prayer circles; if there is someone who is in agony or crisis, we activate it." Praying for another worker is a continuance of what Sharon has learned from one of her favorite public acts of Jesus' ministry: "The marriage at Cana. Not that I have turned water into wine. [But] there is one lesson that I have learned from this—serve the best that you can possibly serve."[34] Sharon explains that serving others means "give everyone 110 percent because they deserve it," whether the offer is a prayer or flight information. And what would happen if Sharon served the equivalent of old wine in new bottles? "I think that God is not really thrilled when we do not work to our capabilities."

Holy Angels Church attendee Rebecca Danforth not only has a God-inspired work ethic, but she finds a more instrumental role for her labors. Rebecca has worked for over twenty-seven years with a telecommunication company answering people's questions about their bills. "On my job, it is communication and okay, you have a telephone and the bill has to be paid and I am there to communicate what the amount of the bill is to be paid, then that is helping the customer. Now, if I was at work and slouching on the job and not doing my job, no, that is not doing God's work. But doing your job in a proficient and accurate manner to get the job done, yes, that is being helpful to God." Notice Rebecca's belief that she can assist God in some earthly endeavor. Her work is not just agreeable to God, but if done with gusto and efficiency, Rebecca's work is helpful to God.

Acting as a partner with God meant more often than not being inspired by a communal purpose for work. In these cases workers stressed a driven attraction to a particular form of work and an appreciation of how work served the needs of others. No working-class believer better exemplified the vocational spirit than Ed Carille. Ed has two lifelong loves. He has been a carpenter for over twenty years and he has been singing with a guitar on his lap for as long as he has been building furniture. The two crafts actually come together nicely when he sings spirituals during worship services at St. Denis Catholic Church. Ed describes himself as "a singing carpenter." He feels called by God to work as a carpenter and to sing songs; the hymn "Yahweh, You Are Near" is one of his favorites. "I have always been good with my hands and have been blessed with a good eye for color." Transforming a raw material like wood into a finished cabinet brings pure joy to Ed. His deep satisfaction comes from a belief that his work is an expression of what God wants him to do with his talents. To hear Ed talk about his work as a calling strongly suggests that he feels "gifted" with a skill. While it is true that his skills have been cultivated over two decades of work and that Ed has adopted the virtues of craftsmanship, the ability to create with his hands appears to be a fortunate disposition. Armand Larive would credit Ed's natural talents to the "fruits" of the Holy Spirit. Skills, like Paul's virtues of "love, joy, peace, patience, kindness, goodness, faithfulness, gentleness, and self-control" (Galatians 5:22), are gifts from God's Spirit. Miroslav Volf further argues that "the gifts of the Spirit are related to the specific tasks or function to which God calls" and fits each person.[35] The Spirit of God, according to Miroslav,"calls, endows, and empowers Christians to work in their various vocations."[36]

When he makes something beautiful and functional, Ed feels that he has given something of himself to the world. "If you are able to give of yourself, I think that is what it's all about." Ed's giving of his talents as an offering to the world underscored the common thread among faith community members in this book of seeing their work as addressing the well-being of others. Work certainly filled self-interested needs, but when considering the spiritual nature of their labors, workers were covetous of a socially uplifting occupation. Working for others even equated for some with being a faithful Christian. Take Family in Faith Church congregant Todd Macdonald. He admits that during busy work periods he does not always keep the obligation of attending Sunday church worship services. But he does faithfully go to work as a painter. Did he then consider himself a good Christian? "I thought I was good, could have been better, but when I did a job and the people were happy, that made me feel like I had done something for somebody."

Pat Glatz of St. Denis Parish echoed Todd's communal view of work. She is an experienced special education teacher who feels closest to God when working with children and their parents. "When a parent has a child that has a problem and they get to the point where they are kind of against a brick wall and you can give them ammunition, it directly impacts their kids' life, their life at home, in the neighborhood. It's a good feeling to be able to do that." Whether it was painting or teaching, working-class Christians seemed to abide by the apostle Paul's reminder of Jesus' message that "In all things I have shown you that by so toiling one must help the weak" (Acts 20:35). As Pat and other workers described their jobs, it was clear that work has a spiritual purpose beyond doing well for oneself. Christian ethicist Gilbert Meilaender sees work as a service that is intended to benefit others. "God calls each of us to some work in life and by his providential governance uses our work to serve the needs of many neighbors."[37] Contrary to modern social relations of production and cultural biases toward "individualism," work to Pat Glatz is not a solitary exchange for daily bread.

The way a person defines what he or she does for a living is often shaped by how transformative that work turns out to be in an individual's life. In George Gennardo's case, it was as if God had put the mop right into his hands. George presently attends Family and Faith Church and works as a custodian for a Chicago school. He believes he is doing God's work by keeping the school clean and safe for children. But his work did not always invoke such spiritual feelings. George worked for a factory for twenty years before it shut down and relocated, ultimately to China. About three-quarters of the way into his time with the company George had an awakening. "It was right at that time I was ready to kill my best friend. I almost beat him to death while he slept. When he woke up and saw me over him, he asked me to forgive him. Something came over me." George was in a violent mood because, like his friend, he was badly abusing drugs and alcohol. "It was right then and there that I left his apartment and got on my hands and knees and said to God that if He was really there, you need to help me."

George admits that his addictions fed a rapidly deteriorating work ethic. But since the day he raised his fists against a friend, everything has changed. "I came to work fifteen minutes early everyday, sometimes half hour early. I would stay late when no one else wanted to and did extra work when nobody else wanted to. I just put the extra effort in. I feel God had a hand in that and in changing me." In George's mind, God used the workplace to ground George in a life of a meaning and respectability. The actual work, though identical to before, had now become a means to redeem George's life. He now saw the job as a gift from his Creator, and if it was God's will to give him the opportunity and strength to work, then George would "do my best." It was not easy giving up a dependence on cocaine and drinking, but George slowly realized that "with God I could do whatever I wanted to."

Unfortunately, a new-found relationship with the Lord did not deter the company from taking advantage of cheaper labor markets and from building a second plant in Tijuana, Mexico. "After then it got tougher for the company, so they built in China which did it in for us." The loss of his job would have sent George spiraling back into a $1,500 a week drug habit if not for his new-found faith. "Actually, I think God was working because the move to China gave me the opportunity to do the stuff that I had wanted to do but had not had a chance." One thing George did that many workers in their thirties and forties do when they have been involuntarily unemployed was to go back to school. In George's case he took and completed a course in home inspection. The class did not lead to a new job, but by chance George met the principal of a north side Chicago school who suggested that he put an application in for a janitor's position. George filled the application out in the morning of the last day in which they were being accepted. "I filled it out, turned it in, and by the time that I got home, I had a telephone call and the school wanted to interview me." Two days later, George was hired to keep clean the very high school he had once sold drugs in.

"It's hard work, actually, and it's humbling me in a way, but my wife mentioned to me one time that God had put me there for a reason." What reason? "To help other people." But George had more in mind than a simple scrub and shine. "The son of God was a carpenter. He probably did a little bit of everything to basically help people out. If you need this done, then you have to do this. I think that God puts us in different positions and different work to help people out. I think that it's a service. The work serves a purpose, someone, and a need. It's like being a missionary." George's custodial relationship with the school feels to him like he's doing godly work. "You have to consider what Christ went through. Anytime you can serve someone or in this case if you look at the school, I am doing this so that kids can learn without having to worry about trash on the floor or sitting with vandalism on the wall, so yes it's godly work." Listening to George describe the act of cleaning up someone else's mess as if it were an enviable task that more people should aspire to reminded me of the Last Supper story where Jesus "poured water into a basin, and began to wash the disciples' feet and to wipe them with the towel with which he was girded" (John 13:5). In George's work activity it is possible to literally see the broom, scrub brush, bucket, cloth, and mop as the tools of a truly faithful man.

The work of a janitor can be physically tasking and, ironically, always unsanitary. George did not describe his job as pleasant, fun, or easy. But was work meant to be pleasant or distasteful? More succinctly, did God intend for work to be punishment or blessing? Donna Schiavone is a massage therapist who feels that through her work the Holy Spirit is speaking directly to her. Donna went to school to study occupational therapy, but after repeated failures dropped out. "So I am sitting in the library one day trying to figure out what I wanted to do while looking at an occupational outlook handbook and the Holy Spirit just said, 'Do massage therapy.' I'm not kidding; I am not making this up. I had never even had a massage in my life." Eighteen years later Donna is still doing ten to fifteen massages a week and each one is part of a genuine Christian ministry. "Jesus went around helping people and this [massage therapy] is a healing profession." Donna offers a persuasive explanation for considering her work as a ministry. "He [Jesus] tells us not to be stressed, don't worry, don't fret, so whatever I can do to help people to stay calm, centered, and focused and have a life that is not pained and stressed, then that has to be a good thing." Laying her hands on people suffering with chronic pain provides Donna with the opportunity to reduce the anxiety that Jesus counseled against in each of the Gospels.[38] Her hands become the instrument by which a person's anxiety is reduced and life returned to a more pleasant state. Work to Donna "is a fact of life," but "not a punishment even if it gets in the way of some family and other stuff."

But as she has conventionally understood it, the story of creation told in the book of Genesis challenges Donna's own uplifting experience as a massage therapist. Donna was taught that the story of God's creation imposed upon the world an idea of work as toil, drudgery, and suffering. Because Adam had not obeyed God, humankind was doomed to make a living the hard way: "In the sweat of your face you shall eat bread till you return to the ground." Genesis seemed only a more poetic way of saying, "You work hard all your life, then you die." And in the end you have little to show for your labors. "[F]or out of the dust you were taken; you are dust and dust you shall return" (Genesis 3:19). This bleak version of the creation story does not leave a Christian with much hope for a life of ministerial labor. But then again we have Donna's healing hands. When she considers the "fall" of Adam and Eve, Donna accepts that paradise does not exist on earth because of "original sin."[39] One bite of the forbidden fruit established the sinfulness of human beings and necessitated a life of hard labor. But Donna rejects the idea that hard work means unprosperous, unsatisfying, or even insignificant work. "Yes, God threw Adam and Eve out and he told Adam that he was going to work the soil and it was going to be hard, but God also promised the fruits of work." Not only that, but as Donna points out, God gave Adam the job of tilling paradise before Adam strayed (Genesis 2:15). It would seem that God anticipated and even required work before "sin" was even born.

Donna is reflecting what Goran Agrell called the ambivalent nature of work.[40] As phrased by Armand Larive, "It is partly toil, but it is partly service to God in creation."[41] Larive explains that in Eden, Adam "tilled and cared for" God's creation. Maintaining the earth would not be easy, but by "tilling, harvesting, and husbanding the gifts of God" humans would be co-workers with God in taking care of creation.[42] Donna relates her manipulation of soft tissue for the purpose of facilitating comfort as protecting God's creation, but also knows her limitations. "We are created in the image of God so we have characteristics that are the same, but I cannot create out of nothing—that is the only difference." If creating out of nothing is beyond Donna's power, working with joy and fulfillment are not. It is a theme repeated over and over again by the working-class faithful in this book.

"No form of work is a punishment," declares Mohammed Khan, a fifty-four-year-old Muslim taxi driver. Even if a good job is taken away, the next one is still a gift from God. Khan notes that "[i]f I get fired and lose my job, the best way that I have to be a good Muslim is to be patient." Replacing one job with another is often how God maneuvers you away from "sin" and into a holier position. "The prophet Muhammad, he teaches us that if you are fired or you lose your job, you thank Allah for this problem because a better job than this job will come to you." Either way, Khan sees his work as more than about money. "Money is not really why you are working; it is to do your best to help others. To do good where Allah has brought you." Khan adds that Muhammad said, "work on this world and you will never die," but also "worship Allah as if you were to die tomorrow." Work and worship, then, are part of a unified structure of religious belief and action. Muhammad's message is strikingly similar to Jesus': "God desires ease for you and desires not hardship."[43]

Josie Winston has known hardships on the job, but she is driven by a firm faith that her work is called by God. Josie attends the Church of Our Lord and Savior Jesus Christ and has worked nearly thirty years as a social worker for the Chicago public schools. While her employment has been mostly steady, there have been times of reduced hours and extended layoffs. Josie exhibits an abiding passion for working with the elementary school children put in her care. The job has featured moments of terrific elation and frightening despair. The extremes suggest to her that work was meant to be more than a way to make a buck and a burden in our lives. The secret, Josie reveals, is to be the Lord's caregiver. "The one thing that has been consistent in the thirty years that I have been with the Chicago schools and it is always in my mind and it has brought me through the years, is that scripture says when you do something, you do it as if you are doing it unto the Lord. No matter how much I'm doing, I am doing this as if I am doing it for the Lord. That has really been my foundation." Josie's labors on behalf of God are also works done with God's cooperation. She admits to never working alone or "outside of the Holy Spirit." God and Josie are, as the apostle Paul wrote, "fellow workers" (1 Corinthians 3:9).

Voluntary leisure is, of course, valued as a chance to rest, to pursue cultural interests, and to enjoy nonwork time with family and friends. But forced unemployment or underemployment makes it terribly difficult for a person to provide for a household, community, or their own body. And sustaining a quality of life is crucial to being able to live in the image of God. Armand Larive points out that the God of Israel was not a "resident king" but assumed the role of worker, and Douglas Meeks referred to the Lord as the one who sustains "households."[44] Caroline Garcia of Immaculate Conception Church has taken the idea of sustenance beyond her own home. As a processing clerk for a bank located in a stable but decidedly working-class community, she witnesses the efforts of hard-working people trying to improve their living conditions. Some of the decisions of her employer have so deeply troubled Caroline that she believes the Holy Spirit compels her to act at work. "You have to use your faith where I work because it is a corporation that sometime steps on the little man." Caroline recognizes her rather lowly formal status with the bank, but sees her job as a way to protect people who are in pursuit of the American dream. "You have to speak up for them and that's what I do. A lot of times I get into trouble but I don't care."

Rudy Ramirez also attends Immaculate Conception Church and has his own way of providing. Rudy's job as a unionized food service aide at a Chicago hospital requires him to prepare food plates for the patients. He believes that God places great value in the work that he and his coworkers perform. "We all play our parts whether it is fixing the plates or cleaning a pot or mixing gravy. It doesn't matter how menial the job is, we all play our part." Rudy once aspired to a cook's job in the hospital because it paid more, but he has settled into the food service aide position. "It is better for me to be on the bottom and to be raised up—God will be there." Besides, he still performs a little distribution "miracle" each day. "I feed whoever needs to be fed at the time. If not for me and my co-workers, how would that hospital's patients get fed?" Rudy's coparishioner Caroline Ramirez assertively reminds me that Rudy is "dividing the fish and feeding the hungry." Caroline's reference to the stories of Jesus feeding the multitude raises the possibility that it is only because of people like Rudy that God can continuously care for his creation.[45]

Feeding and caring for the patients at Chicago's hospitals is a demanding and labor-intensive job; unfortunately, large hospital systems like Advocate Health Care and Resurrection Health Care have not seen fit to properly reward and protect their most ministerial employees. Both hospital chains rely on a large cadre of low-paid workers that serve many poorer communities. In an effort to improve the quality of health care delivered to poor and working-class citizens and to raise the living standards of hospital employees, a coalition of labor unions, community groups, and religious institutions have united behind the ethic of Proverbs 14:31: "Those who oppress the poor insult the Maker, but those who are kind to the needy honor God." Organized by the Service Employees International Union (SEIU), the Hospital Accountability Project has brought together workers, patient activists, and religious leaders to adopt a "Protocol for Agreement" to provide a framework to resolve racial and class issues at Advocate. The protocols are built upon a strong scriptural foundation of persistent petition for economic justice.[46]

A second campaign directed at Resurrection Health (the city's second-largest hospital system) by the American Federation of State, County and Municipal Employees (AFSCME) has likewise been a community effort to advocate for improved health services for the city's neediest people and for the rights of hospital workers to organize into a union.[47] The union has documented many cases of low-wage immigrant workers being told by Resurrection supervisors that if they support the union they will be fired. Union efforts to expose the hospital system's poor quality of services and treatment of workers has led to a petition of support signed by thirty-seven priests in the Archdiocese of Chicago urging hospital management to meet with the union. But despite corporate resistance to both union-inspired efforts, Rudy keeps feeding the sick. In doing so he helps to sustain the lives of his patients by delivering little miracles on food trays three times a day.

Rudy's experience at a non-union hospital highlights the underappreciated and unvervalued role that unions can play in bringing dignity to the workplace. Too narrowly treated in popular and scholarly media as a mere economic agent, unions have the capacity to contribute to the kind of earthly existence that would honor God's creation. As uncommon as it is to see a public acknowledgment of organized labor's positive contribution to the social good, it is rarer still to find a union leader who addresses the relationship between faith and union activity. One exception is Bob Gunter. As president of the Illinois State Postal Workers Union Local

854, Gunter used his column in the union's newsletter to ask a provocative question of his membership: "When was the last time you went to church?"

The question was actually generated by an aunt who found Bob's support for liberal causes and politicians to be contrary to the teachings of Jesus. Agitated by the exchange with his aunt, Gunter wrote an essay to his members about the unity of faith and unionism. "I believe unions are doing God's work by protecting workers' rights, which are really human rights." Gunter also expressed disappointment that "many ministers and priests today know nothing about work or unions, and the TV evangelists are even less knowledgeable." Bob went on to remind his aunt and the local's members, "Jesus was the most famous 'liberal' and a carpenter by trade." The postal union president ended his brief essay by declaring that "work" is more prominently featured in the Bible than sin."[48] While it would undoubtedly be a challenging intellectual parlor game to determine what Jesus' contemporary political ideology would be, Gunter more importantly draws attention to a spirituality that unites personal salvation and social justice. Doing your job is doing God's work, and a collective body of workers organized to protect the dignity of that work, as well as the workers, projects a creative, communal, and compassionate image of God into the world.[49]

Sometimes the approach a person takes to her or his secular work even undercuts the value of spiritual caregiving. Church of Our Lord and Savior Jesus Christ congregant Ron McCracken (no relationship to Pastor McCracken) sees a basic contradiction between being a faithful Christian and a Christian with little regard for his secular occupation. "How can you be faithful when you are lazy?" Ron refers to people like this as "religious fanatics; all heavenly good and no earthly good." In Ron's theology, doing earthly good requires that each person realize that there is "work to do down here." By work he does not mean evangelizing. "There are things you have to do to survive on a daily basis, there are real issues here." St. Denis parishioner Laura Dawson also sees the false dichotomy between spiritual "good works" and work "down here." "Good works, I guess I think of church-type stuff right away, but then I think, good works can be people who do their jobs every day and they can be ordinary jobs, but the people can be working very hard and doing the best that they can and that can be good works." Ron and Laura are both critical of an unfortunate tendency for people of faith "to discount the value of work and yourself as a worker in deference to the higher realm of religion."[50] Ordinary work is not typically valued as possessing any inherent spiritual qualities. At best a person's job can have some instrumental purpose in advancing a walk in faith. But as Sherman and Hendricks matter-of-factly point out, "[I]f God were only interested in soul-work, then He needn't have created a physical universe."[51] Ron McCracken and Laura Dawson understand that spiritual things and secular work are not relationally oppositional.

Barbara Bebus has attended St. Bruno Catholic Church since moving at age five to within one mile of Midway Airport on the city's South Side. Her salt-and-pepper hair confirms a twenty-six-year career as a billing clerk for a large retailer. Growing up, she helped her mom keep the books of a small family business and today even pitches in and helps the church out during festival season. "I have been working with numbers all of my life." To work with numbers, Barb notes, "requires stern moral fiber" and she makes it known to me that she is not a dishonest woman. "I feel called to do this." Barb's vocational devotion to working with numbers significantly contributes to her spirituality. She desires to spend eternity with God, and faithfully worships, but salvation demands more than that; it literally takes work. "I would say my work is part of my path to salvation." Barbara does not expect a person to be a paragon of righteous acts like "Mother Teresa" to be pleasing to God, but something more than just passive faith is needed. In her case, that something extra is getting the numbers to add up correctly.

Hispanic-Latino workers attending Our Lady of Guadalupe Church have also scaled the heights of Martin Luther's theological barrier. Rosaria Morales works part-time as a secretary. She speaks powerfully of recognizing God's presence at work and believes that she "serves Him better by being there." Curiously, Rosaria is thankful for the work but attaches its significance to how well it allows her to be a good Christian. "Serving God is first and work is next." So as long as she feels comfortable that God is being honored by her labors, then Rosaria will continue in the job. In other words, the job must bring her into a closer relationship with God. Gabriel Padilla, Javier Castro, and Manuel Murillo all toil in scrap yards and the dangerous nature of their work makes the presence of the Holy Spirit palpable. Javier, a union laborer, claims that "my work is the method that God has chosen to help me approach people." Manuel explains that "there are many divisions and envies in the company, but God has presented me with an opportunity to help others by showing my faith." Gabriel adds that "God is always watching at work, how you use your talents." Nena Barajas finds her work as a teacher's aide in a preschool to be very rewarding and she "gets closer to God by doing a good job." Mateo Reyes is a salesman and declares "that if you don't work when you have the capacity to do so, it's a sin." The sin for Mateo is that God's salvific work can only continue if human beings use their hands and feet.

"What this means is that we are here on earth to do His mission. To feed the hungry. To comfort the one who is crying. We are here for a mission and that is why we are His feet."

These working-class south Chicago Hispanic-Latino Catholics have each found something sacred about their work. It is not only that work is doing service to God or is a way to get closer to God. It is not only about a morally just way to behave at work or seeing our labors as falling under God's watchful eye. Work is more holy than that: "we are His feet." Our Lady of Guadalupe parishioners expect, as Luther commanded, that their faith alone will open up heaven's gates, but they equally believe that God acts in the world through their labors. They describe a God that is not aloof, merely bestowing saving grace on some and denying it to others according to some inscrutable sovereign plan or election. Instead, God appears as one who delights in the work we do and encourages the efforts of people to conduct meaningful labor. Indeed, God needs our labors to till an earthly garden. This may not be the conventional Lutheran route to salvation, but it is inconceivable to me that Rosaria, Gabriel, or Mateo would expect to enjoy heavenly bliss if they did damage to God's feet and hands. It is obvious by their commitment to *work as Christians* that it is not enough to solely express their faith by attending church or prayer groups. Members of Our Lady of Guadalupe fully acknowledged that without God's constant, preserving, and sustaining grace, no work would be possible. But with equal weight and personal obligation they also accepted that without joyfully performing the work that God has given, the Lord's mission "to save the world" (John 13:47) cannot be accomplished.

Andy Schutt expressed the exuberance with which he believed that a person should carry out his or her work. But doing so required understanding the co-creative nature of work. Andy, a truck driver for a cement company, believed his job afforded him the opportunity to cooperate with God in turning raw material into a finished product. "Everything that we have now was created; I mean the means of processing cement and making it available and useful." He offered up a brief history of cement. "First there was fire and they burned the rock and then ground it up and added a little gypsum and there was concrete." The result was a constructed world mixed with human labor. It is true that "God made the earth," but it "all was created to help us grow and it works." Andy described a spiritual celebration of the power of honest work. "I tell you, there is nothing more rewarding than at the end of the day and everything went well and you sit down and you are tired and you are home having a good meal—now that was a great day." God's creation added to and made better through cooperative human labor. This was the kind of work that the apostle Paul was commending when he spoke harshly against alienated and objectionable labor, treated merely as a commodity: "Whatever your task, work heartily, as serving the Lord and not men, knowing that from the Lord you will receive the inheritance as your reward; you are serving the Lord Christ" (Colossians 3:23–24). In Andy's two-ton truck the fruits of the Holy Spirit were carried from cement processing plant to construction sites all over the city. It may not have been heard as a worship sermon, but the message of human beings loving God by "serving life in God's creation" was delivered with exquisite craftsmanship.[52]

Andy's Schutt's instrumentalist approach to godly work was not shared by everyone interviewed. Fellow Park Lane Christian Reform Church member Marilyn Vanden Bout worked tirelessly as a hospital secretary in a high-risk pregnancy unit. "It is God's grace that so many babies are born healthy and alive. The pain of women crying is very painful. There is a lot of crying." While Marilyn acknowledged the critical role that she plays in making it possible for the doctors to save a woman's child, she did not recognize her job as advancing God's mission on earth. She was certain that God was present at each pregnancy, but her clerical duties didn't measure up to the godly work of the ancient apostles or the medical staff who depended on her. Even after the religious-based hospital brought in a priest to bless the hands of everyone in the prenatal unit, Marilyn did not see her work as a sacred ministry. The work may have been what God wanted her to do but, nonetheless, it did not add up to Christian "good works." "I guess I do not think of it [work] in that respect."

Jim Estrada of Our Lady of Guadalupe Parish is a construction worker and he also fails to see how his job or any job (short of the priesthood) can get him closer to God. For Jim, prayer groups, worship services, and other church activities are the only avenues to God. He would, however, be very comfortable working for an employer who had sponsored or allowed a work-based ministry.[53] John Schiavone also struggles to see God's presence where he works. But his difficulties have more to do with the unsatisfying nature of his work than with the spiritual potentiality of work. John reluctantly enters data into a computer. He is blunt in announcing that "[m]y work only relates to money." As a result, John needs prayer and worship to escape those places in his life that are defined by his need to earn a living. But ironically his soulless work experience has caused him to spiritually reach out. "I have prayed a little bit to God to show me where I should be, to help me find the right job."

Stephanie Baron had not found the right job yet, but when we spoke she had high hopes for what and where it would be. She was only twenty-one at the time and was enrolled in the Chicago Police Academy.

Stephanie was the kind of person who always stepped up to help. She had taught CCD (i.e., Catholic Christian Doctrine) classes for a while at St. Bruno Parish where her father was a Sunday mass usher. Stephanie also filled in as an usher and spent most weekends doing some type of service for the parish. Her commitment to the church came from a steady diet of Catholic education. As a third-generation Polish Catholic she had been a student at St. Bruno's Elementary School and Chicago's Mother McCauley High School. She grew up with reverence for spiritual work and particularly for the job that priests and nuns performed. What she learned along the way was that religion should help to solve some basic human problem. For Stephanie that problem was the "unfairness of people living on the streets that have nothing and then there are people that have so much that they don't know what to do with it all . . . the inequality in that." So she decided to become a cop.

Homelessness is society's sin, according to Stephanie, and walking a beat is one way to address that sin. "I really don't think that going to church and praying to God for the guy on the corner downtown will really do much." It is not that she rejects the value of prayer, but that her faith compels her to work at the problem. In Stephanie's eyes, she can best do that by working as an officer of the law. And police work may be her best road to salvation. "I think [my road to salvation] is to help people. That is my biggest goal." I wondered out loud about how arresting people equaled salvation? "While you have to catch the bad guys, I think it is more to help people, to serve and protect. I know that I cannot go out saving or helping everybody, but what I can do, I am hoping to do just so people can have some hope." In her chosen occupation, hope can come at a steep price because workers run a high risk of being hurt or even worse. "Yeah, but I think it is very noble to die for something that you believe in. The resurrection of Christ was great and amazing, but I think actually dying for something that you believe in is really something that you have to give somebody credit for. Jesus dying was the greatest gift. Anyone who will die for something that they believe in, I really admire. I think that would be it for me personally."

I believed Stephanie when she said she was ready to give her life for a cause. She seemed to have found a job that would allow her to be faithful to the principles embodied in the life of Jesus. Here was a vision of Jesus as the community's protector; the one who snatches the criminal and gets a runaway off the street. But that raised the question: did Stephanie believe that as one of Chicago's finest she would be doing God's work? Her answer was a definite yes, but in a curiously limited way. She noted that "of God's work, I believe [a] priest did more, but both jobs are important in saving people or coming to peoples' assistance." The work a priest did appeared to accompany something more than "protect and serve." What was it about policing that did not encompass God's work? Upon reflection, Stephanie recognized that she had used "God's work" to connote the conventional sacramental tasks of a priest. True, a police officer would not say mass, but is there more to God's work than what transpires under a chapel roof? Stephanie was certain there was and offered a clarification: "The police officer does more physical [God] work and the priest would do more [God work] emotionally." Maybe, but no matter how Stephanie parses the distinctions, there seem to be holes in Luther's wall.

CHAPTER 6

A Taste of Heaven

ACCORDING TO Christian, Jewish, and Islamic tradition, a day of final reckoning will come to pass for all believers and nonbelievers. Some form of messianism or culminating end point of history has significantly influenced each of the world's great monotheistic Abrahamic religions. The accounts of messianic transformation widely diverge from one another even within the traditions, but what each religion shares is the idea that only through faith can a person enter the kingdom of heaven. Judgment day will surely come and therefore salvation to each of my workers was a gift from God. But if belief alone was sufficient to attain everlasting life, then what does God expect from the lives we live? Robert Wuthnow emphasized that John Calvin and Martin Luther "played a major role in sacralizing work," but labor itself, no matter how noble, could not secure God's grace.[1] Miroslav Volf, however, counters that Thomas Carlyle infused work with explicit religious overtones. Mundane work for Carlyle "replaced prayer to God and became a means of secular salvation."[2] Islamic religious scholar Karen Armstrong points out that when Muslims recite the Qur'an "they become aware of the history of their own being, rather than an objective history of salvation."[3] Rabbis of the Talmudic era stressed that the individual was accountable to "the world-to-come" for their actions here on earth. They also taught that "better one hour spent in repentance and good deeds in this world than the whole life in the world-to-come." Attention to the eternal effects of a life well lived underscores a popular aphorism from one of the most important figures in Jewish history, Hillel: "If not now, when?"[4]

"By what means shall I become righteous and acceptable to God?" was the beguiling question that Luther raised.[5] The question of human labor's contribution to salvation also fully animated the discussions in this book and significantly shaped the relationship between a worker's faith and occupation. In the book of Genesis there is the story of "Jacobs' Ladder." Jacob, one of two sons of Isaac (son of Abraham) flees his home in fear that he will be killed by his brother Esau. One night while sleeping, Jacob dreamt "that there was a ladder set up on the earth, and the top of it reached to heaven." The ladder was occupied by "angels of God" who were "ascending and descending on it." When Jacob awoke, he concluded that this place where he slept was the "gate of heaven" (Genesis 28:10–17). Each worker believed in an attainable heaven, but what heaven was exactly and, most important, what the best road to travel to get there were subject to debate.

Do you have a conception of heaven?

ANGELA BLUNT: I cannot even imagine some of the things that are there.

Believing in a place where righteous individuals spend eternity with God is a basic religious principle that goes hand in hand with each person's faith that God is real. To believe in God or Allah is to imagine a heaven. God and heaven are a package. But that is where the agreement mostly ends. While heaven is a goal for every believer, the interviewees were very uncertain and reluctant to describe what they thought it would be. The difficulty people had was a bit surprising given that everyone admitted that they had thought for many years about heaven and had been educated to conceive of an eternity with God in a variety of forms. Heaven equaled salvation, but what salvation would be was no more than a mystery. Still, Angela Blunt had some pretty good ideas.

"When you talk about heaven itself, the heavenly place where God has built for us, that is not on earth." To Angela and many others, there was an earth–heaven dichotomy. We lived in our bodies on earth, but after certain physical death those humans who are judged by God as faithful would be raised in likely spiritual form to reside in a new home called heaven. The body was reserved for earthly living and the soul for spiritual rest. There also appeared to be a sharp body–soul separation. But the boundary line between the here and now and the hereafter was apparently a little permeable. Angela believes she witnesses a glimpse of heaven all the time. "Whenever I am with God, I am in the presence of what heaven can only be." It's not the real thing, but when a person acknowledges God's presence, the physical world is transformed into what heaven "can only be." Angela cannot find the words to describe what *the* place called heaven would look like, but she knows that when she acknowledges God's presence, it lends a heavenly quality to her earthly space. Here is certainly not heaven, but heaven can be partially realized even while our hearts continue to beat.

Cheryl Lawrence agrees with her fellow Church of Our Lord and Savior Jesus Christ congregant Angela that heaven is mostly beyond human existence. But while she attends worship regularly, Cheryl is not dogmatic about how a person gets to heaven. Can you get to heaven without going to church? "Wherever you are you can make do." Worship services are important, but they are not required for salvation. Well, can you be saved without prayer? Now, communicating with God was something entirely different. Cheryl and everyone else at the Church of Our Lord and Savior Jesus Christ emphatically declared "No"! What was it about prayer that made it so essential for salvation? Florence Joseph put it nicely by stating forthrightly that "if you have a relationship with God, there is an interaction." Prayer is communicating with God. Worship is also, but as the folks at this small congregation pointed out, people of good faith do not need a congregational worship service to establish a relationship with God. There is much to be spiritually gained by worshiping with others, but salvation requires a relationship with God, and prayer—as a form of personal communication—is a more critical practice to keeping a life in the spirit.

The congregants at the Church of Our Lord and Savior Jesus Christ echoed the feelings of nearly everyone I spoke with about prayer and salvation. Salvation was first and foremost "a gift of God." Pastor McCracken explained that "[w]e are not saved by what we do or who we are. We are saved by what He has done and *by accepting him*" (emphasis in original). Prayer appears to be a principal vehicle for "accepting him." In prayer an individual can express thanks, petition for help, express fears and anxieties, and, most important, declare love and obedience to God. Prayer can also be a powerful sign of God's presence. Each of the Muslim cabdrivers was insistent that abiding by Islamic law in praying five times a day was critical to recognizing the presence of Allah in the world. Prayer sessions could be hard to accommodate while steering patrons around the city, but somehow a cabbie made do. It could have been worse. According to Karen Armstrong, legend has it that God initially told Muhammad on the Temple Mount that Muslims would have to "make *salat* fifty times a day." But after repeated requests for leniency from the Prophet, "al-Llah" relented and reduced the command to a more manageable, if still disciplined, five times a day.[6]

Working-class believers particularly liked the idea that prayer can be done at any time, anywhere, and either with or without someone else. In this way, the beloved and respected congregational leader is helpful, but not as important to the individual's salvation as their own private prayer-bound relationship with God. But isn't prayer an act? If we pray, don't we "accept" salvation by something we do? As explained by many workers from multiple faith traditions, prayer is indeed an act of faith, but it is not the prayer itself that saves us. Jewish kosher deli supervisor Barry Blaustein stressed the centrality of faith as being about "man's relationship to God, and man's relationship to man." Prayer, it seems, played a powerful role in developing both relationships because it allows a person to see the transcendent quality of a mundane life. God is reaching out to the world and prayer is a believer's reaching back. In David Ariel's terms, prayer is "the highest form of intimacy between humans and god."[7]

Talking with God allows a person to get close to God, and once in a personal relationship with God, right behavior toward others will necessarily follow. Florence Joseph again speaks plainly but insightfully about the power of prayer to set into motion a relationship with God. "If you have a relationship with God, and you are borrowing and begging [to get by] every day and then sitting in church every Sunday, you would not be robbing banks on Monday through Friday." "Begging and borrowing" will not get you into heaven, but "begging and borrowing" instead of robbery and plunder may be reflections of a person in a right relationship with God. As Florence noted, "You should know better [than to steal] if you have a relationship with God." And that relationship is not only dynamically shaped every day through prayer, it is also the key to a heavenly promised land.

St. Denis parishioner Laura Dawson, an English as a Second Language teacher, also recognized that "prayer can be done even by people who are physically unable to do anything else." But she thought salvation warranted something more than communicating with God. "Faith and acting on faith is the way into heaven . . . you need to put your faith into practice." Apparently, personal salvation is not assured by God's act alone. Nor does worship, Bible reading, or prayer come with a guarantee. Instead, salvation demands putting your faith into practice. In Laura's life, practicing her faith could mean reading from a prayer book, but it more often takes an uncommon shape. When asked how she put her faith into practice, Laura gave an answer not likely heard in most of the Sunday school classes she attended as a kid:

LAURA: Well, I get up in the morning when I do not feel like it and go to work.

Why would going to work be an act of faith?

LAURA: Because I would rather stay in bed for a while, but there are things and obligations that I need to do to take care of, like, my family and others.

How about teaching the ESL class?

LAURA: Yes, oh yeah. Some people could say that is a way to express your faith.

In what way?

LAURA: You know, through your work.

Laura is a believer who goes to church and prays, but she believes that none of the conventional "churchy things" is the path to eternal bliss with God. Armand Larive agrees that "getting out of bed is a religious act" because it reveals a "primary meaning people give themselves for facing the day."[8] The writer of the brief but stern book of James agrees: "What does it profit, my brethren, if a man says he has faith but has not works? Can his faith save him? . . . So faith by itself, if it has no works is dead" (James 2:14–18). Perhaps Laura's mundane ministry of daily toils is shaped by her view of heaven.

"When we talk about the kingdom of heaven, I believe it is in heaven and it is also on earth." Laura perceives no boundary between the everlasting joys of heaven and the ups and downs of human existence. But how does a world full of suffering and pain become not just like heaven, but heaven itself? "That is our mission as Christians—to start to bring a little bit of heaven to earth now by doing some of these good works. I feel that it is not just about the next life, but it's also about this life." Laura believes in an afterlife where God waits, but as a Christian, she is not waiting for salvation. She is acting now out of gratitude for what God has done in her life. Heaven is "my health, freedom, life, family, good food, good relationships, and satisfaction in helping people." To Laura, heaven can be partially realized here on earth. Whatever greater peace awaits her after death she feels certain that there is an approximation of God's kingdom among the living. In the words of the twentieth-century Jewish theologian Abraham Joshua Heschel, a meaningful spiritual life requires "the ability to feel the taste of heaven."[9]

Laura and many other members of faith communities identified things like good health, shelter, a job, and friendship as the fruits of salvation. The benefits of a life well lived and well provisioned were not simply opportunities to prove a spiritual worthiness to God. A child's laughter, a loved one's recovery from illness, and the satisfaction of a job well done were not just preliminary blessings provided by a munificent power. Instead, folks like Laura saw heaven unfolding as they lived and breathed. To be sure, as imagined upon the body's death, a spiritual heaven offered Laura unknowable and wondrous blessings, but she was equally adamant about defining heaven in earthly terms. Most significant, these material and temporal riches were not rewards for being a believer. By Laura's account, God gave us just enough heaven on earth for everyone to live well, regardless of a person's religious conviction. It appears, then, that experiencing heaven in the present tense does not require faith in a metaphysical God. On the contrary, to Laura, clean air, a safe neighborhood, and clothes on your back are examples of a heaven freely given to believer and nonbeliever alike by a loving God. In gratitude, Laura gives thanks "to God for the rewards that we have."

But what about *the* heaven after the body and soul have separated? After hearing Christian and non-Christian workers wrestle with the concept of a spiritual nirvana it would seem that a culminating salvation amounts to a promise and belief in an undefined eternal life in the actual presence of God. But that promise for most is conditional upon faith. It is a belief shared by Somalia-born cabdriver Mohammad Saba. "As Muslims, we believe that if we do not accept Allah, we are not going to go to heaven." No matter how you live on earth? "Yes, you have to believe in Allah and all the prophets." But actions on earth are not without influence. *Chicago Tribune* columnist John Kass wrote about Muslim cabbie Ziarat Khan's sincere efforts to return a wallet left in his taxi. After finding the owner and insisting that the owner check the billfold to be certain that no credit cards or money were missing, Khan was offered a $100 reward from a very grateful person. But he refused the offer. When asked by Kass why he turned the money down, the cabbie answered, "If you help somebody, if you do good things, the day after judgment you will get rewarded."[10]

Nonetheless, Saba's belief in the absolute necessity of faith to gain access to "the Garden of Eternity that is promised to the God-fearing" contrasted with his uncertainly over determining the value of earthly behavior.[11] "No one can say who is going to heaven." Certainly righteous acts of kindness or charity are blessed by Allah because "God loves the good doer," and evildoers by contrast "are given up to destruction for what they have earned," but neither way of behaving is a certain predictor of eternal salvation.[12] "The knowledge is with God," but according to Saba's humble understanding, without faith in Allah salvation is impossible.[13] And how much better is Allah's promised paradise than the one Saba presently enjoys? For an answer, Saba directed me to a remarkably understated but meaningful passage in the Qur'an: "Yet the enjoyment of this present life, compared with the world to come, is a little thing."[14]

Saba and Laura both acknowledged being faithful to the "kingdom of the heavens and the earth."[15] In practical terms, both accept that eternal salvation works out to be God's promised gift to those who believe. They also further agree that the blessings of heaven, at least a fair piece of it, are attainable now and can be lived minute by minute. But there is some difference as to whether faith alone is sufficient to ensure God's salvation. Saba claims a hegemonic role for faith, while Laura believes "people are supposed to act out their faith and put it into practice." Faith, it seems, is just the beginning of Laura's road to salvation. It was also a good place to start for Katie Jordan, a parishioner at Holy Angels Parish. She spent years as a garment worker and can attest to the fact that the inside of a textile shop is an unlikely sanctuary for God to dwell. But when asked where she found heaven to be, Katie's response was immediate: "We find God here [on earth], the same place we find each other."

According to Katie, there was no being with God that did not involve embracing the needs of another woman on the factory floor. Katie reminded me of scriptures "where Jesus quotes about being in prison, for being sick, for being hungry, and if you did this to my people then you have done it for me."[16] In other words, salvation in Katie's life was earned by serving others. "I firmly believe that we are here for each other, not just for ourselves, because God tells us that whatever gifts we have are not for us but to give to others to help somebody." In serving others Katie experienced, in part, the heaven God planned for everyone. Heaven was made real wherever God's plan for a loving community took form. But more important, Katie revealed that "to minister to another is to minister to God." Heaven and salvation are realized in the act of washing, feeding, healing, protecting, and loving others because to do so is to love God. In Katie's theology, that is heaven enough.

Painter Todd Macdonald of Family in Faith Lutheran Church spends most of his days working with brushes. He feels that heaven gets closer each time he does his craft well. He believes in a nonworldly heaven that is to some degree earned by what he does for his customers. But like Katie Jordan's work, Todd also experiences God's salvation with every stroke of his paintbrush. It seems that the work brings him closer to God. "I think it is more so than just coming to church. I just know that it is doing something good for Jesus Christ and the customers." Here again a worker finds the blessings of heaven and an expected approval from God by honoring God through earthly acts. Not simply prayers or worship services or Bible readings, but occupational acts. Todd was in a very literal way working his way into heaven. More important than holding the right religious ideas or exhibiting correct dogmatic behavior, Todd wielded a brush to color a ladder to God. But it was not always why he worked. "Before renewing my faith I was just doing my job well, but it was really not doing something good for Christ." Now Todd paints an edifice for a customer who in the painter's eyes embodies the spirit of God. "Maybe every job has some type of religious thing where they are trying to get to heaven in some way." In Todd's work he is preparing a place for God to dwell.

Jerry Logisz has been doing prep work for Jesus since he was sixteen years old. "[I work] for a food service company. I started in 1988 working in the credit department for $1.50 an hour part-time in high school and I just kept on working there." Jerry has been a lifelong member of St. Bruno Catholic Parish and he believes he was given a talent for numbers from God. In time Jerry made a lateral move within the company. "I said I would like to get a job working with computers so I just switched departments." Jerry sees the transition as something more than a wise managerial use of personnel. "The way I see it is that everybody has a talent for something and I guess this is what my talent is. I am not going to say that it is fun going to work every day, because many times it is not . . . there is the bureaucracy and the time sheets and the e-mails and all of that stuff, but I think if you were given a talent for something then you should go ahead and use it. I think that it is what is expected of you." Who is the subject that expects you to use your talents? Jerry offers a big smile and his shining eyes open wide as he answers joyfully, "God."

While Jerry's Catholicism prioritizes God's grace as the only salvation for "sinners," the stone path to heaven is apparently constructed with more than righteous beliefs. Jerry emphatically acknowledges that there is a relationship between his work and how God will ultimately judge him. "One guy is not going to have it all. God is going to divvy it [talents] up so that is why I think you are going to have to account for your talents. I think that I am using my talents in the way that they were intended." The purpose for which talents and skills are exercised is critical to how Jerry relates his earthly toil to an opportunity for a life everlasting. "I am not just using them for myself. I am using them for my family and charity." Jerry is very clear that using talents for *someone else* and on behalf of *others* in need of charitable help is the way that God intended human skills to be deployed. Jerry believes in a final "Judgment Day" and how a person's talents were put to work will be important to both sinner and Lord.

> You can either use or squander what you have . . . [but] He is going to ask you to tell Him what you did with your life. If you did all of that cheating people and suppose that made you as healthy as a horse and gave you plenty of means so that you don't even have to work and you had all the money in the world at your disposal and there was a Little League baseball team that needed a manager and you were a great baseball player because that is how you got your millions, do you coach that Little League team? God will ask you. If you said no, God will ask you what you did instead. You will have to explain that you got a big screen TV and home theater and you had every video game in the world. God will ask you what you thought was more important and that is where I think the justice will come.

Jerry's example of a superstar baseball player forced to explain to God why he invested in expensive electronic toys instead of teaching kids how to play the game comes from his own love of the Chicago Cubs. His passion for the Cubbies has even survived his presence at the infamous sixth game of the 2003 National League Championship Series. Despite the annual rite of disappointment that Cubs fans have learned to live with, Jerry has no intention of standing before God with a television remote in his hand. He has coached Little League baseball for many years. Time spent on a baseball field and charitable donations to St. Bruno Parish are simple ways that he allows his talent for math to be profitable. In Jerry's theology, talents are not meant to accumulate wealth for personal gain but should become a service to others.

> I think that over the long run . . . if you have wealth you should make yourself unrich. Rather than squander it on yourself or make sure that your descendants get it, maybe you should be providing for someone else. If you were a millionaire that was sitting there with your million dollars you could have helped balance and offset a bunch of evil. There could have been a lot of people who would not have to eat dog food if you had not bought that big screen TV. There are a lot of people who could have been cured of disease but there was no money for research because you gambled away $20,000 that you could have given to research.

Jerry believes that every talent counts and every talent counts equally. But he was not always so sure. "For a while I wrestled with wondering if I was worth as much to God as the pope or even Father Killian [the pastor at St. Bruno]. Obviously, this guy is more valuable to God—well, then I thought that maybe that's not true. If I told God that I went into the priesthood because I thought being a priest was more valuable than a computer programmer, I think God would not be happy. I think that we have been given the ability to find out what it is that we are good at." And once we have found out what our talents are and put them into practice for the good of others, is God pleased with us? "I think that's true. You work yours and I work mine." Jerry had one particular Gospel story (Matthew 25:14–30) that he liked to point to as support for the importance of wisely using God's gifts. It is the account of the man who called forth his three servants and "entrusted to them his property." To the first servant he gave five talents (i.e., a small amount of money), to the second he gave two, and to the third he gave only one. The talents were distributed "to each according to his ability." After a while the man conducted an accounting of what the servants had done with their talents. The first two servants had used their talents to multiply their wealth, but the last servant had done nothing more than bury his talent in the ground. The master was pleased with the servants who put their talents into action and invited them to "enter into the joy of your master." But for the inactive servant, the master had only harsh words "and cast the worthless servant into the outer darkness" (Matthew 25:14–30). In Jerry's interpretation, salvation may not be earned, but if a final accounting is to be made before the presence of God, then the work we have done or failed to do will not be dismissed in the supplicant whisper of "I believed."

When talking about salvation, working-class believers often pointed out the contradiction between possessing financial or material wealth and righteousness. As revealed in chapter 4, people graciously held open the gates of heaven for a faithful person of wealth, but suggested that earthly riches can distort a person's understanding of what God desires. St. Bruno parishioner Sharon Aftab offered a particularly trenchant analysis of the difference the money makes to eternal salvation. "I think when people get more money than they really need they have no place for God in their life." Did she know anyone like that? "Yeah, I think about my friends who are loan officers and before the low mortgage rates and everything, they were in church all the time. Now that we have low mortgage rates and they are making money hand over fist, I don't think any of them have been in church." Has money replaced God in their heart? "I think they are worshiping the Golden Calf."

Sharon's comments drew me to an inexplicable question: does God then favor the poor or working person? "I think He does because the poor are more realistic. They are cleaning floors and they are going to work on a daily basis." Sharon then starkly contrasted the divergent ways the wealthy and working people experienced life. "They [the poor and working people] are not paying for people to tend to all their daily needs—they are actually living life as opposed to paying for a life." Here, class perceptions of salvation could not be more significant. Getting to heaven requires doing work in your life—gardening, weeding, cutting grass, sweeping the floor, acting as a steward over creation. People of lesser means are compelled to do God's grunt work on earth; the wealthy are not. Sharon claims the riches of the upper class buy them relief from human toils, but "when you have a little bit too much disposable income, you inadvertently lose most of your ties to God." In the end, "What good will it be for a man if he gains the whole world, yet forfeits his soul? Or what can a man give in exchange for his soul?" (Matthew 16:26).

St. Bruno parishioner Bernice Feltz also believes that salvation's road is made up of something more than faith. "Trying to be a fair person is part of the path." She trusts that heaven exists: "I think there is someplace that my soul is going to go." But getting Bernice's soul to a preferred final destination is a little tougher than just accepting Jesus into her life. It apparently includes responsibly earning eight hours' pay for eight hours' work. "If I can get through the day and do something that keeps me from losing it and being nasty and plotting revenge, then I am on the path." The path Bernice speaks of is constructed of the talents God has given us. "God puts you on this path and then He gives us the intelligence to discover shoes that when you are walking that path you are not cutting your feet. You make a decision every time you get out of bed. Do I go to work today or not? Do I do a good job or do I not do a good job?" Bernice accepts that Jesus' death on the cross has made salvation possible, yet she underscores that "you have control." Faith is essential, work is necessary, but faith lived through work is the best route to God.

It demands, according to Holy Angels parishioners Rebecca Danforth and Michael Morman, much more than being prayerful and attending church. While Rebecca "cannot describe heaven," salvation requires being attentive "to many things you have to do in life." Michael agrees that salvation is realized by building heaven on earth. "I think that heaven is a lifestyle. I really think that it is not something that you bring to church or leave there. It is how you live your home life, your work life, social life, how you deal with other people, how you handle problems, how you handle stress, how you raise your children. It's definitely not something you can find in one place." The heaven Michael describes includes an array of interpersonal relationships conducted over a lifetime under the guidance of the commandment that Jesus called the second greatest: "You shall love your neighbor as yourself" (Mark 12:31). For Rebecca and Michael salvation comes less from "personal piety and morals" than by turning their walk in faith into a lifetime of loving social relationships.

Rebecca further adds that God's redemption is also inherent in how she does her telecommunication job. "Now if I was at work slouching on the job and not doing my job, I would not be doing God's work. But doing your job in a proficient and accurate manner, yes, that is being helpful to God." Rebecca's and Michael's comments underscored their understanding that a connection existed between salvation and knowing that God is present within workday activities. Work itself may not ensure salvation, but at least in Rebecca's faith, if it is done as an honor to God, then the job you do will help God do His or Hers. Acting as Jesus would toward others would not only advance an earthly kingdom, but as other believers have suggested about using their work to meet the needs of others, it would mean actually doing good to God. However, failing to minister to God would be a certain sign of damnation. Wheaton College professor of ethics Lindy Scott foretells the scriptural destinies of those who neglect God in their relationships: "They would have to depart from God's presence, accursed and eternally punished in the eternal fire prepared for the devil and his angels."[17] In other words, acting contrary to Jesus' teachings about the needs of others is a sure road to hell. Salvation follows a different path.

Rebecca and Michael also gained insight about "eternal life" with God from how Jesus died. When asked to talk about Jesus' crucifixion and resurrection, Rebecca and Michael were quick to announce that they were inspired to be better Christians because of the painful way the Son of God was killed. "To be nailed to a cross," Rebecca paused, then continued, "This man actually gave up his life by being nailed to the cross." Jesus' agonizing ordeal on the cross not only cleansed humankind of their sins, but set an example for Rebecca and Michael of what the children of God would have to do to enter God's kingdom. Arthur Reliford, also of Holy Angels, found the same meaning in Christ's death. Both Rebecca and Michael agreed with Arthur's explanation that "the self-sacrificing, giving it all up . . . the cascading effect two thousand years later has made a huge difference when people actually use this [Jesus' death] as an example of how they can live their lives. He made the ultimate sacrifice and he gave up his life." In living and dying for the love of humankind, Jesus pointed the way to the Father. So how exactly does Jesus' death teach us about how to live rightly and gain salvation? Arthur leaned closer to me and authoritatively explained, "We have to sacrifice our own desires so that we can be more present for others."

Police officer and Family in Faith congregant Craig Rutz would not argue with the connection between his salvation and sacrifice. In fact, while he does not "disbelieve the resurrection," he has drawn the conclusion that whether it did or did not happen was not really important. "The important thing is that Jesus died." Why is death more inspiring than being reborn? "Dying was the sacrifice. That is where God let his son die to make the sacrifice. Whether he took him back and physically raised the body or raised the spirit is not important." In death Jesus sealed the deal that if people took care of one another and were willing to put the needs of others ahead of their own, people would then be acting like Jesus and would, therefore, fulfill God's original plan for the world. In essence, through the work people did for others heaven would be created on earth. Craig's police work, for instance, is a primary means for acquiring the "ability to feel the taste of heaven."[18] If there is eternal life in a heaven after physical death, Craig would be very happy, but "it is irrelevant because the only thing that matters to us right now is our lives with one another right now." And what if a spiritual heaven does exist, how then is Craig's salvation assured? Simply put, by "doing the right things for the right reason, if we have lived in the way of Jesus."

In her seventy-nine years Shirley Haveck has had many opportunities to conduct her life in a way that would please God. She has attended Mennonite Community Church since the early 1960s and during World War II worked as a blue-print "tracer" for a company that built earth-moving equipment. Over the following years Shirley has also made cold cut sandwiches at a convenience store and worked as a lunch hostess at an elementary school. A lot of her days are now spent volunteering at the church and at a local senior citizen center. Over her lifetime, one of the few jobs Shirley has not done is that of a minister. But by her accounting, if she had been a pastor, her chance of being eternally rewarded would have likely improved. Shirley believes that a minister is the best occupation for performing "good works." In her way of thinking, good works (i.e., acts that extend God's message) can be done in "a lot of jobs," but the highest form of labor is direct service to the church. Despite her decades of secular paid labor, when asked to identify an example of "good works" from her life, Shirley answered, "When I get the communion ready for here [worship service]." Preparing a weekly spiritual supper of bread and wine for the company of seventy other parishioners was a higher-order "good work" than preparing deli sandwiches, keeping the school lunchroom orderly, and laboring on the home front during World War II.

Shirley's continuum of "good works" is important to consider because she believes that all her paid jobs, as well as her volunteering at the church, are consistent with what God expects from her. "I am just living my life the way I hope that God wants me to." With each paper tracing during the war, for every ring of the store cash register, and with each communion host taken and eaten, salvation draws nearer to Shirley. God judges it all, but Shirley lets on that service to the church is better and preaching the Word is probably best. Nonetheless, she sees her efforts to "follow the Ten Commandments and try to be uplifting to other people" as her personal course of salvation. Shirley's capacity to believe in a life everlasting was once clouded by the cancer deaths of her mom and sister. She now acknowledges that her life has had its curses and its blessings. But rewards for good acts committed on behalf of a manufacturer of earth-moving equipment, national chain store, elementary school, and Mennonite Church are coming. When? "I think probably when you die. I don't think that I will receive them in this world." Apparently heaven is unimaginable, but a way to get there is not.

Family in Faith Church congregant Donna Schiavone does a lot of healing work as a massage therapist, but she does not expect any of it to open heaven's pearly gates. She refers to a scriptural passage that she remembers saying: "all your good works are as filthy rags to me . . . what I [God] want is obedience." Donna wants God to be happy with her life activities, but in the end, being a faithful servant of God is all that matters. Salvation is possible only through submission to "the Ten Commandments which everyone knows and the first one is love God with all your heart, your mind, and your soul." Loving God unconditionally is Donna's path to salvation, no matter how pleasing God finds her work. Carpenter Ed Carrile would agree with Donna's single-factor approach to redemption. He thinks salvation is made much too complicated. "If you love yourself and love others, as you love yourself and love God, then everything else will be taken care of."

The sentiment expressed by Donna, Ed, and many other workers is to love yourself, others, and God. But what is not initially said is how to do that. For example, is praying adequate for loving God? Does not committing any willful acts of harm to others suffice as loving others? Or is something more affirmative needed for obeying God's cherished two greatest commandments? Upon further discussion Ed revealed that there is more to staying on the road to salvation then just pietistic expressions of brotherly and sisterly affection. "For me to stay on the road to salvation is to know that I am flawed. But I have gifts to give." And what is the connection to salvation? "I think that God expects me to use those gifts. Work is a medium in which I use my gifts and talents." Ed eventually acknowledged that everyone "needs something to facilitate the things that you do," and most critically, "to be the person God made you."

While every faithful worker agreed that salvation requires obedience to God's first and second commandments, for Ed it was hard to imagine an eternal life with God after a misspent one on earth. "I actually believe that we are here to be God's hands, eyes, and ears. He works through us, I truly believe that. It's not like he is going to come down and do a miracle every time. I think he uses people and that is why he gives certain people certain gifts." Ed expresses a strong desire to use the talents he has been provided with to do what he believes is God's work on earth. That work includes the time Jesus spent during his brief public ministry. Ed explained that the most important lesson from Jesus' adult life was that "he was always with the lepers, the tax collectors, and the people who were shunned by the community." It was Jesus' inspiring life and death that directed Ed to a way of life that would bring him into a right relationship with God. "The whole fact that he was human and went through all of that suffering proves that we can do it, too, because he was here. We need to use his example to see what we need in our daily lives." Ed stressed that to do God's work is to honor God.

While most workers could not conceptualize a heavenly kingdom, Sandra Houston did have one clear image: "It would be a place with people that meant so much to me." Sandra attends Holy Angels Church and during worship always prays to the mother she lost when Sandra was very young. "I would imagine that no matter how you appeared in heaven, because she was my mother that I would know her." In going to a place where her mother would be waiting, Sandra describes a heaven where new beginnings are celebrated. Her mom gave birth to Sandra and once called to heaven by God, Sandra will be reunited with her mother. "Heaven is like being reborn, where everyone is waiting for you and waiting to love you." In this sense heaven is a journey back to a comforting state of being, unfettered by the flaws of human existence.

What will it take to be reborn again? Sandra claims to have no idea, but simply trusts in God's guidance. "I don't really know. But God is constantly directing me and teaching me." Prayer, worship, Bible reading, volunteering at the church, acts of kindness, and doing her job well are all included in the ways that Sandra feels that God is directing her life. Salvation, however, still remains a mystery. "It's up to God," Sandra shrugs, but then admits that heaven can seem very close when she follows her faith. "I love it when God gets in my spirit and tells me what I have to do and then I do it." Whatever "it" may be, Sandra's trust in an eternal life is predicated on being moved by the Spirit of God to act. Miroslav Volf has written that "from the perspective of the new covenant . . . all God's people are gifted and called to various tasks by the Spirit."[19] Volf is exploring the inspirational quality of human labor and contends that when work is done in accordance with the will of God "it must be understood as *cooperation with God*" (emphasis in original).[20] Consequently, it would appear that Sandra has a strong if unidentified sense that acting in a way consonant with the Holy Spirit will lead her to salvation. The apostle Paul appears to agree: "Whatever your task, work heartily, as serving the Lord and not men, knowing that from the Lord you will receive the inheritance as your reward; you are serving the Lord Christ" (Colossians 3:23–25).

Azmat Ali expects to be rewarded for his faith "only after the death." Born in Pakistan, Ali has driven a Chicago city cab and worked in a restaurant to support his wife and three children. In his life he has been blessed by Allah with many wonderful opportunities to live as a good Muslim. But "whatever you do now, your work let's say, you get money now, only money." Here on earth, Ali stresses, our human activities can only earn us the enjoyments of the present life. "But later on you will be rewarded for your faith and good deeds." Azmat has an example from his work as a taxi driver. "Somebody left a cell phone in the back of my cab and I got it back to him. The reward for me is not now, but later. I am talking to this guy that left the cell phone and he wanted to give me some money and I said no. My reward will be in the hereafter, not now." Azmat feels obligated to act morally, in accordance with the Qur'an, but Allah's final judgment of his worthiness will come only after the body has withered away. But is doing righteous acts sufficient to get you into heaven? "We must accept Allah; if not, the Qur'an says heaven will be denied." Azmat may have been referring to the following dire passage: "But those who disbelieve, and die disbelieving, upon them shall rest the curse of God and the angels, and of men altogether, therein dwelling forever; the chastisement shall not be lightened for them; no respite shall be given them."[21]

Salvation will surely be withheld from the disbelievers, but paradise is no less likely if a person has acted immorally. Azmat makes clear that "Allah is always with us. He is watching us at any time; whatever you do, bad or good. He watches us, and he will not stop us from doing wrong things, but we believe that we will be punished later on when we die. After we die and we wake up, we will be punished for bad things." Passages from the Qur'an which note the severity of Allah's judgment of the wicked are common throughout the holy book. One such warning message spoken to Muhammad declares, "For He admits into His mercy whomsoever He will; as for the evildoers, He has prepared for them a painful chastisement."[22] Azmat, like every other Muslim cabdriver, did not claim an absolute awareness of who is and who is not a worthy Muslim. Each spoke of the Qur'an as a kind of rule book for correct living, but no one was willing to say under what conditions a faithful Muslim (meaning one who accepted Allah) would or would not go to heaven. Their hesitation notwithstanding, it was imperative as an article of faith that they live a good life, and that doing positive acts would indeed return dividends in the afterlife. Even the language of the Qur'an symbolically suggested a payoff: "Whatever good you shall forward to your souls' account, you shall find it with God as better and mightier a wage."[23]

Death and its aftermath is a common denominator for understanding how most workers feel about their chances for salvation. June Sargent, Eileen Foggie, and Rosemary Sykes, all of Holy Angels Parish, point to Jesus' crucifixion for inspiration about what a Christian life demands.

JUNE: To put himself as a human and to take all of that.

EILEEN: It helps me not make judgments because He never said a word. He never made anybody judge anybody either.

ROSEMARY: The crucifixion is a constant reminder of the sacrifice and what God has done and what he will do for us.

EILEEN: That is what it took to cleanse and pave our way to heaven.

JUNE: It is just like if we are doing these great jobs and then the next week, we may be homeless.

EILEEN: We are all going to be crucified in a certain way.

Over and over again the faithful women of Holy Angels Parish expressed awe over Jesus' sacrifice and suffering. But instead of feeling saddened by his passion and death, they hold on to the crucifixion as a climactic victory over evil and sin. Jesus' death happens in a particularly cruel way because he is unwavering in his love for the Father and he has presented a revolutionary challenge to a corrupt Roman and Jewish power structure. Eileen, June, and Rosemary remind me that Jesus was returned to the Father because of the sacrifices he made in a fully human life. In other words, God raised him up because he lived and died as a righteous *person*. If the resurrection of the Son of God was predicated on a life of human activity, then perhaps June, Eileen, and Rosemary are correct to expect no less from their time on earth.

The small numbers of people who participate in the services of the New Garden Community Universalist-Unitarian Church do expect less. Unlike the other religious representatives I spoke to, the dozen or so folks at New Garden are not influenced by conventional religious dogma. The church was started by Reverend Jean Siegfried Darling, a onetime freelance media artist and community activist with a Masters in Divinity Studies who also serves as the group's pastor. Darling had previously been a member of a UU congregation, but left to form a faith-based group that could achieve two complementary objectives. "One is that it would be committed to social justice," Darling recounts, "and the other would be that it would have services that felt spiritually nourishing and not like lectures." Attracting a small number of people of different religious denominations, New Garden held its first worship service on Labor Day 2002. Groups have met every Sunday in the historic United Electrical, Radio and Machine Workers (UE) Union Hall on Ashland Street, in an area of Chicago once called "Union Row."

The church's services are held in a sparse, spacious, second-floor room. Typically a circle of metal folding chairs is arranged around a small brown table adorned with a checkered brown cloth, small candles, and a silver chalice. Darling has little need for an altar, sanctuary, stained-glass windows, pews, or larger-than-life religious icons. She wears no religious vestments. Reverend Darling does, however, usually have a compact disc player and an array of inspiring books resting at her elbow. Participants in a New Garden service are often greeted by a musical prelude, followed by a lighting of the candles. After some brief opening remarks from the attendees, everyone joins in singing a song. As the singing fades, everyone greets one another and then listens to a selection of readings. On the day I attended, the readings were not from a recognized holy book. They were from a collection of poems by Langston Hughes on race and equality. Darling's sermon built upon the theme of race and work by focusing on the role of "Black Inventors" in America. Her short sermon was followed by a responsive reading, which included the following expression of gratitude: "For co-workers, we give thanks, for the merging of labors, in which goods of prosperity are brought to us all. Things made by another's hands establish us in gratitude." Following the reading, jazz pianist Thelonious Monk's "Straight, No Chaser" welcomed participants to make a good-will offering to pay for the coffee and potluck lunch at the conclusion of the service.

Darling is atypical because she envisioned organizing an explicitly "labor–peace" church that would be comfortable and welcoming to working people. Jean had been a speaker in the National Interfaith Committee on Worker Issues' "Labor in the Pulpits" Labor Day celebrations. During the Labor Day weekend, people of all walks of life visited religious institutions across the city to speak about the importance of organized labor to the goals of living a faithful life.[24] In Reverend Darling, a knowledge of worker issues and a deep wellspring of faith came together to imagine a congregation that would reach God through its fellowship with people who labored to build a "new garden" paradise. New Garden Community would be a place for people to open their minds and hearts to the Divine in their presence. To do so meant adhering to the principles of pacifism and economic justice. Wars, prisons, and shameful economic inequality constituted a violent assault on the nation and the people hurt the most were those who labored for the least.

Addressing itself to the liberal UU principals of equality, compassion, human potential, and God's benevolence, New Garden Community adopted a complementary mission, approach, and personality: it would be *introverted* with a spiritual focus during worship but *extroverted* with a social justice focus toward the world.[25] Faith and social action were not just separate ideas, but part of an integrated, moral life. It was Darling's objective to bridge the tensions between humanism (head) and spirituality (heart) that have always existed within Unitarian Universalism. In her conception, spiritual connectedness to the Divine was not assured through ritualistic acts of personal salvation, but realized by living an ethical life. And an ethical life meant participating in social action.

New Garden's guiding principle is to transform lives through art and action. Consequently, worship services are not conventional religious moments that normatively give thanks to a divine God. Most services are more like the above or like the one dedicated to the responsibility of nonprofit hospitals to care for the poor, or a "service Sunday" where lunches and clothes are distributed to the poor at the Pacific Garden Mission.[26] Darling and others are committed to celebrating life "whose foundation and purpose is love."[27] When New Garden congregants speak of God, they have in mind the collective human potential to make the world in the image of a nonviolent and peaceful place. That place could be called heaven. While some attendees hold views of a spiritual heaven, none are particularly worried about eternally resting there. It is here on earth where a kingdom of peace should reign.

Dave Karchar, a substitute teacher and part-time employee with a computer firm, explains that it is an eternal connectedness that best describes New Garden's UU idea of God and salvation. "I think one of the typical human things is that we assume that for a power to be greater than ourselves, it must be great enough to create the whole universe." This power is easily called "God." But Dave goes on to clarify that the "sum total of everything done and communicated by humanity over the years" has been produced by human acts of curiosity, hatred, love, and confusion. The world, in other words, did not need a divine power greater than its inhabitants to take shape. If salvation is going to come, according to Dave, it will be through the acts of a very fallible, but collective human spirit capable of "miracle-like" achievements. What the people at New Garden most opposed was a view of heaven and salvation that was autocratic. Again, Dave Karcher offered the following metaphoric explanation for New Garden's discomfort with conventional religious notions of salvation:

> Part of what happens is like if there was a board game called "Heaven" with 6.2 billion players. You have one coach and one referee that happens to be the same person. So what happens is that the coach sends inspiration to individuals who can react any way that they want toward achieving the end of the game, which is of course "heaven." But if the player does not play the way the referee expects him or her to play, the referee calls a foul and punishes the player, while for the other players the game continues.

Reverend Darling rarely speaks of a heaven or hell, but she does preach about salvation. Her idea of salvation, however, is not the kind that awaits the righteous soul when the body returns to dust. "Salvation," she explains, "or what saves us, what damns us, and what happens as a result . . . is about life on Earth."[28] Salvation is not a universal inheritance for all believers paid by the blood of Christ, but comes instead from a life that moves in the direction of greater individual consciousness. According to Reverend Darling, the consciousness that can save each of us is a realization that everyone has a responsibility to the common good. God, for Jean, lies within each person and it is there where a purpose-driven life toward community is formed. Not to be found in dogma or ritual, God is a "creative intelligent consciousness intrinsic to all beings."[29] To seek God is to reach out for the "thread that winds through all of existence, that links everything, that envelops everything, that moves toward health, toward love, toward connectedness."[30]

Once imbued with how interconnected creation is, a person interested in salvation will accept the imperative to make the world a better place. At times that may mean resistance to evil. Jean is adamant that salvation is "freedom achieved [peacefully] through rebellion against illegitimate and dominating authority, either overtly or stealthy."[31] A person's faith should guide his or her ethical behavior in the face of injustice. The road to salvation is just as Isaiah said: "remove the evil of your doings from below my eyes; cease to do evil, learn to do good; seek justice, correct oppression" (Isaiah 1:16–17). Jean sees God's potentiality on the morning news and is called to act. "Salvation is here and now" and the goal of religion is to transform this world, "not the next."[32] In Jean's theology, "being saved" requires speaking to the "unnamable force that imbues all growing things, that inhabits the urge to grow, to gain in complexity and consciousness."[33] Here, then, is where salvation begins and ends. To know that God's "work is helped or hurt by the actions of human beings" and whenever people consciously share their lives, "it is never too late for redemption."[34]

Not surprisingly, New Garden members found the idea of a God who punishes as bizarre. While the Christian and non-Christian workers I spoke with held differing views of God's sense of justice, no believer embraced a description of a painful life after death in a place called "hell." Heaven was believable if not describable, but hell in any form was harder to find. Workers struggled with a sense of eternal damnation because the notion of hell carried with it the baggage of a cruel God who would finally abandon His or Her children. Leaving any human being created in the image of God to an eternity of suffering was radically inconsistent with working-class believers' fundamental notions of God as all loving. Virginia Coleman of Holy Angels Parish whimsically fantasized about an otherworldly heaven where she will gently rest among "waterfalls and rivers." In this place there is "no animosity, no hate, just contentment." But if there is a heaven after death, then does a hell also exist? Coleman, and nearly all believers, will testify to the existence of evil in the world, even to Satan, but inexplicably not to hell as an alternative destiny for our souls.

However, Coleman and fellow Holy Angel parishioner Vince Washington will work for the blessings of an earthly heaven where both spirit and body are healed. Washington makes very clear that "there is heaven on earth because there is peace and serenity here." A heaven in the midst of human fallibility can be realized as a place of tranquility because God is present in the spirit of all people. Here heaven is a state of being and human consciousness. It is experienced in the world created by God, but only internally realized. Vince added, "[H]eaven on earth comes from within a person. From your spirit and how you feel and how you perceive things." It is not an earthly heaven of three-dimensional reality, visible to the naked eye. Nor, according to Coleman and Washington, should heaven be spoken of as just "the ultimate." Instead, there is a heaven *right here and right now,* which emanates from a personal philosophy of life that allows the individual to live in harmony with the world. Heaven is a feeling of contentment about life, but does a euphoric feeling of contentment mean salvation after death?

"I believe the Lord wants us to act out our faith. He wants us to help our fellow man," Washington argues. Feeling comfortable with others is not the same as sharing your comforts with others. Virginia Coleman's motivation for reaching out to the afflicted begins with the Genesis story. "For me it is that everyone on this earth is a child of God." So how does faith inspire her to act? "Helping someone else to become better or help them to open their eyes and realize that they do not necessarily have to be in the bad situation that they are in." But the action she recommends is not the type of sharing Jesus taught when he discouraged his followers from possessive materialism ("from him who takes away your coat do not withhold even your shirt" [Luke 6:29]). Instead Coleman believes that assisting in a person's spiritual development will fulfill her mission on earth and, by implication, prepare her for an eternity of peace. "If I can take the blinder off someone else, that is what I feel the Lord wants me to do. This is His work and I am going to do his work." Virginia is prepared to share her faith with those who need to be with God. She believes "His work" is evangelization. Coleman's and Washington's faith compels them first and foremost "to save others." They are deeply attentive to the material needs of God's children but feel that "ultimate" salvation is earned by bringing disbelievers to God; in Coleman's words, "To drive people closer in faith and try to act and talk about the Lord more."

St. Denis parishioner Ellen Kilmurry has been attending church for forty-five years and she has grown impatient waiting for the kingdom of God to come. "I am trying to get it here." And Ellen sees no middle ground for believers. "Either you are building the kingdom or you are not." Bringing heaven into people's lives is as simple as choosing to act Christ-like, and "every action is part of learning how to be a kingdom builder." What Ellen means by kingdom building is visible in her life activities: she administers to the poor. Religious practices have been a part of her life for nearly a half century, but she is certain that churchgoing alone will not get heaven built. "I don't think you are given free will and you are given a brain in order to just go to church on Sunday and sing a few songs." Salvation includes becoming the person that God created and "being able to express freely all the gifts that you were given." But to use God-given talents a person must be fed, clothed, educated, sheltered, protected, encouraged, fairly compensated, and loved. To Ellen, God's work requires helping people to be fully human.

She equates fulfilling basic needs with creating the conditions that permit a person to be fully realized in the image of God. An individual's talents are like a hard-wired program that, once completely mastered, brings him or her into a closer relationship with God. Ellen has never understood any other purpose for God's gifts to us. "Why would they be used in the next life?" Yes, she conceives of a next life: "a large community, not much different from what we are doing now." But heaven on earth will never happen "if all you did was sing and read the Bible." Ellen Kilmurry has been marching and organizing against injustice and for the downtrodden since the day she could recite the Rosary. At the age of fifteen she met Cesar Chavez, and while attending St. John's Church, she was strongly influenced by Father John Barlow, who had worked with Martin Luther King Jr. in Selma, Alabama. Ellen and a few of her friends at the church also traveled on buses to Gary, Indiana, to work for Senator Robert Kennedy on an antipoverty campaign. Her walk-in-faith has literally covered miles of sidewalks, thoroughfares, and neighborhoods. It has also provided for the material needs of others through her work with the Chicago Port Ministries and as a participant in the religious-community-labor coalition United Power for Action and Justice.

On Pentecost Sunday, May 26, 1985, Father Augustin Milton, O.F.M., and a few people committed to bringing the church to the streets opened up a soup kitchen in Chicago at 5058 South Ashland. Inspired by a section of the Portiuncula Church in Assisi, Italy, the small group renamed the space "The Port." Over the next twenty-plus years, the initial humble effort to feed a couple dozen of the city's hungry grew into the "Port Ministries." Ellen Kilmurry now helps to service a multifaceted ministry to the poor that includes a mobile soup kitchen, a restaurant-style feeding ministry, food and clothing donations, a nonresidential program for children and educational opportunities for adults, a health-care clinic, a recreational facility for children ages eight to eighteen, and a full-family shelter. The Port's mission to "find Jesus in the 'distressing disguise of the poor' and to serve him" aligns with Ellen's own walk of faith.[35] It also explains her participation with United Power for Action and Justice.

Formed in 1997 as a dream fulfilled of the late Monsignor Jack Egan of the archdiocese of Chicago, United Power is an assembly of secular and multidenominational institutions that organized to concentrate grassroots power on behalf of social justice.[36] On October 19, 1997, over ten thousand people from 320 different institutions joined forces to create the new metropolitan-wide citizens' organization. Dedicated to "building a politics of the common good," the organizations' leaders addressed "pressing issues in their communities—violence, downsizing, high housing costs—and emphasized their regional nature."[37] With the support of the late Cardinal Joseph Bernardin, a large committee of African American religious leaders, white Protestant denominations, Jewish organizations,

Islamic institutions, and labor unions raised over $2 million and hired the Saul Alinsky–created Industrial Areas Foundation to organize the new citizens' group. Since its impressive founding assembly, United Power has participated in social movements focused on universal health care, affordable housing, leadership development, and institutional building. The organization has over 230 institutional members, including St. Denis Church, where Ellen Kilmurry passionately integrates her faith with secular struggle.

Ellen is an advocate for social justice in the name of a living Christ. In her life, faith and work are not separate domains. She admits that she may be an exception, but then "not everyone is going to be on picket lines, but everyone can vote, everyone can read the newspaper." As she explains, "[T]here are many things in between advocacy and radicalism than just attending church." The bottom line is: "You have to be on the path toward action to get to heaven." Ellen is acting for social justice and for an end to what she considers the biggest problem that human beings have in the world: "the fact that we are all compartmentalized." People are divided by race, ethnicity, age, gender, class, language, and religious beliefs. She also recognizes that there are powerful economic interests that benefit from a divided human community of less fortunate means. But Ellen has tremendous confidence in a universal faith-based community that "can let us connect with other people" and build a social movement to eradicate poverty, homelessness, joblessness, and human exploitation. Ellen could not imagine a more righteous road to heaven. "Let's say that God offered me the path and I chose it."

Uniting all people around Jesus' principle of economic sharing or "koinonia" is a theme that has been repeated by many of the Christians interviewed. As interpreted from religious texts by Wheaton College professor Lindy Scott, koinonia emphasizes "the sharing of one's possessions with the poor and the needy of the land."[38] Scott cites the following passage from the Old Testament to explain what koinonia demands of Jews and Christian alike: "If there is among you a poor man, one of your brethren, in any of your towns in your land which the Lord your God gives you, you shall not harden your heart, or shut your hand against your poor brother; but you shall open your hand to him, and lend him sufficient for his need, whatever it may be" (Deuteronomy 15:7–9). Working-class Catholics like Caroline Garcia and Rudy Ramirez not only believed in the principle, but expected their path to salvation to be paved by it.

Garcia and Ramirez both attend the largely Hispanic-Latino Immaculate Conception Church on Chicago's southeast side. Caroline, a processing clerk in a bank, and Rudy, a food service aide in a hospital, are both articulate advocates for a life of Christian social action. They both believe that as Christians they have a sacred duty to speak out against injustice and to act in affirmative ways to improve the world. Evil is something both recognize. Caroline sees it in the actions of nations. "I think evil is war in Bosnia, evil is war in Somalia, evil is war in Iraq, evil was the Holocaust." Rudy offers a more personal accountability approach to the existence of evil. "Evil for me begins in what I choose to accept. I know right from wrong." Rudy is dismissive of claims from people that the "Devil made people to do badly." Good or bad happens, he insists, only because "my thinking leads me to my actions." So in a world of evil where people have the freedom to choose poorly or wisely, what does a Christian need to do to get to heaven? Rudy is confident that "believing is not enough." The nature of a world characterized by wars and a host of economic deprivations places serious obligations on the faithful. Salvation is unlikely, according to Rudy, "without reaching out and helping other people and caring for other people." Caroline adds that "there are many ways to help and not necessarily with the money, but with listening and visiting."

Caroline believes that God will be pleased with you "as long as you follow through on your faith." Church attendance, prayer, and "being in the Word" are all helpful in knowing God, but to Rudy the key to heaven is "in following in His footsteps." Not so much in "doing what He said," but in doing "what He has done." Caroline and Rudy always focus their faith on what happens after they stop praying. They see God in the homeless, the poor, the war victim, the lonely person in need of a friend, and especially the sick. Caroline grew very animated as she sketched out a contemporary story of rejecting the biblical lepers:

> Look at now, people get sick with AIDS. Lots of people did not want to get near people who had AIDS. If Jesus was here, He would have gotten near them. This is where religion comes in. If you do not practice your faith every day, how can you call it your faith? If you are going to be judging and going to be ignoring someone who is really ill, or passing someone who needs help, how can you say that you are a good practicing Catholic or whatever? You go to church on Sunday, but yet you come out of church and on Monday you are doing the same thing over again? I don't know what kind of religion that is.

Perhaps it can be called a false or dead faith. Rudy referred to the biblical passage warning that "faith apart from works is dead" (James 2:26) to express disdain for "Sunday Christians." And if living as a good person is, as Caroline says, "all that matters to God," then it matters most how a person acts in life. A person should act, according to Caroline, like the

Jesus who "sat with lepers and died on the cross to save us." Again the importance of social fellowship, taking care of the needy, and bearing the weight of the cross is tremendously influential to how a working-class Christian views the path to salvation. "When we die," Rudy ruefully notes, "we are going to get judged and what you do now is what is going to count up there [heaven]." Why else, he wonders, would we be given one life to live?

Kim and Gerry Vargas think they know why. The married congregants of Family in Faith Lutheran Church describe themselves as devout born-again Christians. God's gift of life, Gerry explains, is why Christians know so little about heaven. "Probably the reason why the Lord does not want to tell us much about heaven is because He wants us to enjoy the things that he has created for us on earth. Nature and this beautiful earth. I don't think it is probably as beautiful as heaven can be, but I can just imagine." Kim agrees that earth is in the image of heaven and where God wants us to place our attention. It is the Lord's design that offers "the birds and the flowers, how unique they are." But heaven is greater yet, and Kim takes great joy in knowing that the Lord says, "I go to prepare a place for you." While uncertain what will happen when she dies, Kim expresses no fears about death. She and her husband are avid readers of the Bible and believe in the book's inerrancy. "We have to have faith, and just the fact that the Lord is preparing a place for us and that the Lord loves us as much as he does, there is comfort in that." Trusting in God means opening oneself to the Spirit of God. As we discussed heaven, Kim and Gerry stressed that salvation requires a receptive heart.

Do you believe there is a particular path to salvation for you?

GERRY: Yes, there are a couple of things. The first one is that you have to acknowledge that the Lord Christ has died and given you the gift of eternal life. You have to acknowledge that.

KIM: You have to accept the gift.

GERRY: Yes, you have to accept His gift. You also have to be born again. When you accept His gift you have to be born again in the Spirit. You must be born of the Spirit. When you are born of the Spirit, the human within you is dead because walking in the Spirit is putting aside your pride; putting aside your ego; putting aside everything that makes you that pile of man that separates you from God by accepting the gift that the Lord Jesus gave us.

KIM: It is by allowing the Holy Spirit to be in charge of every step you take. You have to invite Him in to live in your heart.

In Gerry and Kim's religious mindset salvation is not earned by a life oriented to righteous action. To believe in God fundamentally requires an acceptance of God as Lord, Creator, and Savior. It means being a "soldier of Christ"—a Christian grunt who reads and believes in biblical prophecy and who travels by "faith and not by sight" (2 Corinthians 5:7). The Vargases' confidence in attaining heaven solely by *right belief*, however, does not prevent Kim from writing letters of concern to a United States senator and toy company, and speaking out against the building of a community waste-transfer site. In these cases Kim explains that she was acting in furtherance of God's kingdom and as such was acting like a good Christian soldier. Fighting the righteous fight also meant voting against John Kerry in the 2004 presidential election. "I have heard John Kerry say in so many words that he is personally against abortion and yet he is for a woman's right to choose. I think one of the greatest issues in any election is the politicians' views on abortion because that is the greatest tragedy to ever come about in our nation or any nation." Kim and Gerry could not support any candidate who would permit legalized abortions, so "to be His [God's] follower" meant voting for George W. Bush. In the Vargases' theology, it was also an action consistent with accepting the Spirit of God into your life. To have acted otherwise would have been a rejection of the Holy Spirit and would have triggered a fast descent into hell.

Tom Cahill, recently retired after forty years as a union typesetter, has developed an ecclesiastical interpretation of human labors and spiritual worship. Along with his job and extended family, Tom's deepest lifetime commitment has been to the Irish Catholicism of his childhood. He proudly refers to himself as a "seven-day Catholic" who "doesn't go to church and then do something [i.e., contrary to his faith] the rest of the week." On Sunday Tom worships at St. Denis Church and feels that salvation requires working within and as the body of Christ. Tom views a person's physical existence as God's manifested presence on earth. In others words, God's work can only get done on earth when people like Tom choose to be in co-creation with God. Eternity with God, he notes, begins with a purpose. "God did not put me here to do bad. The purpose was to bring good into other peoples' lives." Caring for others requires saying devout prayers and faithfully worshiping, but also "I believe that good works are necessary because Jesus went among the people and talked and actually consorted with people that other people did not really like. You have to look at how He led His life [and] we basically carry on His life on earth." Jesus was the model for how an Irish typesetter worked and lived. Salvation was promised to Tom if he worked and worshiped as a part of the eternal God. "We are members of His [spiritual and physical] body. You may be a finger or an arm, but God is the body and we are the extensions of it. He works through us so collectively as a unit we are there."

Tom's belief that each individual fits together to construct the presence of God on earth was nicely reflected in Paul's letter to the Ephesians: "And his gifts were that some should be apostles, some prophets, some evangelists, some pastors and teachers, to equip the saints for the work of ministry, for building up the body of Christ" (Ephesians 4:11–12). In Tom's lived theology the ministry is shared by pastor and typesetter alike. Each reveals "that there is a God." God works through the church congregation and the masses producing in the marketplace. In both, salvation is fully in reach.

Sandra McDowell has worked for over sixteen years assisting pregnant teenagers in a county public health program. She has dedicated long hours to a job she reflexively calls "her life." On many occasions Sandra has made a difference in the lives of girls sixteen years and younger. When her work leads to helping a young mother, she is grateful for God's blessing, but when Sandra's help comes too late, she realizes how far away heaven remains. "There was a baby who was paralyzed because the girl's boyfriend, the baby wouldn't stop crying and he threw it down on the table." During the tragic moments Sandra yearns for God's merciful intervention, but no matter the course of events, she is reluctant to believe in a heaven on earth. "I just feel that it's not heaven because I still have to, you know, go through the bad parts of town [in Chicago] and drug dealers and police and all that kind of stuff, so it's sure not heaven down here."

Sandra readily declares that "God should be first in her life," and while she faithfully attends worship services at Community Mennonite Church, she strongly contends that her work is a path to salvation. In order to be redeemed, Sandra holds that "you have to live right . . . make [your life] pleasing to God by trying to help people in need." According to Sandra, getting to heaven will take more than riding on wings of right belief. People "would [need] to be kinder to each other and want to help people instead of trying to destroy 'em and destroy property. So many who need to be helped . . . God would appreciate helping the less fortunate." Sandra recounts helping one particular girl with a two-year-old daughter by asking the Mennonite church to answer a prayer. "She didn't have any heat and we prayed that the family would come up with the money, plus with the help of the church to get heat into the house, and they finally did, after three or four months." Her labors at the county health department provide

Sandra with the chance to "live rightly," but she also acts as a Christian disciple. "I'm trying to help the girls to be, to live the right way, to get to heaven, OK." Sandra believes in spreading the word of God, but she also knows that getting the heat turned on for a single teenage mother is another way to inch a person closer to God's kingdom.

"Like a lot of flowers and sunshine" is how lab technician Krystyna Bogdanowicz describes her vision of heaven. "It's something great, it's gonna be good and happy." In an English language strongly influenced by her Polish upbringing, Krystyna declares her belief in the kingdom promised by God. She faithfully attends St. Bruno Church, prays daily, believes fervently in the idea of mortal sin, and is inspired by the biblical story of Christ's resurrection. Krystyna expects to find heaven when she dies and to share eternal bliss in God's glory. But despite her fundamental adherence to a life after death, salvation is not likely to be found in faith alone. "You can't just pray, pray, pray. I mean it's good to go to church because I personally like to go to church, but church is just an institution, it's just a place that was built by tradition. It's not like, when Jesus was around, there wasn't a church."

Krystyna retains a deep-seated old country reverence for the miraculous potential of faith, yet she has a decidedly pragmatic approach to salvation. She learned to be an action-oriented Catholic in Poland and has never forgotten. "To help people you know. Because I am only here with my daughter and my husband, so [we] help people in Poland or here, like we have a neighbor, she's older. . . . [In this country] it maybe different because you cannot go to neighbors without asking them, this is a different world here, but in Poland, you go to neighbor because you know them forever and you can help them." Krystyna's favorite Gospel story is the nativity of Jesus because it makes her feel happy and provides the very real possibility of personal redemption. Jesus' birth sets into motion a model way of life that is a blueprint for how a person can attain salvation. Every Sunday Krystyna humbly prays to God on her knees, but Monday through Friday she tends to the needs of her family, neighbors, and patients. "Like with your actions, you are pretty much supporting faith. Like your faith is known through your actions." I suspect that Krystyna's God would find favor in the gospel she teaches. "Do good with your life, don't do bad things to people" and heaven will take care of itself.

Achieving an eternal life with God can seem a very arduous and unpredictable task. Most working-class believers offered ideas about the paths that lead to salvation but then humbly admitted uncertainty about God's judgment. There were individuals, though, like Community Mennonite congregant Paul Mares, who saw the gates of heaven swung wide open. It was just a matter of walking through. As a Christian, Paul imagines that heaven lies within reach for those who are "trying to be Christ-like." By Christ-like Paul does not mean to be in a regular state of worship or praise, or to adhere to doctrinaire beliefs. "Being Christ-like is being a servant, not to be served, but to serve." Service to others is how Paul describes his current work as a carpenter and cites a litany of past occupations as evidence of how he has climbed the heavenly staircase. "I had worked in this community as a day-care teacher, as a driver for a sheltered care workshop, and . . . [in] a home repair program." Paul's service through paid and volunteer labor is how he describes "being aware of other people's needs." He also prays that the needs of others are fulfilled, but prayer is not the same as "actually trying to fulfill those needs." Talking to God helps, but picking up a hammer is how you build a ladder.

Or you can open the gates of heaven by playing beautiful music. Mira Sojka-Topor does more than attend church at St. Bruno. Truth be told, the thirty-one-year-old Polish mother of two children ministers during nearly every weekend worship service. Mira plays the church organ and sings the worship hymns. She calls her church job a sacred "duty": God has placed this classically trained musician behind an organ at St. Bruno. According to Mira, the Holy Spirit "comes through the music, through me, and goes back to God." Salvation is God's judgment and Mira has little idea about the nature of heaven, but she is confident that Jacob's Ladder is climbed one note at a time. "[God] will choose that kind of a person . . . someone who had a good life and was a good person, and give him heaven." Heaven is awarded to people after death "who had a good life and made the right choices." In Mira's case, making right choices inspires her to "think about others and be helpful, and do many good stuff." Mira believes that God is very pleased about her willingness to answer the church call to music ministry, and that her sacred gift of music is a regular way that she can transcend the space between flesh and bone, and pure heavenly spirit.

If believers like Mira have a special talent that fulfills God's plan for them on earth, there are also people like Deborah Hindelewicz who have no idea what talents God wants her to use. Deborah, along with her husband, John, attends St. Bruno Church. She works in the research department for an information technology company. Deborah believes in a life after death with God, but has more questions than answers about what personal salvation requires. She is, however, certain about one thing. "The path to salvation is for me to strive to be all that God intended me to be." Desiring to know God's purpose inspires Deborah to constantly "pray for His will and guidance as to what talents that I am supposed to be using here." Deborah muses that the object of her labors must be for more than individual gain. "What is His plan for me to make my part to make this world a better place to be? I ask what I am here for. I ask what He would have me do." These fundamental questions are common among believers of all faith traditions, but in Deborah's theology the answers determine her eternal fate.

> If I go to church and I do not do anything during the week to reflect how I am a Christian, then my faith is nothing. There are a few people who just go to church and feel that all that they have to do is go to church and then they will get into heaven. But I do not believe that. I believe that you have to go outside of just going to church and you have to reach out and help other people. That you have to go outside of yourself and not only think of yourself but to think of other people or a cause that speaks out to you. That you know that you should be there or you know that you should be helping someone less fortunate.

John Hindelewicz, a longtime union welder and now part-time welding instructor at a business school, sums up his wife's and his own views on the path to salvation: "Faith without works is dead." And Deborah is reminded of an example of how a very powerful and publicly faithful man did his job "sinfully" and hurt thousands of people. "[President] Clinton signs the NAFTA bill and these big corporations, you hear on the news every day, [start] laying off people. For him to sign that bill is just so wrong. It is wrong to use people as cheap labor or just slaves. This cheap labor is just using humans in such a wrong and awful way. He had greed in mind. He did not have the right heart." What may or may not have been in William Jefferson Clinton's heart is unknowable, but to Catholics Deborah and John Hindelewicz the ex-president's free-trade love affair did not lift him up Jacob's Ladder.

Andy Schutt of Park Lane Christian Reform Church agrees that belief in Christ is essential to salvation, but goes further to allow for a dispensation for a person who lives a sinful life. First of all, "you will not go to heaven if you do not believe that Jesus died for you. That is the only way to heaven." To Andy the path to salvation cannot be paved with good or even heroic deeds. Andy quotes the following from John's Gospel to punctuate his point: "I am the way and the truth, and the life; no one comes to the Father, but by me" (John 14:6). But what of the person who lives sinfully? Can you be abusive to people during life and still be saved after death? "Yes, regardless of how you acted." Andy sees salvation available for even the most evil of beings by drawing deeply from the meaning of Jesus' crucifixion. "He made a way for me to be covered from all my sins.

Jesus died and took my place [i.e., suffered for the sins of the world]. But I have to accept Him as savior. I don't know if good works will do you any good." Andy is uncertain about what heaven will be like, but he is not doubtful about where it is. "Our ultimate reward is not in this life. Man rejected God; we disobeyed him." Now only a death accompanied by the acceptance of Jesus Christ as your savior will bring the ultimate rewards of faith. "This is only a little short journey that I have on earth here." Andy is comfortable waiting for his time.

CONCLUSION

God and Working-Class Lives

MARTIN BUBER, one of the most renowned Jewish thinkers of the twentieth century, had an understanding of God that I believe working-class congregants implicitly endorsed in the way that they *lived their faith*. Buber stressed that God was an all-encompassing presence who engaged humanity through the experience of living in the world. God was not inaccessible or one to be spoken of in the third person. God does not "command law, nor can he be sought after through rituals."[1] But more important was what Buber had to say about human beings experiencing God in their life: "Man cannot reach the divine by reaching beyond the human."[2] The working-class Christians, Jews, and Muslims that I spoke with described a living faith that was realized in God's name, but was all about finding God in the relationship with others. While making no claims to a grand theology, I found the daily relational nature of spirituality to be a central tenet of working-class faith. Faith to workers was not a solitary show of personal piety, but an act of community building.

Going to church, temple, or mosque were just the tips of a faith-influenced working-class life; while important, it is less relevant to being faithful than the actions of working-class believers after worship service ends. Believers talked about their lives as if they considered them communion with God. God seems to be everywhere to the painter, nurse, bus driver, massage therapist, butcher, processing clerk, cemetery worker, and teacher. God's quiet and steady presence reflects the unified quality of a working-class spiritual life. Faith neither begins nor ends with going to temple, reciting the Lord's Prayer, or saying salut. To the working-class Catholics, Lutherans, Mennonites, Baptists, Muslims, and Jews featured in this book the sacred and secular are integrated. The presence of a spiritual being is just about all that holds together a world of struggle and service for people living paycheck to paycheck. Struggle is paramount and comes with the territory. Being human means experiencing illness, accident, and misfortune as well as joy, elation, and good health. God is not to blame for the pain. Somehow the Almighty is responsible for everything, but not for the particular bad that befalls human beings. Rather, the horrible and tragic is woven into a grand strategy of universal salvation that no one is capable of understanding. What working-class believers did know was that without suffering and sacrifice God is not known. Worker after worker found inspiration and redemption from responding to the agonies of life. Struggle was a physical, social, economic, and psychic state where working people realized the grace of God. In struggle they found hope, gained courage, endured doubt, and fought evil. By the blessing of struggle they were saved.

Few saw miracles of divine intervention, although turning to God in prayer for help was a common practice. There was nothing formal or doctrinaire about the prayers. They were more like brief, unstructured one-way conversations with God. Sometimes giving praise, other times pleading for help. In times of duress workers did not expect their prayers to produce magical cures, although they could, if God willed it so. Some had moments of abandonment and cried out, "My God, my God, why hast thou forsaken me?" (Mark 15:34). But the typical cry of suffering was not expected to earn any quid pro quo dividend. At best it sought out only God's wisdom and protection. Prayers of thanks were most often about personal and familial continued good health and for the blessing of "having a job." Petitions happened more often in ordinary places (i.e., the car, the kitchen, and nearly always at work) than during weekly worship.

Workers rarely asked for God's mercy for themselves. There was a belief that a prayer said for personal assistance was less likely to be answered than one said for another. The prayer or petition to God was a way that working-class believers identified with other people who had experienced distress and to seek help for others. I imagine that's why, despite her own ill health, my mother insisted on always talking to God about everyone but herself. In the immediate days before she was to get the results of a breast screening, my mother made an entry in a private journal expressing her fears but added that she was talking to God about my own postsurgical health.

> DECEMBER 11, 2002
> We got some hail and then we got snow. Just an inch or so. Slag trucks salted the streets and traffic was moving . . . I baked chocolate chip cookies. Tomorrow I'll make more. I don't bake like I did when you boys were home. Dad doesn't need all those sweets! I'm still hanging in there. Very, very hard. I'm trying honey. . . . A little scared what they will find when I go to this doctor. The 2 black spots. Know what I mean? When I know, you'll know. I promise. Love you. I'm praying that your health improves. *It just has to!* (emphasis in original)

Mom made at least eight entries where she mentions praying for me. There were none about petitions to God on her own behalf. She had an enormous capacity to understand the pain of others and even in prayer her personal agonies were not brought before God. Mom's prayers for an end to suffering, like so many of the people I interviewed, reflected "a conviction that things are better off where they are: in the hands of God."[3]

Most of their prayers were said somewhere other than in a house of worship and were privately uttered in silence. Only a small minority of workers had ever been part of a prayer group or even a prayer chain. Talking to God on the way to work or over a coffee mug was very common. Workers actually prayed to themselves a lot at work, but few kept visible religious icons around them to announce their faith. In some workplaces public displays of faith could be tricky, but in truth no worker thought it was necessary to drape themselves in religious accessories. At most a Bible or devotional book sat close by and maybe a printed prayer taped to a cubicle. For some, talking about God during work breaks was pretty common. A few even shared prayers publicly at work before the day's grind commenced. When praying, Muslim, Jew, Catholic, and Protestant used essentially the same words and addressed common topics.

When, if, or how God would make things better was an alluring mystery, but no person of faith believed that God willed suffering or wanted people to hurt. Nobody was being punished for living in a state of sin. Few people even felt comfortable defining what a sin might be or when a sin had occurred. One strong exception was St. Denis parishioner Larry Hill, who offered an explanation that resonated with me: "If you put yourself in a position where you can assist people or treat them morally and do not, then that is sinful." For most others sin was something that simply displeased God. But in the end, that was for God to determine. However, individual acts were easier than corporate acts to characterize as sinful. It seems, according to most working-class believers, that despite the forceful critique of abusive authority emblazoned in the Qur'an, Hebrew Bible, and Christian scriptures, individuals are far more susceptible to displeasing God than corporations or governments.

As interpreted by working-class believers, the actions of business leaders were cloaked in uncertainty over whether corporate behavior was driven by necessary economic forces (not sinful, no matter the consequences to workers, consumers, or citizens) or greed (voluntary and probably sinful). For instance, a farm labor contractor who hires homeless people and then drives down their wage by selling them crack cocaine, beer, and cigarettes from a "company store" is the devil in the flesh. But the contractor who pays the workers just pennies for every bushel of tomatoes picked and then calls the Immigration Control and Enforcement service when the workers talk about unionizing is a more redeemable character.[4] Now, the guys who engineered the financial meltdown of employee retirement incomes at Enron appeared sinful; working-class believers saw what they did as pure theft.[5] After all, there are Christian, Judaic, and Islamic commandments against stealing. But when the chief executive officer at General Motors demands that retired auto workers pay more for their health care, or company officers at United Airlines use a bankruptcy court to dump their obligations to pay retirement benefits to thousands of workers, or Wal-Mart's business strategy erodes local revenue streams vital for schools and public hospitals, or the ten largest investment banks pay over $1 billion in fines, working-class members of faith communities are less certain of what religious principle had been violated.[6] Despite the fact that large numbers of working-class and poor families are most often badly victimized by corporate economic decisions, it is harder to call the logic of capitalism or the particular market moves of a CEO sinful than it is to point an accusatory finger at an individual who claims an illegal tax deduction.

The legal distinction is significant. While no worker would say so, it seemed that sinful activity and illegal actions were often, though not always (e.g., abortion) the same. It is certainly horrible when thousands of workers lose their income, health care, and the kitchen sink, but if the cause of such dislocation was market-driven forces and not criminal corporate activity then it passes the "temptation test."[7] Where making more money at the expense of workers and pursuing rational profits for the stockholders diverged was unclear. Working-class Christians, Muslims, and Jews agreed that everyone was sinful; but except for the personal decisions we make that injure others, sin was an abstract concept better accepted than understood. Despite some religious education on the occasions for sin, working-class believers were more accepting of their own sinful natures than of the existence of evil in the world. Most thought evil was real, but few had an idea of how it was made manifest in the world. Perhaps evil would have been a more pressing concern if congregants had been more worried about an eschatological judgment day.

To the working-class Christian, Jews, and Muslims I spoke with, the heaven promised to believers after death probably exists. Yet, no one, particularly the Jewish believers, was obsessed about getting there and the focus of life did not revolve around some unclear "end-times." Workers universally agreed that they should be doing more to create a more God-like world than testifying to righteousness with an eye to eternal life. Few were active in any civic associations dedicated to social causes and only a handful had ever done more politically than to cast a vote. Not that eternal life was not desired, but that was, after all, in God's power. What was, however, in each individual's power was the means and opportunity to participate in and contribute to a kind of heaven on earth. The value of life was that it gave everyone the opportunity to experience a "taste of heaven." Unlike God's Kingdom in heaven, believers thought they knew the parameters of His or Her domain on earth. But if eternal life was possible, then the work we did would have something to say about our final judgment. Workers' belief that God cared about and measured our labors suggests an eschatological purpose for work. It also recalled the words of a poem on resurrection and work by the Sufi poet Rumi:

> On Resurrection Day God will say,
> What did you do with the strength and the energy
> that your food gave you on earth?
> How did you use your eyes?
> What did you make with your five senses
> while they were dimming and playing out?
> I gave you hands and feet as tools
> for preparing the ground for planting.
> Did you in the health I gave, do the plowing?[8]

The faithful saw beauty all around them and felt blessed by one opportunity after another to do God's will. Most expected a final reward to follow a life clothed in muscle and bone. But no one minimized the value and presence of God's Kingdom evolving on earth. Life was no mere practice session or testing ground for salvation. It may not be the only life we have, but it was a life given by God with no less significance or value than any promised. Walt Whitman, the quintessential nineteenth-century U.S. poet of the artisan working class, saw God similarly in the simple spaces occupied by others:

> Why should I wish to see God better than this day?
> I see something of God each hour of the twenty-four, and each
> moment then,
> In the faces of men and women I see God, and in my own face in the
> glass;
> I find letters from God dropped in the street, and every one is signed
> by God's name,
> And I leave them where they are, for I know that others will
> punctually come forever and ever.[9]

If today is truly the Lord's Day, then the working class were not living a lesser life in anticipation of life eternal. In fact, to live as if human beings had no work to do and no obligations to one another was to commit the greatest of all sins. Avoiding the opportunity to do good work on earth was a terrible rejection of the talents God gave everyone. Working-class believers worshiped for eternal life, but acted as if "earth's crammed with Heaven."[10]

Believers made very clear that they are on the earth for an earthly purpose. Surprisingly, everyone knew of a purpose that they all shared: to take care of one another. What many did not know was how they would personally contribute to serving the needs of others. Some people thought they had discovered their personal contribution. Those who did referred to it as a "calling." For those believers, work brought happiness and fulfillment. They noted how much of their life revolved around the day's labors and accepted Thomas Aquinas's warning that "there can be no joy in living without joy in work."[11] Everyone also accepted that God had plans for the world and everyone inhabiting it. The plan included everything that happened to us and all that we did. Unfortunately, how that plan made sense was beyond human comprehension. For every worker it came down to simple faith. God has a purpose for you and, more important, your life has a purpose for others.

No other message was more compelling about the role of faith in the mundane experiences of working-class believers than that a faithful life necessarily involved doing services for others. In referring to the message in Matthew's Gospel, Donald Spoto indicates that "the standard of judgment for all of us will be the extent to which we have found some personal means of alleviating human misery when we see it."[12] This was not, however, a commitment to saintly acts of charity or hours of selfless volunteerism, or political stands in the gap between God's vision and earthy disparities. By reflecting on the subtle dual interpretations of the command passage from the prophet Micah (6:8), we can articulate how the vast majority of believers served the stranger along the road. In answering what the Lord required of a person, the prophet began by asserting the need "to do justice." Now it was clear that all the workers attempted to refrain from committing unjust acts. Acting justly meant avoiding sinful behavior; according to St. Bruno parishioner Bernice Feltz, it came down to personal accountability: "Did you treat people fairly?" In other words, acting justly meant not being racist, mean, unkind, dishonest, greedy, selfish, intolerant, or uncaring. Believers recounted how they had been good Samaritans and often helped someone less fortunate than themselves. But with notable exceptions, few acted outwardly "to do justice" for others. Instead, Micah's affirmative-action call "*to do* justice" in the world was heard as a subjective identity claim "*to be* just." The former likely requires acting politically on behalf of the sojourner; the latter does not. The latter is a private commitment to God to behave; the former is a pledge to publicly assist the less fortunate. For most congregants, faith had primarily made them aware of their own obligation to be just (by avoiding doing what is bad), but not necessarily to do justice (by acting politically to eliminate the bad).

Still, acting according to God's commands transformed the merely temporal movements of daily life into something sacred. Being faithful to God simply meant making sure your daily actions, very often remunerated ones but including everything a person did, contributed to the well-being of others. The process of expanding physical, emotional, and intellectual labor in paid work not only helped others (no matter the job), but did for God what God wanted done by us. The Muslims, Jews, and Christians interviewed became partners with God because they eased a muscle pain, solved a billing problem, transported someone, painted a room, sawed a piece of wood, taught a class, or cut a piece of kosher meat. They were not certain what God intended for them or even how to stay on the righteous path, but they believed that the jobs they did were particularly important vehicles for fulfilling God's plan. In Matthew Fox's imagining of meaningful human activity, the work we do is an instrument of physical and spiritual agency that "becomes our true worship."[13] Life may happen because God wills it. No one thought otherwise. But life is maintained, nourished, and changed because God's only hands (i.e., you and me) work the earth. In the metaphorical words of Pastor Reginald McCracken, if "it's cold, we have a fireplace. Outside are plenty of trees and we have a saw, yet you're complaining we're cold. Get up! Take that saw (faith). Because you believe it will cut. And cut some wood [work]."[14]

According to the testimonies of workers, we are active doers in the Liturgy of God. Work is as sacred as the prayers we offer in silence and in public assembly with others. The separation between being holy, devout, and religious and acting in the secular world as creative human beings is an illusion. Godly work and good works are not distinct entities; it is impossible to act justly and not act as God, Jesus, or Muhammad preached. Workers of different faiths would embrace Dorothy Sayers's claim that "the only Christian work is good work well done . . . whether it is Church embroidery, or sewage-farming."[15] While conventional insistence that only God's grace can ultimately afford us salvation is not quarreled with, the way many believers spoke of their work as placing them in a co-creative relationship with the Almighty suggested that work is more salvific than church attendance, prayer, reading holy texts, and self-proclamations of faith.

Believing in God is, of course, paramount, but acting as a good Christian, Jew, or Muslim required more than right belief; it demanded acts that made the world more like heaven. "If you believe in God," according to Bernice Feltz, then "you cannot turn around and cheat on your wife." To the working-class faithful I talked with there was no long list of religious commands required to satiate an unforgiving lawgiver and judge. In fact, God was more a partner, parent, teacher, builder, healer, and doer than a cosmic ruler. Justice after death might ultimately get done, but most workers were more focused on how they were living in the "here and now." Few failed to see a heaven among God's creation. Day by day, believers asked God to help them to get by and live righteously. They sought guidance for a myriad of everyday occasions and drew spiritual satisfaction by pleasing their Creator one work hour at a time. A transcendent heaven may or may not exist, and it was up to God whether anyone got there. But workers were here now, on earth, with the hands, feet, heart, and intellect necessary to serve. Formal congregational worship rejuvenated a person's spiritual batteries and allowed believers an uninterrupted time of corporal rest to be only with God. Most also found inspiration and insight in the sermons and homilies of their religious leaders. Now and then a small number of parishioners and congregants read from a holy book and a few could cite a favorite verse. But no faith community member thought a steady diet of overt religious practices was sufficient to live in accordance with God's desire that we live in the service of others. On the other hand, the days between worship services were not to be treated dismissively. God's real work got done in the rise and shine of each workday.

When first approached about the intersection of work and faith, most working-class believers responded like disciples who should either evangelize their workmates or merely act toward them with humility and kindness. Faith seemed principally a guide for social interaction and a set of rules for ethical work performance. The idea that a well-painted room or an efficiently processed phone bill could be an expression of spiritual service was at first an odd notion. I was not surprised by the initial hesitation. Most workers had never heard a worship homily or sermon about their jobs (St. Denis Church being the major exception) or read a religious book about work and the Holy Spirit. No matter the faith tradition, Muslim, Jew, and Christian workers alike knew more about the importance of keeping the sacraments than they did the role of work in allowing people to cooperate with God in transforming the world. It was also true that most knew very little about the formal teachings of their faith. With rare exception, the working-class faithful did not profess a theoretical understanding of their faith. They knew rather skeletal or common things about Jesus, Muhammad, or Yahweh and loosely held scattered, undeveloped thoughts about their own religion's founding or precepts.

Most Christian, Jewish, and Muslim workers were simply obedient to God or at least to what they believed God commanded. In nearly all cases, when they discussed the real practical meaning of faith in their lives, it was nearly impossible to distinguish a person's faith affiliation. Putting formal doctrine aside (something most workers emphatically claimed no real understanding of), there was little significant *religious difference* in how working-class believers lived out their faith. People approached suffering, injustice, God's will, work, and salvation differently, but with few exceptions these differences were not primarily because of their religious membership. By all accounts, in the day-to-day practice of faith there is only one religion: belief in God. All else appears as just a lot of spiritual accessorizing with no significance (except for an Orthodox Jew) in the lives of working people. Ironically, I found working-class believers to be devout followers of the grand idea of a loving, all-powerful Creator and of little else that was religiously doctrinaire.

The claims made here about how working-class people use their faith to find meaning in their lives may of course not be much different from how middle- or upper-class believers put their faith to work. Without asking people of faith from different class identities about how faith informs their lives, it is not possible to claim something definitively unique about a working-class perspective. But even so, it is necessary to understand how working people live out their faith. I further contend that the difference faith makes to the lives of working-class people is even more important to comprehend than it is for middle- and upper-income class believers. Consider for a moment the overwhelming numbers of poor (i.e., once working, sometimes working, working off and on) and working-class congregational members who support rural, storefront, community corner and megachurches, mosques, and synagogues. By every standard of formal religious observance, it is the nation's lower-income groups which not only represent a numerical majority of worshipers, but they also tithe a higher proportion of their incomes than any other religious constituents. In a very real sense, the working class makes it possible for a vibrant and diverse congregational religious observance to flourish in America.

But it is not all about the congregational numbers or financial offerings. The work of numerous religious scholars has documented the heightened way that lower-income groups are drawn to intense religious appeals. In addition, while Christianity, Islam, and Judaism are open to all, they each make special offers to help and redeem the lowliest stationed of God's children. Religion may be a luxury for the wealthy, but it is often a lifeline for the needy. As many of my workers stated, it is those who have an excess of wealth and education who "think they don't need God." In fact, many of the workers recognized a tension between a life of luxury and a commitment to God. Wealth in itself was not a bad thing, but it was nearly always distracting. Christian, Muslim, and Jewish workers pointed out that if you possessed a vast store of riches, it was unlikely that you were being attentive to a spiritual life. Poor and working-class folks were seen as having a deeper commitment to God and a truer understanding of what the Creator required of people.

Jesus, after all, dressed in a simple cloth robe, and when commissioning disciples to spread the word of God throughout the land, he commanded them to "carry no purse, no bag, no sandals" (Luke 10:4). It was the actions of "radical missionaries" who preached to the "ordinary people a message both by what they said and how they lived."[16] The message was an unconditional rejection of society's dominant material values. There was no getting around it; being the "salt of the earth" was impossible when you owned the salt mine. However, possessing wealth did not automatically disqualify a person from entering the kingdom of heaven. The key for working-class believers was what an individual did with his or her material blessings. Riches hoarded or simply left to children carried no spiritual weight. But donations to charities, paying a fair day's wage, and a commitment to humanitarian causes opened up the needle's eye allegorized in the Christian Gospels.[17] Again, service to others was the behavior that marked you as deserving of God's grace.

It is certainly a broad overstatement about the appeal of faith to upper-income groups to suggest that faith and wealth cannot be reconciled. Even the most faithful of the working class is unlikely to have given away all of their worldly possessions. The truth is that Muhammad and Jesus set a standard that none of us are equipped to follow. But nonetheless, it is hard to deny that Christianity was forged among the enslaved, downtrodden, and lost. Islam and Judaism equally provide a worldview of ultimate liberation and salvation for generations of people victimized by oppressive rulers and invaders. Religious scholar Elaine Pagels's citation of the "Gospel of Truth" found at Nag Hammadi wonderfully boils down the message and teachings of the Bible, Torah, and Qur'an: "Speak the truth to those who seek it, and speak of understanding to those who have committed sin through error; Strengthen the feet of those who have stumbled; extend your hands to those who are sick; Feed those who are hungry; Give rest to those who are weary; And raise up those who wish to rise."[18] Despite the universal benefits of spiritual atonement or the shameful abuses of religious leadership, these religions were not found for the powerful and wealthy. While the workers I interviewed claimed no monopolistic ownership over their faith, they did see themselves, as people of modest means, as living closer to the image of their Creator than people who live as if they are gods.

Listening to the voices of working-class believers is also critically important for one final reason. Religion promises salvation, redemption, and eternal happiness. It suggests a vision of life that is beyond hate, suffering, inequality, and sadness. Under God everyone is equal. But in our secular society violence, despair, hurt, and inequality abound. In socioeconomic terms it is the poor and the working class that are exploited for the advantages of more powerful groups. The paradox of an American society flowing with milk and honey, yet saddled with shameful poverty and class exploitation, seriously challenges the relevancy of a "take care of others" faith. When approximately 1 percent of the population can own nearly 40 percent of the nation's net financial wealth, it is an open question just how godly a place America really is.[19]

Anyone who genuinely believes in an all-knowing, all-loving God cannot avoid asking profound questions of American life. How do you explain a modern wealthy society of God-fearing, God-loving people where 22 million other God-fearing, God-loving people live in poverty?[20] By what stretch of rationality can we explain the presence of God's houses of worship all over the American landscape while 3.5 million people are living on the street or in temporary housing?[21] Is it really possible to believe in the healing power of faith when 46 million American people have inadequate medical care?[22] Can the life-giving power of the Lord be respected by a nation that ranks first among the wealthiest countries in the world in infant mortality?[23] What can faith possibly offer by way of explanation for a near 400 percent income disparity between a company's average worker and a Fortune 500 chief executive officer?[24] If we are a nation that submits to a God of justice, then what justice is there when 25 percent of employers illegally fire at least one worker for union activity?[25] At a time when 98 percent of Americans say they believe in God, but 46 percent of those who are actually working state they are "dispirited," how can the religious views of working Americans be ignored?[26]

Yet in the face of abundant economic exploitation Bruce Springsteen can sing that "at the end of every hard-earned day" working-class people "find a reason to believe."[27] Faith, unfortunately, can be easily exploited. Perhaps no belief system lends itself more readily to the manipulative purposes of charlatans, dictators, presidents, corporate heads, foundation directors, media pundits, and would-be spiritual leaders than religion. Because of their economic vulnerability, working-class people are usually the targets of religious fraud. The woman who cleans the office space and the guy who repairs the train tracks believe in God no matter the reality of their socioeconomic situation. Neither low pay nor inadequate benefits shake their spiritual resolve. Redemption is still coming and God's grace is liberatory. Holding doggedly to a belief in a metaphysical entity with the power to return the world to paradise while you balance your life on an economic high wire is either an incredible act of faith or pure insanity. I'm no expert in these matters, but the people who spoke openly with me were decidedly not crazy. It was clear, however, that their faith above all else was strongly shaping the way they interpreted their station in life. Confronted with a force so ubiquitous and unyielding, it makes sense to ask working-class believers how they use their faith to find meaning in life. Does a person's religious identity compel them to upend the moneychangers' tables or capitulate to a society divided by class disparities? It is not enough to say that religion should arouse the consciousness of people to "do justice and love kindness" (Micah 6:8).

All religions declare that people should be treated as God's children. Very often these faiths come together to speak on behalf of exploited workers. In the late summer of 2006 a coalition of four hundred Chicago religious leaders spoke out in support of a hospitality union negotiating a new contract for thousands of hotel workers. The group, including Father Larry Dowling and Ahmed Rehab, the executive director of the Council on American Islamic Relations, signed a "Hospitality and Human Dignity Scroll." Rabbi Victor Mirelman, president of the Chicago Board of Rabbis, also signed the document and clearly stated what is true of every Abrahamic faith: "To exploit or oppress a worker because one has the power to do so is to offend God."[28] Yet what the religious texts pronounce and leaders pontificate about is not the best source of faith's impact on a person's life. To know the difference that faith actually makes in someone's life requires asking believers to talk about their spirituality between daily prayer sessions, and after Saturday temple or Sunday services.

In the final analysis, a comparison of how faith and secular life merge among different socioeconomic groups is very likely to reveal important class differences. Tex Sample has already admonished the Christian church for not responding to the economic and social realities that assault working people everyday. He writes that "blue-collar Americans are caught in a web of ideology and relative powerlessness," and insists that the Christian church needs to "take seriously the empowerment of working-class people and the poor."[29] Luminary Catholic priests from the "Right Reverend New Dealer" John A. Ryan to the beloved Jack Egan and Monsignor George Higgins of the Chicago archdiocese were also fiery partisans for the working class. Higgins was a familiar presence in union halls because he believed that by being there the "church signals its support for the legitimate aspirations of working people."[30]

Chicago's "labor priest" concretely integrated into his ministry the profound meaning of God's relationship to human work as expressed powerfully in the 1981 Encyclical Letter of Pope John Paul II, *Labor Exercens*. The Catholic pontiff annunciated that the Spirit, values, and freedom are not introduced into the world through humankind's pious relationship to a higher presence, but as Gregory Baum explains, the Holy Spirit "emerges from the exigencies of labor itself."[31] John Paul II reconfirmed the "fundamental truth that man, created in the image of God, shares by his work in the activity of the Creator and that, within the limits of his own human capabilities, man in a sense continues to develop that activity, and perfects it as he advances further and further in the discovery of the resources and values contained in the whole of creation."[32]

Religious support for labor and the people who do the world's creative work was also enumerated numerous times in the Old and New Testaments. An Internet Bible search of the word "work" returned over four hundred matching verses.[33] While not all of them address work in the sense of labor, most references, like "I will render to the man according to his works" (Proverbs 24:29) and "the Lord thy God may bless thee in all the works of thine hand which thou doest" (Deuteronomy 14:29), connote an unconditional moral obligation to act justly toward workers. The theological turn to work as a co-creative act with God was represented by the way many workers spoke of their employment. Work was part of the earth's stewardship and it unfolded in the "sacred space" that Verna Dozier pragmatically defined as "where mothers tend their children, teachers guide their students, police officers patrol the streets, doctors care for their patients, [and] laborers ply their trade."[34]

In support of a Christian gospel of work is the National Center for the Laity. The center was formed in 1978 to perpetuate the principles of the Second Vatican Council and to promote the importance of Christian ministries in daily life. The Center for the Laity's founding charter declared that the organization sought "to redirect the church's strategic approach to social action and to urban ministry; to refocus attention on the secular role of the laity." One of its primary endeavors is the publication of a national newsletter, *Initiatives*. The monthly publication features information and resources chronicling the numerous ways that everyday life calls up opportunities to defend and promote Christian principles by supporting the work that people perform. Newsletters published between 2003 and 2005 addressed "taking the initiative" in health care, the classroom, against global poverty, in business ethics, in meat processing, in the labor movement, assisting the unemployed, on wages, among farmworkers, for human rights, on pay disparity, on the global economy, and against materialism.[35] Consistently the National Center for the Laity has asked rank-and-file Christians and pastoral leaders to examine how their faith informed their vocation.

Jewish religious law (*Halachah*) and writings have also long acknowledged respect for the dignity of labor.[36] As Michael Perry, chairman of the Chicago Jewish Labor Committee details in *Labor Rights in the Jewish Tradition*, Jewish teaching has for centuries comprehensively recognized labor rights. From Exodus' "six days thou shalt do thy work" to Talmudic passages like "Love labor and hate mastery and seek no acquaintance with the ruling power," work in the Jewish faith has been highly valued.[37] Talmudic scholars have interpreted passages from the Torah and other documents to provide workers with numerous labor protections. Perry, who is also a staff member of the American Federation of State County and Municipal Employees Union, Council 31, points out that an "entire class of Talmudic labor law deals with conditions of work, establishing rights that in many instances foreshadow modern trade union practices."[38] As evidence of Perry's insights, Jewish community leaders and organized labor in Chicago have built a strong contemporary relationship through an annual Labor Seder.[39]

The Muslim community, and advocates for labor rights as well, share common goals of social justice, economic fairness, and decent treatment for workers. When the prophet Muhammad began teaching in Mecca, he challenged an abusive economic structure that permitted the rich to exploit the poor. The central place reserved in Islam for the unity of faith and good works was highlighted in 2001 as Muslim leaders met in Washington, DC at the "Islam and Labor: Forging Partnerships Conference."

The meeting was convened by the Muslim Public Affairs Council and the National Interfaith Committee for Worker Justice. Muslim imams from around the country pointed out that Islam recognizes the themes of worker justice, equality, the dignity of work, and employer responsibilities toward their employees. Imam Abdul Malik from Minnesota noted that the prophet Muhammad and his companions had ended slavery in Arabia, but that now a new "wage slavery" had emerged in the world. Just as Muhammad had worked 1,400 years ago to unravel an economic structure that held an underclass in bondage, Malik made clear that today's Islam equally holds that "no matter whether you are working in the corporate penthouse, or down in the basement sorting the mail, all people have rights. They're equal before the Lord."[40]

Bringing together the efforts of numerous community, religious, and labor organizations to promote a spiritual message of dignified work is the National Interfaith Committee for Worker Justice (NICWJ). Formed in 1991, NICWJ calls upon shared religious values to mobilize the faithful of all denominations to advocate on behalf of worker rights. It has pursued worker rights in many different forms. The organization has trained seminary students to "witness and engage in struggles for fairness" for workers. It has developed a "Labor in the Pulpit" program bringing people of all faiths into different houses of worship on Labor Day to "preach" a special message about the nexus of faith and work.[41] The Interfaith Committee has sponsored numerous forums on worker rights and social justice. NICWJ has also actively participated in worker campaigns around the country for fair treatment, decent pay, and the right to unionize. In every case the organization has boldly pronounced the inseparable connection between being a faithful servant of God and doing good works in the workplace.[42]

The cumulative effort of faith-based groups to rally believers of all denominations to a collective and individual respect for God's co-creative partnership with human beings is a time-honored moralistic championing of the poor and working class. It is a movement with deep roots in the American cultural tradition. Prophetic traditions (speaking out for what is right as the ancient religious prophets spoke out against the powerful) on behalf of the economically oppressed reach back in American history and parallel the country's nineteenth-century transition from a rural-farming to a twentieth-century urban–manufacturing society.[43] In the twenty-first century, world-shattering economic shifts underway since World War II have now provided faith–community–labor coalitions with a new "world order," where workers confront the destructive imperatives of "one market under God."[44] While the cultural wars waged over the last three decades by religious and secular conservatives against abortion, gay marriage, the theory of evolution, and the constitutional separation of church and state may have come to dominate the public debate over religious values and secular life, I believe that a quieter and more meaningful approach to God is practiced in working-class households.

It is an approach visible in the minutiae of coping with everyday life activities and in the challenges and temptations of human relationships. Working-class believers regularly march off to worship services, put money in the collection plate, and believe in a loving, all-powerful God. If you take the time to ask them, they will also tell you that they, more or less, have ideas about a great number of other religious subjects. But for the most part, their faith begins and ends with God. What happens in between, however, is where working-class faith is really practiced and defined. Faith is shaped by the need to catch the early bus to get to work. Faith is framed by the long hours invested in finishing up the office paperwork. Faith is a carpenter's perfect cut and the teacher's inspiring lesson plan. Faith is stretching a paycheck a little longer, while helping God to keep the building you work in a lot cleaner. Faith is holding a sick person's hand and writing a letter to a politician about bus safety. Faith is tolerating an abusive boss or walking off your job to demand better treatment. Faith is doing your job well. Faith is living with pain, going to work, and being thankful. Faith is ultimately what you do in the name of God. For working-class believers desirous of living a life faithful to God's covenant, "eventually all the theory, the ideals and the well-meaning words must give way to practice, action, the real world and people's concrete situations."[45]

The religion practiced by working-class Christians, Jews, and Muslims comes with all the institutional elements that necessitate a faithful following and provides for those who need to gather in common. For some members their church, mosque, and synagogue offer the only essential teachings about God's essence and will. It is enough to worship and do no harm. Other people of faith find the inspiration to be opponents of social injustice and human exploitation beyond the sacred grounds of formal worship. For them an affirmative collective act to bring justice to the world, including the workplace, is necessary. Some, of course, go regularly to church and fight for things like affordable housing, health care for all, and an end to racism. Despite the differences in how faith was lived, every worker claimed to deeply love God. What it meant to love God, however, included a wide spectrum of beliefs and behaviors. If faith was truly the embodiment of that enduring love, then *actually loving God* should have been practiced in what my late father-in-law called a person's do-gooding." Donald Spoto put it in the following exacting and socially conscious way:

> To care about the plight of the poor, the sick, the victims of war, poverty, epidemics and injustice; to cry out against those who would exploit the disenfranchised and abuse the powerless; to love our friends and those who have a claim on our compassion; to attend wholeheartedly, generously and passionately, in so far as we can, to the needs of others—this is what it means to love God.[46]

While few of the workers in this book lived out their faith in such socially dynamic forms, they did recognize a deepening relationship with God in the service they did for others. Meeting human need and acting for the benefit of others was an act of faith. Perhaps what most working people continue to find in the daily application of their faith was best articulated by Sherwin Epstein, the Jewish meat cutter: "just be good to other people." Amen, brother, amen.

NOTES

Introduction

1. John Russo and Sherry Linkon, *Steel-Town USA: Work and Memory in Youngstown* (Kansas: University Press of Kansas, 2002); Robert Bruno, *Steel Worker Alley: How Class Works in Youngstown* (Ithaca, NY: Cornell University Press, 1997); Terry F. Buss and Steven F. Stevens, *Shutdown at Youngstown: Public Policy for Mass Unemployment* (Albany: State University of New York Press 1983); Staughton Lynd, *The Fight against Shutdowns: Youngstown's Steel Mill Closing* (San Pedro, CA: Singlejack Books 1983).

2. See chapter 2, pp. 43–44 in Robert Bruno, *Steel Worker Alley: How Class Works in Youngstown* (Ithaca, NY: Cornell University Press, 1999).

3. Thomas Fuechtmann and Robin Lovin, *Steeples and Stacks: Religion and the Steel Crisis in Youngstown, Ohio* (Cambridge: Cambridge University Press, 1989).

4. In a Newsweek/BeliefNet Poll, Princeton Survey Research Associates found that 79 percent of Americans were either "spiritual" or "religious" (*Newsweek*, August 29/September 5, 2005, 48); An American Religious Identity Survey conducted in 2001 by the Graduate School of the City University of New York found that 86.8 percent of Americans were religious (www.gc.cuny.edu/studies/aris). According to the Pew Forum on Religion and Public Life, 87 percent of Americans claimed that religion was "very" or "fairly" important in their lives (www.people-press.org/reports).

5. The phrase was from Cale Aardsma, the pastor at Park Lane Reform Christian Church, in Evergreen Park, Illinois.

6. Lori and her husband, Greg, are members of USW Local 1999 in Indianapolis, Indiana.

7. Jeremiah 29:11, 13; all subsequent biblical quotations will be taken from the Revised Standard Version.

8. In his book *Blue Collar Ministry: Facing Economic and Social Realities of Working People* (Valley Forge, PA: Judson Press, 1984), Saint Paul School of Theology Emeritus Professor Tex Sample notes that there are no unambiguously working-class or lower-class denominations. However, citing research from the 1960s and 1980s, Sample records that the highest percentages of working-class congregants regularly attending church (roughly 20 to 30 percent) can be found in Lutheran, Baptist, Methodist, and Roman Catholic denominations. See also: Liston Pope, "Religion and the Class Structure," *Annals of the American Academy of Political and Social Sciences* 256 (March 1948): 84–91; Stan Gaede, "Religious Participation, Socioeconomic Status, and Belief-Orthodoxy," *Journal for the Scientific Study of Religion* 16, no. 3 (September 1977): 245–53; Erich Goode, "Class Styles of Religious Sociation," *British Journal of Sociology* 19, no. 1 (March 1998): 1–16 and "Social Class and Church Participation," *American Journal of Sociology* 72, no. 1 (July 1966): 102–11.

9. H. Richard Niebuhr, *The Social Sources of Denominations* (New York: New Meridian Books, 1957), 26.

10. Wade Clark Roof and William McKinney, *American Mainline Religion: Its Changing Shape and Future* (New Brunswick, NJ: Rutgers University Press, 1987).

11. Christian Smith and Robert Faris, "Socioeconomic Inequality in the American Religious System: An Update and Assessment," *Journal for the Scientific Study of Religion* 44, no. 1 (2005): 95.

12. Erich Goode, "Class Styles of Religious Sociation," *British Journal of Sociology*. 19, no. 1 (March 1998): 5.

13. Ibid., 1.

14. H. Richard Niebuhr, *The Social Sources of Denominations* (New York: New Meridian Books, 1957), 6–7.

15. Quotes are taken from Robert Wuthnow, online interview with Public Broadcasting Service's *Religion and Ethics Newsweekly*, Episode no. 534 (April 26, 2002).

16. Mark Chaves, *Congregations in America* (Cambridge, MA: Harvard University Press, 2004), and Michael Hout and Claude Fischer, "Religious Diversity in America, 1940–2000," paper presented at the American Sociological Association Annual Meeting, Chicago, August 2001.

17. A major publication of the program is Lowell Livezey, editor, *Public Religion and Urban Transformation: Faith in the City* (New York: New York University Press, 2000).

18. Data taken from the 2000 American Religion Data Archive, funded by the Lily Endowment and housed at Pennsylvania State University (www.thearda.com).

19. A brief list of Chicago community works and faith-based institutions would include the following: Albert Hunter, *Symbolic Communities: The Persistence and Change of Chicago's Local Communities* (Chicago: University of Chicago Press, 1974); James R. Barnett, *Work and Community in the Jungle: Chicago's Packinghouse Workers, 1894–1922* (Champaign: University of Illinois Press, 1987); Carolyn Eastwood, *Near West Side Stories: Struggles for Community in Chicago's Maxwell Street Neighborhood* (Forest Park: Lake Claremont Press, 2002); Hartmut Keil and John Jentz, eds., *German Workers in Chicago: A Documentary History of Working-Class Culture from 1850 to WWI* (Champaign: University of Illinois Press, 1988); Dominic Candeloro, *Chicago's Italians: Immigrants, Ethnics, Americans* (Chicago: Arcadia Publishing, 2003); James B. Lagrand, *Indian Metropolis: Native Americans in Chicago, 1945–75* (Champaign: University of Illinois Press, 2002); John Gerard McLaughlin, *Irish Chicago* (Chicago:

Arcadia Publishing, 2003); Eileen M. McMahon, *What Parish Are You From? A Chicago Irish Community and Race Relations* (Lexington: University Press of Kentucky, 1995); Dominic A. Pacyga, *Polish Immigrants and Industrial Chicago: Workers on the South Side, 1880–1922* (Chicago: University of Chicago Press, 2003); Melvin G. Holi and Peter D. Jones, *Ethnic Chicago: A Multicultural Portrait* (Grand Rapids, MI: Wm. B. Eerdmans Publishing, 1995); Mary Pattillo-McCoy, *Black Picket Fences: Privilege and Peril among the Black Middle Class* (Chicago: University of Chicago Press, 2000); Louise Carroll Wade, *Chicago's Pride: The Stockyards, Packingtown, and Environs in the Nineteenth Century* (Champaign: University of Illinois Press, 2003); Rita Arias Jirasek and Carlos Tortolero, *Mexican Chicago. IL* (Chicago: Arcadia, 2002); Joseph C. Bigott, *From Cottage to Bungalow: Houses and the Working Class in Metropolitan Chicago, 1869–1929* (Chicago: University of Chicago Press, 2001); Frances Kostarelos, *Feeling the Spirit: Faith and Hope in an Evangelical Black Storefront Church* (University of South Carolina Press, 1995); Irving Cutler, *The Jews of Chicago: From Shtetl to Suburb* (Champaign: University of Illinois Press, 1996).

20. Liston Pope, *Millhands and Preachers* (New Haven, CT: Yale University Press, 1942).

21. A few of the most recognizable religious studies and sources of congregant beliefs include the following: American Religion Data Archive at Pennsylvania State University (www.thearda.com); 2005 Survey Report, The Pew Forum on Religion and Public Life, the Pew Research Center for the People and the Press (www.people-press.org/reports); 2004 National Opinion Research Center's General Social Survey, University of Chicago; 2004 National Surveys of Religion and Politics, the Bliss Institute of Applied Politics at the University of Akron; 2001 American Religious Identity Survey (ARIS) conducted at the Graduate School of the City University of New York (www.gc.cuny.edu); 2001 Barna Poll on U.S. Religious Belief (www.adherents.com/BarnaPoll).

22. Egon Mayer, Barry A. Kosmin, and Ariela Keysar, *The American Jewish Identity Survey: An Exploration in the Demography and Outlook of a People* (The Center of Cultural Judaism, Graduate Center of the City University of New York, 2001). Available online at http://www.Jewishvirtuallibrary.org

23. Kambiz Ghanea Bassiri, *Competing Visions of Islam in the United States: A Study of Los Angeles* (New York: Greenwood Press, 1997); Charles Kurzman, *Liberal Islam: A Sourcebook* (Oxford: Oxford University Press, 1998); Omid Safi, ed., *Progressive Muslims: On Justice, Gender, and Pluralism* (One World Publications LTD., 2003); Charles Le Gai Eaton, *Islam and the Destiny of Man* (Stony Brook: State University of New York Press, 1986); Seyyed Hossein Nasr, *Ideals and Realities of Islam* (Chicago: Kazi Publications, 2000).

24. Gustavo Gutierrez, *A Theology of Liberation: History, Politics and Salvation* (Maryknoll, NY: Orbis Books, 1988); Phillip Berryman, *Liberation Theology: Essential Facts about the Revolutionary Religious Movement in Latin America and Beyond* (Philadelphia: Temple University Press, 1988); Jon Sobrino, *Christology at the Crossroads: A Latin American Approach* (Maryknoll, NY: Orbis Books, 1978).

25. Mark and Louise Zwick, *The Catholic Worker Movement: The Intellectual and Spiritual Origins* (New York: Paulist Press, 2006); National Conference of Catholic Bishops, *Economic Justice for All: Pastoral Letter on Catholic Social Teaching and the U.S. Economy* (Washington, DC: United States Catholic Conference, 1989); John Coleman, ed., *One Hundred Years of Catholic Social Thought* (Maryknoll, NY: Orbis

Books, 1991); Gregory Baum, *The Priority of Labor: A Commentary on* Laborem Exercens (New York: Paulist Press, 1982); David Byers, *Justice in the Marketplace: Collected Statements of the Vatican and the United States Catholic Bishops on Economic Policy, 1891–1984* (AAA, 1985); Ronald C. White and C. Howard Hopkins, *The Social Gospel: Religion and Reform in Changing America* (Philadelphia: Temple University Press, 1976); Christopher H. Evans, *The Kingdom Is Always But Coming: A Life of Walter Rauschenbusch* (Grand Rapids, MI: Wm. B. Erdmans Publishing, 2004); Steven Fraser, *Labor Will Rule: Sidney Hillman and the Rise of American Labor* (Ithaca, NY: Cornell University Press, 1993); Marc Dollinger, *Quest for Inclusion: Jews and Liberalism in Modern America* (Princeton, NJ: Princeton University Press, 2000).

26. One major exception to the nonworking-class Jewish congregation was the Orthodox North Shore congregation, Agudas Achim. The Rabbi Philip Leftkowitz was very gracious in explaining to me that his members were all elderly nonworking immigrant Russian Jews who spoke no English and were actually surviving on very meager incomes.

27. By comparison Jewish household income in 1996 was $51, 871, Catholic was $35,788, Missouri/Wisconsin Lutheran $37,686, and United Methodist $33,893. See Christian Smith and Robert Faris, "Socioeconomic Inequality in the American Religious System: An Update and Assessment," *Journal for the Scientific Study of Religion* 44, no. 1 (2005): 95–104.

28. According to the *National Jewish Population Survey* and *The American Jewish Identity Survey*, American Jews are asked to self-identify as "secular," "somewhat secular," "somewhat religious," or "religious." The surveys revealed that secular Jews are less likely to be congregational members than religious Jews. In addition, Reform Jews are more likely to have a secular orientation to the world, while Orthodox Jews express a much more religious perspective (2001).

29. Armand Larive, *After Sunday: A Theology of Work* (New York: Continuum Press, 2004).

30. Tex Sample, *Blue Collar Ministry: Facing Economic and Social Realities of Working People* (Valley Forge, PA: Judson Press 1984).

31. Larive, *After Sunday*, ix.

32. Ibid., 1.

33. Ibid., 2.

34. The quote comes from Laurie Beth Jones's *Jesus CEO: Using Ancient Wisdom for Visionary Leadership* (New York: Hyperion 1995). Just a few very other eclectic representative examples from the business-oriented "faith and work" movement are Os Hillman's *The 9 to 5 Window* (Ventura, CA: Regal Books, 2005) and Hillman's International Coalition of Workplace Ministries and Web site, *Marketplace Leaders: Helping You Fulfill God's Calling* (www.icwm.net); The Faith and Work Project (faithandwork@improvement.co.uk); "God and Business," *Fortune Magazine*, July 16, 2001; "Spirituality in the Workplace," *Business Week*, November 1999; Russell Shorto, "Faith at Work," *New York Times Magazine*, October 31, 2004; "God in the Workplace," *Business Reform Magazine*, January/March 2003; *The Professional Association for People Involved with Spirituality in the Workplace* (www.spiritatwork); and Billy Graham's cohosting of the His Presence in the Workplace Conference in Asheville, North Carolina in 2003. Additionally, according to Pat Hammond of Intervarsity Press there were seventy-nine books published on faith and work in 2000 alone.

35. Reference is to Os Hillman's International Coalition of Workplace Miniseries and Web site.

36. For a definition of religious employment discrimination see D. Douglas Shureen, "What Is 'Religion' for Purposes of Employment Discrimination Cases?" *Employees Relations Law Journal* 29, no. 4 (Spring 2004): 34–43.

37. Helen Irvin, "Proselytizing in the Workplace Carries Risk of Religious Harassment Disputes," *Daily Labor Report*, Bureau of National Affairs, Washington, DC, 151 (August 6, 2004): C1–C4.

38. Ibid., C1.

39. Ibid., C4. The bill in 2003 was titled the Workplace Religious Freedom Act.

40. Douglas Sherman and William Hendricks, *Your Work Matters to God* (Colorado Springs, CO: Navspress, 1987).

41. The second quote is from 1 Timothy 5:19 in *The New Oxford Annotated Bible, Revised Standard Version* (New York: Oxford University Press, 1973).

42. Quoted from page 425 of Robert Wuthnow, "Overcoming Status Distinctions? Religious Involvement, Social Class, Race, and Ethnicity in Friendship Patterns," *Sociology of Religion* 64, no. 4 (Winter 2003): 423–42.

43. Sherman and Hendricks, *Your Work Matters to God.*

44. Alan Wolfe, *Transformation of American Religion: How We Actually Live Our Faith* (Chicago: University of Chicago Press, 2003).

45. Larive, *After Sunday*, 3.

46. Joanne Ciulla, *The Working Life: The Promise and Betrayal of Modern Work* (New York: Three Rivers Press, 2000).

47. Ibid., xii.

48. Gregory Augustine Pierce is a founding member of the Business Executives for Economic Justice and author of *Spirituality@ Work: 10 Ways to Balance Your Life on-the-Job* (Skokie, IL: ACTA Publications, 2003). The quote is taken from a letter to the editor published in the *New York Times Magazine* and reprinted on his Web site, Spirituality @ Work Dialogue (gpierce@actpublkications.com).

49. Studs Terkel, *Working* (New York: Avon Books, 1972).

50. C. S. Lewis, *The Problem of Pain* (New York: HarperCollins Books, 2001), 116.

51. *Income, Poverty, and Health Insurance Coverage in the United States: 2004*, United States Census Bureau, Department of Labor, Washington, DC and Kaiser Family Foundation and Health Research and Educational Trust, Employer Health Benefits 2004 Survey (www.kff.org/insurance).

52. A bankruptcy court awarded United Airline executives $45 million in stock as part of a post-bankruptcy reorganization plan. United's workers, however, were forced to accept over $4 billion in pay and benefit cuts. For an overview of the airline industry and United Airline story, see Beth Almeida, "Weathering the Perfect Storm: Defined Benefit Pensions Plans in the Airline Industry," *Labor and Employment Relations Association Series, Proceedings of the 57th Annual Meeting, 2005*. For a history of the steel industry collapse, see Robert Bruno, "USWA-Bargained and State-Oriented Responses to the Recurrent Steel Crisis," *Labor Studies Journal* 30, no. 1 (Spring 2005): 67–91. An overview assessing the economic rationale for these corporate evasions can be found in Roger Lowenstein's "The End of Pensions," *New York Times*, October 30, 2005; Bernard Condon, "The Coming Pension Crisis," *Forbes Magazine*, August 12, 2004; and Douglas V. Orr, "Strategic Bankruptcy and Private Pension Default," *Journal of Economic Issues* 32 (1998): 669–88.

53. A review of each of these accounting and corporate scandals with a special emphasis on the Enron Corporation can be found in David Teather's "Four Years On,

Enron Men Face Their Day of Reckoning," *The Guardian*, January 26, 2006. Also the Ralph Nader-founded Citizen Works provided a criminal police-like blotter of corporate malfeasance and illegality at www.citizenworks.org.

54. Robert Wurthnow, *God and Mammon in America* (New York: Free Press, 1994).

55. Aristotle, *Politics*, trans. H. Rackham (Cambridge, MA: Harvard University Press, 1977).

56. Ciulla, *The Working Life*, 49.

57. James Bernard Murphy, *The Moral Economy of Labor: Aristotelian Themes in Economic Theory* (New Haven, CT: Yale University Press, 1993), and Al Genie, *My Job, My Self: Work and the Creation of the Modern Individual* (London: Routledge Press, 2000).

58. Martin Luther, "The Method and Fruits of Justification," in *The World's Great Sermons, Volume I*, comp. Grenville Kleiser (New York: Funk and Wagnalls Company, 1909), 113–43.

59. Dorothy Sayers, "Why Work?" in *Leading Lives That Matter: What We Should Do and Who We Should Be*, ed. Mark R. Schwehn and Dorothy C. Bass (Grand Rapids, MI: Eerdmans Publishing Company, 2006), 195.

60. Miroslav Volf, *Work in the Spirit: Toward a Theology of Work* (Portland, OR: Wipf and Stock Publishers, 2001), 126.

Chapter 1

1. C. S. Lewis, *The Problem of Pain* (New York: HarperCollins Books, 1996).

2. C. S. Lewis, *A Grief Observed* (New York: Bantam, 1961).

3. My mother accepted her culpability. In her journal entry for December 18, 2002, she wrote, "Can't blame this on anyone. Just me. Started smoking when it was the thing to do. Stupid!!"

4. Quote is from C. S. Lewis, *Surprised by Joy* (New York: Harcourt, Brace Jovanovich, 1955), 20–21. The "thing" refers to his prayers for his dying mother.

5. Lewis, *The Problem of Pain*, 25.

6. Bart D. Ehrman, *God's Problem: How the Bible Fails to Answer Our Most Important Question—Why We Suffer* (New York: Harper One, 2008), 3. Subsequent references to this volume will be by page number within the text.

7. Mike Mason, *The Gospel According to Job: An Honest Look at Pain and Doubt from the Life of One Who Lost Everything* (Wheaton, IL: Crossway Books, 2002), xi.

8. Quoted in Abraham Cohen, *Everyman's Talmud: The Major Teachings of the Rabbinic Sages* (New York: Schocken Books, 1995), 18.

9. Katie was one of the founding members of the Coalition for Labor Union Women (CLUW) formed in 1974. CLUW was organized by women in labor unions to address the critical needs of unorganized women and to make unions more responsive to the needs of all women. CLUW's founding conference took place in Chicago and Katie was the city chapter's first director.

10. Father Robert Miller, "In Memoriam, Rev. Paul Bernard Smith," at www.holyangels.com.

11. In 2005 the black population equaled 85.5 percent of the area (United States Census Bureau, United States Department of Commerce, Washington, DC).

12. For data on unemployment insurance, see the many reports compiled by the Center on Budget and Policy Priorities at www.cbpp.org.

13. Information about Family in Faith's history was taken from the *History of Family in Faith, January 1993–August 2006* (document provided to me from church administrative assistant, Karen Schultz).

14. Volf, *Work in the Spirit*, 114.

15. Wallace Best has written that the "dual themes of captivity and deliverance, or captivities and deliverances, have comprised . . . the most intimate and enduring aspects of black life." See *Passionately Human, No Less Divine* (Princeton, NJ: Princeton University Press, 2005).

16. Quote taken from the church sermon on September 19, 2004.

17. Red Aurebach and John Feinstein, *Let Me Tell You a Story: A Lifetime in the Game* (New York: Little Brown & Co., 2004). Feinstein also told the story in an October 30, 2006 interview on National Public Radio.

18. Lawrence Mishel, Jared Bernstein, and Sylvia Allegretto, *The State of Working America 2004/2005* (Ithaca, NY: Cornell University Press, 2005), 101–2.

19. In this case, both jobs are held by Gerry. But from 1979 to 2000 low- and moderate-income wives increased their working hours by between 60 percent and 70 percent (see Mishel et al., *The State of Working America 2004/2005*, 102).

20. The value of the minimum wage has fallen 22.9 percent since 1967 (see Mishel et al., *The State of Working America 2004/2005*, 198). Rapidly falling unionization rates (24 percent in 1973 to 12.5 percent in 2003), and the economic loss to workers in terms of wages and benefits are detailed in *The State of Working America*, 189–197.

21. A. J. Arberry, trans., *The Koran Interpreted* (New York: Touchstone 1955), vol. II, "Jonah," chapter 105, 237.

Chapter 2

1. Stephen Prothero, *American Jesus: How the Son of God Became a National Icon* (New York: Farrar, Straus and Giroux, 2003), 10.

2. Marcus J. Borg, *Meeting Jesus Again for the First Time* (San Francisco: HarperCollins, 1995), 14.

3. Michael Zweig does a nice job breaking down the working population by class in his book *Working Class Majority: Americas Best Kept Secret* (Ithaca, NY: ILR Press, 2001).

4. Walt Whitman, "Song of Myself," verse 1274, in *Leaves of Grass, The First (1855) Edition*, ed. Malcolm Crowley (New York: Penguin Classics, 1986), 83.

5. While Denise's observation about construction work crews is anecdotal, it is not without historic credibility. The construction industry in the Chicago-metro area has an ugly history of racial and gender discrimination. In most cases it was either a lawsuit or the threat of one that finally opened unionized apprenticeship trade programs to people of color and women.

6. Part I, "Thunder," Sura 13:10, in *The Koran Interpreted*, trans. A. J. Arberry (New York: TouchstoneBooks, 1955), 268.

7. Not working during the time that the employee is being paid to work.

8. Quote is taken from David S. Ariel, *What Do Jews Believe? The Spiritual Foundations of Judaism* (New York: Schocken Books, 1995), 97.

9. Quotes taken from Abraham Cohen, *Everyman's Talmud: The Major Teachings of the Rabbinic Sages* (New York: Schocken Books, 1975), 93–94.

10. Barry Blaustein belonged to Local 1546 of the United Food and Commercial Workers.

11. Ariel, *What Do Jews Believe?* 173–74.

12. In *What Do Jews Believe?* David S. Ariel defines *mitzvot* "as laws based on God's commandments and the practices developed by our sages specifically in order to implement God's will." *Mitzvots* "characterize the Jewish way of life in which actions and behavior are prescribed" (159).

13. According to *Women in the Labor Force: A Databank* (Washington, DC: U.S. Bureau of Labor Statistics, U.S. Department of Labor), the occupational fields with the highest female participation was "education and health services."

14. "The Diversity Project: Stories and Practical Learnings about the Origins of Multicultural Urban Churches," at www.newlifetimeministries-nlm.org.

15. Ibid.

16. The *Story of Community Mennonite, Markham, Illinois,* transcribed by Pastor Chuck Neufeld, October 5, 2001 from a document created in the 1980s.

17. Mennonite Church USA—Online Directory, Congregational Information, Community Mennonite Church, at www.directory.mennoniteusa.org/congregation.

18. This compares to the nearly 20 percent of Mennonites in the United States who are African American, Hispanic, or Asian (*Who Are the Mennonites?–Third Way Café*–Mennonite Media, at www.thirdway.com/mennonite).

19. The complete passage is "for I was hungry and you gave me food, I was thirsty and you gave me drink, I was a stranger and you welcomed me. I was naked and you clothed me, I was sick and you visited me, I was in prison and you came to me. . . . Truly, I say to you as you did it to one of the least of these my brethren, you did it to me" (Matthew 25:40).

20. Jesus' social class is described by John Dominic Crossan in *Jesus: A Revolutionary Biography* (New York: HarperCollins, 1995), 23–28.

21. Golgotha or Calvary is the name given to the hill on which Jesus was crucified. The hill is described as being outside Jerusalem, but its location is not certain. Calvary is mentioned in all four accounts of Jesus' crucifixion in the Christian canonical Gospels.

22. Borg, *Meeting Jesus Again,* 75.

23. Shamus Toomey, "Our Lady of Guadalupe Home to Nation's First St. Jude Shrine," *Chicago Sun-Times,* May 5, 2006, A11.

24. One of those charter members was Wayne Huizenga who went on to own Waste Management Inc., Blockbuster Video, the Florida Marlins major league baseball team, and the Miami Dolphins national football league team. *God's Enduring Faithfulness, Fifty Years, A History of the Park Lane Christian Reform Church, 1953–2003,* ed. Don Sinnema (Park Lane Fiftieth Anniversary Committee, 2003), 75.

25. Ibid., 9.

26. Ibid., 15.

27. Isaiah 65: 21–25.

Chapter 3

1. Jack Miles, *God, A Biography* (New York: Vantage Books, 1995), 123.

2. The trilogy of God's is borrowed from Karen Armstrong's *Muhammad: A Biography of the Prophet* (New York: HarperCollins, 1993), 98.

3. Stephen Hart, *What Does the Lord Require? How American Christians Think about Social Justice* (New Brunswick, NJ: Rutgers University Press 1996).

4. Mark Chaves, *Congregations in America* (Cambridge, MA: Harvard University Press, 2004), 95.

5. Ibid., 95.

6. Rory McVeigh and David Sikkink, "God, Politics, and Protest: Religious Beliefs and the Legitimation of Contentious Tactics," *Social Forces* 79, no. 4 (June 2001): 1425–58.

7. Evan Curry, Jerome R. Kochm, and Paul Chalfant, "Concern for God and Concern for Society: Religiosity and Social Justice," *Sociological Spectrum* 24 (2004): 663.

8. For a compelling analysis of Call to Renewal, see David S. Gutterman's *Prophetic Politics: Christian Social Movements and American Democracy* (Ithaca, NY: Cornell University Press, 2005). Quote from Jim Wallis, *Faith Works: Lessons from the Life of an Activist Preacher* (New York: Random House 2000), xxvii.

9. Jim Wallis, *The Soul of Politics: Beyond "Religious Right" and "Secular Left"* (New York: Harcourt, Brace 1995), 230.

10. William Glantz, "Labor Objects to 'Super Pensions,'" *Washington Times*, April 7, 2006. Available online at: www.vuchannel.net/other-archive/news/Section-8-business-and-finance

11. The Institute for Policy Studies and United for a Fair Economy, Executive Excess 2007: The Staggering Social Cost of U.S. Business Leadership, 14th Annual CEO Compensation Survey. Available online at www.ips-dc.org

12. Glantz, "Labor Objects to 'Super Pensions."

13. Arthur Kennickell, Currents and Undercurrents: Changes in the Distribution of Wealth, 1989–2004, Federal Reserve Board, Washington, DC, 20551, January 30, 2006. Available from Federal Reserve Board.

14. According to the Labor Department's Bureau of Labor Statistics, the "working poor" made up 5.6 percent of the labor force, an increase from 4.7 in 2000. "Working Poor" Number 7.8 Million, *Union Labor Report*, Bureau of National Affairs, Washington, DC, 60, no. 12 (June 16, 2006): 91.

15. Rick Wolf, "The Fallout from Falling Wages," mrzine/MonthlyReview.org/ June 12, 2006.

16. The staff of the university program published its research on St. Bruno and other select Chicago-area religious institutions as *Public Religion Faith in the City and Urban Transformation*, ed. Lowell W. Livezey (New York: New York University Press, 2000). St. Bruno was included in Elfriede Wedam's contribution on Southwest Side churches, "God Doesn't Ask What Language I Pray In," in *Public Religion Faith in the City*, 107–32.

17. Wedam, "God Doesn't Ask What Language I Pray In," 112.

18. Donald Spoto, *In Silence, Why We Pray* (New York: Penguin Group 2004), 71.

19. David S. Gutterman, *Prophetic Politics: Christian Social Movements and American Democracy* (Ithaca, NY: Cornell University Press 2005), 133.

20. Jim Wallis is quoted in Gutterman, *Prophetic Politics*, 139.

21. Since doing the research for this book, Father Dowling was transferred to St. Agatha Parish in Chicago. St. Agatha was the site of yet another case of pastoral sexual misconduct and the archbishop of Chicago removed the incumbent pastor. Father Dowling was installed as the parish's new spiritual leader.

22. Margaret Ramirez, "As Activist Rally, Priests Show Support by Fasting," *Chicago Tribune*, April 11, 2006.

23. A provision in the airline's reorganization plan granted an estimated $15 million in equity to Tilton (see Reuters News Service, "United Airlines Emerges from Bankruptcy," February 1, 2006).

24. McCracken is a longstanding, accomplished, and respected union member and steward of the International Brotherhood of Teamsters, Chicago Local 743.

25. Immaculate Conception Parish Diamond Jubilee Commemorative, 1882–1957 available at the Archdiocese of Chicago's Joseph Cardinal Bernardin Archives and Records Center, Chicago, Illinois, 8–21.

26. Ibid., 21–26.

27. The church's commitment to class equality was further enforced after Pope Pius XI published the pro-labor papal encyclical *Quadragesimo Anno*. In 1931 a "triduum of supplication" was held at the parish to bring attention to the plight of workers and to improving labor conditions. See *Immaculate Conception Parish Diamond Jubilee Commemorative, 1882–1957*, 83.

28. Ibid., 433–34.

29. Froma Harrop, "Why the Minimum Wage Wins," www.TomPaine.com, April 13, 2006.

30. Karen Armstrong, *Muhammad: A Biography of the Prophet* (New York: HarperCollins, 1993), 91.

31. "The Forenoon," Sura 93: 6–8, in *The Koran Interpreted*, 342, trans. A. J. Arberry (New York: Touchstone Books, 1955).

32. Karen Armstrong, *Muhammad: A Biography of the Prophet* (New York: HarperCollins, 1993), 229.

33. Ibid., 92.

34. "Distinguished," Sura 51: 5, Arberry, trans., 185.

35. Ibid.

36. Quotes taken from Abraham Cohen's *Everyman's Talmud: The Major Teachings of the Rabbinic Sages* (New York: Schocken Books, 1975), 196–97.

37. David S. Ariel, *What Do Jews Believe? The Spiritual Foundations of Judaism* (New York: Schocken Books, 1995), 62.

38. Cohen, *Everyman's Talmud*, 101.

39. For the "ten words" that express a person's duties toward God and his/her neighbor, see Exodus 20:1–17.

40. Jane Sasseen and David Polek, "White-Collar Crime: Who Does Time?" *Business Week online*, www.businessweek.com, Special Report, February 6, 2006.

41. Ford Motors took advantage of a loophole in the 2004 American Jobs Creation Act which allowed them to reduce their tax on profits repatriated from overseas from the normal 35 percent to 5.25 percent. The law never required the company to create a single job. The statistic was reported in *Newsweek*, February 6, 2006, 14.

42. The story of "Daniel in the Lions' Den" is covered in Daniel 6:6–24.

43. Darren Cushman Wood, *Blue Collar Jesus: How Christianity Supports Workers' Rights* (Santa Ana, CA: Seven Locks Press, 2004), 29.

44. Unfortunately, Katie's activism is still needed. According to a 1999 study of working conditions in Chicago by the Midwest Center in Labor and Community Research, 34.4 percent of all workers were employed in jobs that met the Department of Labor definition of a sweatshop (see Midwest Center in Study at 222.clcr.org).

45. Stephen Franklin, "Two Lines in Caterpillar Strike: Frustration, Hope," *Chicago Tribune*, June 23, 1994, Business Page 1.

46. Reverend Miller has since left the church and taken a sabbatical at Notre Dame University.

47. Genesis data taken from Genesis Housing Development Corporation, 2004 Annual Report.

48. Homelessness data was taken from the Urban Institute, *1996 National Survey of Homeless Assistance Providers and Clients*, accessed October 23, 2006, at http://www.urban.org/publications/410496.html. Poverty data were taken from Amy Glasmeirer's *An Atlas of Poverty in America: One Nation, Pulling Apart 1960–2003* (New York: Routledge Press, 2005). Unemployment figures come from the "The Employment Situation: September 2005," Bureau of Labor Statistics, United States Department of Labor.

49. The story of Jesus feeding the five thousand was taken from Mark 6:30–44.

50. Quote taken from a church flyer celebrating Black History Month titled "Moving Forth with Pride," February 29, 2004.

51. Wood, *Blue Collar Jesus*, 152.

52. William Mirola, "Fighting in the Pews and Fighting in the Streets: Protestantism, Consciousness and the Eight-Hour Movement in Chicago, 1867–1912" (Ph.D. diss., Indiana University, 1995), quoted in Wood, *Blue Collar Jesus*, 158.

53. Kim Vargas, "Put Seatbelts on Buses to Save Lives," Letter to the Editor, *Press Publications/Northwest DuPage*, July 5, 2001.

54. Letter from Ann Marie Ferrini, Consumer Affairs Representative, Hasbro Toys, to Mrs. Kim R. Vargas, March 20, 2004.

Chapter 4

1. Mark Chaves uses the term "repertoire" to describe specific ways that congregations behave at worship services. I think, however, the term is flexible enough so that it can be easily used to speak about broader forms of religious practice. *Congregations in America* (Cambridge, MA: Harvard University Press, 2004).

2. K. L. Ladd and B. Spilka found intercessory prayers to be a prominent form of prayer. See "Inward, Outward, and Upward: Cognitive Aspects of Prayer," *Journal for the Scientific Study of Religion* 41 (2002): 475–84.

3. The title is "Prayer before Work" and is not authored.

4. Leonard Fleming, "Muslim Cabbies Get Tickets While Praying," *Chicago Sun Times*, September 16, 2007, Metro 3A.

5. The Council of Islamic Organizations of Greater Chicago, at www.ciogc.org.

6. Ibid.

7. "City Worker Charged in Cab Driver's Death," CBS2 News Report, February 7, 2005, at cbs2chicago.com and "Update on Haroon Paryani Case," The Council of Islamic Organizations of Greater Chicago, at www.ciogc.org.

8. "Update on Haroon Paryani Case," The Council of Islamic Organizations of Greater Chicago, at www.ciogc.org.

9. Jewish synagogues hold ownership services on Friday evenings to commemorate the start of the Jewish shabbat or sabbath, which extends from sundown Friday to sundown Saturday. Jews also understand this period as a time to refrain from all

useful or creative work and other prohibited activities that distract the believer from fully commemorating God's creation of the universe. A good primer on the subject is Mark Dov Shapiro and Neil Waldman's *Gates of Sabbath: A Guide for Observing Shabbat* (New York: Central Conference of American Rabbis, 1991).

10. A mezuzah is a piece of parchment inscribed with Hebrew verses from the Torah.

11. Quote is taken from Abraham Cohen's *Everyman's Talmud: The Major Teachings of the Rabbinic Sages* (New York: Schocken Books, 1975), 41.

12. The dietary laws (as many others) were laid out in the Old Testament's book of Deuteronomy ("book of laws"), particularly 14:1–22.

13. Mark Chaves, *Congregations in America* (Cambridge, MA: Harvard University Press, 2004), 5.

14. John Dominic Crossan, *Jesus: A Revolutionary Biography*, 71.

15. Quote taken from the church sermon on "Faith," September 24, 2006.

16. Armand Larive, *After Sunday: A Theology of Work* (New York: Continuum Press, 2004), 3.

17. Chaves, *Congregations in America*, 169.

18. The reference is from Matthew 5:13. In cultural terms the description "salt of the earth" has come to be applied to working people of simple means and modest wealth.

19. Edward N. Wolff, *Top Heavy: A Study of the Increasing Inequality of Wealth in America* (New York: New Press, 2001).

20. The reference to "eternal life" is from John 4:14.

21. Michael Harrington, *The Other America* (New York: Scribner, 1997).

22. Crossan, *Jesus: A Revolutionary Biography*, 68.

23. Tex Sample, *Blue Collar Ministry: Facing Economic and Social Realities of Working People* (Valley, Forge, PA: Judson Press, 1984), 108.

24. Ibid.

25. United Power for Action and Justice is an independent Chicago-area organization of religious bodies, neighborhood groups, and labor unions formed in 1997 to fight for the "common good."

26. Larry Dowling, interviewed by author, October 8, 2005, Chicago, IL.

27. Ibid.

28. Ibid.

29. Ibid.

30. Catholic teachings on the economy and workplace come from many different papal and church documents. A good summary of church principles is found in a Statement of the U.S. Bishops, Economic Justice for All: A Catholic Framework for Economic Life. Catholic and non-Christian positions on economics, workers, and unions are available online from the National Interfaith Committee for Worker Justice at www.igc.org/nicj.

31. For Eight-Hour Day and Solidarity Forever lyrics, see Edith Fowke, *Songs of Work and Protest* (New York: Dover Publications, 1973).

32. Dowling, interviewed by author, October 8, 2005, Chicago, IL.

33. *Initiatives* 169 (January 2008): 4.

34. Steven C. Warner, *Christ Has No Body Now But Yours* (Franklin Park, IL: World Library Publications, 2003).

35. The word "liturgy" means "work of the people." From St. Denis worship on the Fourth Sunday of Lent, March 21, 2004.

36. One example of real protection was the church's use as a "sanctuary" for workers employed at a nearby Home Depot who were looking for a safe place to meet with union organizers. The church formed a "workers' rights committee" to welcome and assist the union. An account of the event was shared in an e-mail from William J. Black of the Southwest Organizing Project on February 12, 2004.

37. Dietrich Bonhoeffer, *The Cost of Discipleship* (New York: Touchstone Books, 1995).

38. Dowling, interviewed by author, October 8, 2005, Chicago, IL.

39. Ibid.

40. Ibid.

41. Ibid.

42. The Advocate Health Care system was created in 1995 through a merger of the Evangelical Health Systems Corporation and Lutheran General Health Systems. According to the company's Web site (www.advocatehealth.com), Advocate is the largest not-for-profit health-care delivery system in metropolitan Chicago and employs nearly 25,000 people.

43. "Faith in Action," *Hospitality Accountability Project, Report No. 5*, Service Employees International Union, at www.hospitalmonitor.org.

44. Ibid.

45. Standard and Poor's, "Advocate Health Care Network, Illinois," May 2004 quarterly ratings update; online at www.ratingsdirect.com.

46. For the immediate quote see Leviticus 25:10. The entire Jubilee passage is 25:1–55.

47. See Robert Wuthnow and J. H. Evans, eds., *The Quiet Hand of God: Faith-based Activism and the Public Role of Mainline Protestantism* (Berkeley: University of California Press, 2002), and Robert Wuthnow, "Mobilizing Civic Engagement: The Changing Impact of Religious Involvement," in *Civic Engagement in American Democracy*, ed. M. Fiorina and Theda Skocpol (Washington, DC: Brookings Institution, 1988).

48. Donald Spoto, *In Silence, Why We Pray* (New York: Penguin Group, 2005), 130.

Chapter 5

1. Miroslav Volf, *Work in the Spirit: Toward a Theology of Work* (Eugene, OR: Wipf and Stock, 2001), 126.

2. Thomas Carlyle, *Past and Present* (Boston: Riverside Press, 1965), 196, 294.

3. Volf, *Work in the Spirit*, 126.

4. Larive, *After Sunday*, 25.

5. Quoted in Joane Ciulla, *The Working Life* (New York: Three Rivers Press, 2000), 51.

6. Ibid., 26.

7. Quote is from Wally Kroeker, reprinted in *Initiatives* 155 (April 2006): 1.

8. Juliet Schor, *The Overworked American: The Unexpected Decline of Leisure* (New York: Basic Books, 1991).

9. Lawrence Mishel, Jared Bernstein, and Sylvia Allegretto, *The State of Working America, 2004–2005*, Economic Policy Institute (Ithaca, NY: ILR Press, 2005).

10. James Bernard Murphy, *The Moral Economy of Labor: Aristotelian Themes in Economic Theory* (New Haven, CT: Yale University Press, 1993), 1.

11. Al Gini, *My Job, My Self: Work and the Creation of the Modern Individual* (New York: Routledge, 2001), preface.

12. Arlie Hochschild, *The Second Shift* (New York: Penguin Books, 2003).

13. Larive, *After Sunday*, 1.

14. The idea of a "calling" was best popularized by sociologist Max Weber's *The Protestant Ethic and the Spirit of Capitalism* (New York: Scribner's Press, 1958).

15. United States Department of Health, Education, and Welfare, *Work in America: Report of a Special Task Force to the Secretary of Health, Education, and Welfare* (Cambridge, MA: MIT Press, 1973).

16. General Social Survey, University of Chicago.

17. Eugene McCarraher was quoted in "A Catholic Work Ethic," *Initiatives* 159 (October 2006): 1.

18. John 14:12. The verse is completed by "and greater works than these will he do, because I go to the Father."

19. The full passage is at Isaiah 44:9–17.

20. Started in 1984 as a soup kitchen, over these past twenty years "The Port" has grown into the "Port Ministries." As described on its Web site (www.theportministries.org), "The Port" is

> a multi-faceted ministry to the poor, homeless, families and children (currently housed in 5 buildings) that still continues its mission in the simple ways of our beginnings. As we pray and trust, we vividly see and experience the Lord's presence, care and love daily . . . in the people we serve and in the many benefactors and volunteers that respond and give from their hearts to serve those in need. We see the secondary mission of Port Ministries fulfilled: giving others the opportunity to touch and serve Jesus in His "distressing disguise."

21. "Enwrapped," chapter 73, verse 15, in *The Koran Interpreted*, trans. A. J. Arberry (New York: Simon and Schuster, 1996), 309.

22. David Jensen, *Responsive Labor: A Theology of Work* (Louisville: Westminster John Knox Press, 2006), 47–48.

23. Al Gini, *My Job, My Self: Work and the Creation of the Modern Individual* (New York: Routledge, 2001), 5. Sherwin is actually part of a crew that daily cuts approximately 1,500 pounds of meat a day.

24. Abraham Cohen, *Everyman's Talmud: The Major Teachings of the Rabbinic Sages* (New York: Schocken Books, 1975), 193.

25. Volf, *Work in the Spirit*, 189.

26. Matthew Fox, *The Reinvention of Work: A New Vision of Livelihood for Our Time* (New York: HarperCollins, 1994), 125.

27. Ibid., 126.

28. David S. Ariel, *What Do Jews Believe? The Spiritual Foundations of Judaism* (New York: Schocken Books, 1995), 47.

29. Volf, *Work in the Spirit*, 108.

30. When Robert Wuthnow asked people in the labor force if they agreed with the statement "I feel God called me to the particular line of work I am in," only 32 percent did ("The Changing Nature of Work in the United States: Implications for Vocation, Ethics, and Faith," *Cresset* [Michaelmas 2003]: 11).

31. Quote taken from Sarah Stockton, reprinted in *Initiatives* 155 (April 2006): 2.

32. Sharon is a member of the International Association of Machinists.

33. There have been numerous books, magazine articles, and newspaper stories written about the much-debated conservative Catholic order. The official Web site of Opus Dei is www.opusdei.org.

34. For the Marriage at Cana story, see John 2:9–10.

35. Volf, *Work in the Spirit*, 111.

36. Ibid., 113.

37. Gilbert Meilaender, "Friendship and Vocation," in *Leading Lives That Matter: What We Should Do and Who We Should Be*, ed. Mark R. Schwehn and Dorothy C. Bass (Grand Rapids, MI: Eerdmans Publishing Company, 2006), 231.

38. See Mark 4:35–40; Matthew 6:25–34; Luke 12:22–32; John 14:1, 14: 27.

39. A reference to Adam and Eve's disobeying God's direction not to eat from the "tree of the knowledge of good and evil" in Genesis 2:15–17.

40. Goren Agrell, *Work, Toil and Sustenance: An Examination of the Views of Work in the New Testament, Taking into Consideration Views Found in Old Testament, Intertestamental, and Early Rabbinic Writings*, trans. Stephen Westerholm (Lund: Verbum H. Olsson, 1976), 7–13.

41. Larive, *After Sunday*, 11.

42. Ibid., 11.

43. "The Cow," chapter 2, verse 180, in *The Koran Interpreted*, 52.

44. Larive, *After Sunday*, 13, and Douglas Meeks, *God the Economist: The Doctrine of God and Political Economy* (Minneapolis, MN: Fortress Press, 1989).

45. For instance, in John 6:1–14.

46. Considerable information, history, and the Protocols of Agreement, along with assorted articles about SEIU's Hospital Accountability Project, can be found at the union's Web site, www.hospitalmonitor.org.

47. See "The High Price of Growth at Resurrection Health Care: Corporatization of Quality Care," AFSCME Council 31 (November 2005). More information about AFSCME's campaign at Resurrection Hospital can be found at www.afscmeorganizers.org.

48. Bob Gunter, "When Was the Last Time You went to Church?" *Heartbeat*, Illinois State Postal Workers Union Local 854, June 23, 2007, 7–8.

49. Darren Cushman Wood identifies creativity, communalism, and compassion as "those aspects of the imagery of God in every human being that shows how we should view work" (*Blue Collar Jesus*, 148).

50. Douglas Sherman and William Hendricks, *Your Work Matters to God* (Colorado Springs, CO: Navpress, 1987), 49.

51. Ibid., 21.

52. The quote is from Meeks, *God the Economist*, 146.

53. Barbara Rose, "Religious Faith Finding Place in Workplace," *Chicago Tribune*, October 23, 2005, 1.

Chapter 6

1. Robert Wuthnow, "The Changing Nature of Work in the United States: Implications for Vocation, Ethics, and Faith," *Cresset* (Michaelmas 2003): 11.

2. Miroslav Volf, *Work in the Spirit: Toward a Theology of Work* (Portland, OR: Wipf and Stock Publishers, 2001), 126.

3. Karen Armstrong, *Muhammad: A Biography of the Prophet* (New York: HarperCollins, 1993), 99.

4. Quotes are taken from David S. Ariel, *What Do Jews Believe? The Spiritual Foundations of Judaism* (New York: Schocken Books, 1995), 74.

5. Martin Luther, "The Method and Fruits of Justification," in *The World's Great Sermons, Volume I*, comp. Grenville Kleiser (New York: Funk and Wagnalls Company, 1909), 113–43.

6. Armstrong, *Muhammad: A Biography of the Prophet*, 139.

7. Quote is from Ariel, *What Do Jews Believe?* 209.

8. Armand Larive, *After Sunday: A Theology of Work* (New York: Continuum Publishing, 2004), 1.

9. Quote is from Ariel, *What Do Jews Believe?* 208.

10. John Kass, "Decency Drives Cabbie to Do the Right Thing," *Chicago Tribune*, February 15, 2007, sec. 1, p. 2.

11. "Salvation," chapter 25, verse 15, in *The Koran Interpreted*, trans. A. J. Arberry (New York: Simon and Schuster, 1955), II:57.

12. "The House of Imran," chapter 3, verse 140, in *The Koran Interpreted*, I:91; "Cattle," chapter 6, verse 65, ibid., 157.

13. "The Kingdom," chapter 67, verse 25, ibid., II:292.

14. "Repentance," chapter 9, verse 35, ibid., I:211.

15. "Salvation," chapter 25, Ibid., II:56.

16. Matthew 25:35–37; Mark, Luke.

17. Lindy Scott, *Economic Koinonia within the Body of Christ* (Mexico City: Editorial Kyrios, 1980), 21.

18. Ariel, *What Do Jews Believe?* 48.

19. Volf, *Work in the Spirit*, 114.

20. Ibid., 114.

21. "The Cow," chapter 2, verse 155, in *The Koran Interpreted*, I:48.

22. "Man," chapter 76, verse 30, ibid., II:316.

23. "Enwrapped," chapter 63, verse 15, ibid., II:309.

24. I have also participated as a speaker on many occasions.

25. For a brief history of U-U, see Peter W. Williams, *America's Religions: From Their Origins to the Twenty-First Century* (Urbana: University of Illinois Press, 2002), 220–25.

26. To be aware of worship themes or to attend New Garden Community Church services, go to www.NewGardenUU.org.

27. New Garden Community Church service program, February 6, 2005.

28. Reverend Jean Siegfried Darling sermon for New Garden Community Church, "A Middle Way," September 17, 2006.

29. Reverend Jean Siegfried Darling sermon for New Garden Community Church, "Origins," September 10, 2006.

30. Ibid.

31. Ibid.

32. Siegfried Darling sermon for New Garden Community Church, "A Middle Way," September 17, 2006.

33. Ibid.

34. Ibid.

35. For a fuller description of the Port Ministries, go to www.theportministries.org.

36. For a fuller description of United Power for Action and Justice, go to www.united-power.org.

37. Thomas J. Lenz, "Building a Force for the Common Good: United Power for Action and Justice," *Shelterforce Online*, 101, September/October 1998, at www.nhi.org.

38. Scott, *Economic Koinonia within the Body of Christ*, 21.

Conclusion

1. David S. Ariel, *What Do Jews Believe? The Spiritual Foundations of Judaism* (New York: Schocken Books, 1995), 47.

2. Martin Buber, *Hasidism and Modern Man* (New York: Humanities Press, 1956), 42.

3. Donald Spoto, *In Silence, Why We Pray* (New York: Penguin Group, 2005), 135.

4. A federal jury in Jacksonville, Florida actually returned a guilty verdict against a farm labor contractor and his wife on charges that they recruited homeless persons and then manipulated them into trading their earned wages for drugs (*Daily Labor Report*, Bureau of National Affairs, 168 [August 30, 2006], A-7).

5. David Teather, "Four Years On, Enron Men Face Their Day of Reckoning," *Guardian* (U.K), January 26, 2006.

6. Derrick Z. Jackson, "As Goes GM, So Goes the Nation," *Chicago Tribune*, October 24, 2005, 19; John Bogle, *The Battle for the Soul of Capitalism* (New Haven, CT: Yale University Press, 2005).

7. Christian workers referred to the biblical story of Jesus' time in the desert fighting off the devil's offers of earthly delights (see Matthew 4:1–11).

8. Rumi, *One-Handed Basket Weaving*, trans. Coleman Barks (Athens, GA: Maypop, 1991), 40–41.

9. Walt Whitman, "Song of Myself," verses 1276–80, in *Leaves of Grass, The First (1855) Edition*, ed. Malcolm Crowley (New York: Penguin Classics, 1986), 83.

10. The phrase is taken from a line from an Elizabeth Barrett Browning poem quoted in Elizabeth Dreyer, *Earth Crammed with Heaven: A Spirituality of Everyday Life* (New York: Paulist, 1994), page facing the Introduction.

11. Thomas Aquinas, *Summa Theologica* I.

12. Spoto, *In Silence, Why We Pray*, 73.

13. Matthew Fox, *The Reinvention of Work: A New Vision of Livelihood for Our Time* (New York: HarperCollins, 1994), 127.

14. Pastor Reginald Earl McCracken Jr., sermon on "Faith," Our Lord and Savior Jesus Christ, September 24, 2006.

15. Dorothy Sayers, "Why Work?" in *Leading Lives That Matter: What We Should Do and Who We Should Be*, ed. Mark R. Schwehn and Dorothy C. Bass (Grand Rapids, MI: Eerdmans Publishing Company, 2006), 195.

16. Dominic Crossan, *Jesus: A Revolutionary Biography* (New York: HarperCollins, 1995), 114.

17. Scott, *Economic Koinonia within the Body of Christ*, 63.

18. Elaine Pagels, *Beyond Belief: The Secret Gospel of Thomas* (New York: Vintage Books, 2003), 122.

19. G. William Domhoff, *Who Rules in America? Wealth, Income and Power*, www.sociology.ucsc.edu/whorulesamerica/power/wealth, February 2006.

20. Martin Crutsinger writes that according to the Federal Reserve Bank's "Survey of Consumer Finances," in 2004 the top 10 percent of "households saw their net worth rise by 6.1 percent to an average of $3.11 million while the bottom 25 percent suffered a decline from a net worth in which their assets equaled their liabilities in 2001 to owing $1,400 more than their total assets in 2004" (Associated Press, "Average American Family Income Declines," February 23, 2006).

21. "How Many People Experience Homelessness?" National Coalition for the Homeless, NCH Fact Sheet #3 (June 2005); "Homelessness in the United States and the Human Right to Housing," National Law Center on Homelessness and Poverty (January 2004); *A Status Report on Hunger and Homelessness in American Cities, 2004* Washington, DC:, U.S. Conference of Mayors).

22. Income, Poverty, and Health Insurance Coverage in the United States: 2006 Report, released August 28, 2007.

23. *Infant Mortality Rates and Rankings, World Health Report*, World Health Organization at www.who.int (2005); *Morbidity and Mortality Report*, Centers for Disease Control and Prevention (Washington, DC: U.S. Government Printing Office, March 15, 1996); Factor *Contributing to the Infant Mortality Ranking of the United States*, Congressional Budget Office (Washington, DC: U.S. Government Printing Office, February 1992).

24. Institute for Policy Studies and United for a Fair Economy Report, U.S. Census Bureau, U.S. Department of Commerce, Washington, DC, 2006.

25. Kate Bonfenbrenner, "Uneasy Terrain: The Impact of Capital Mobility on Workers, Wages and Union Organizing," a report (monograph) available from Cornell University, September 6, 2000. Also see John Logan, "Consultant, Lawyers, and the 'Union Free' Movement in the USA since 1970s," *Industrial Relations Journal* 33, no. 3 (2002): 38–51, and Richard Freeman and Morris Kliener, "Employer Behavior in the Face of Union Organizing Drives," *Industrial Relations Review* 36, no. 4 (1990): 351–65.

26. www.msnbc.msn.com (October 28, 2005).

27. The quote is from the lyrics to Bruce Springsteen's song "Reason to Believe" (Sony BMG Music Entertainment, 2005, at www.brucespringsteen.net/songs).

28. "Key Religious Leaders Launch Coalition with Chicago Hotel Workers (UNITE HERE); Crucial Support Comes on Eve of Hilton, Hyatt Strike Votes," *Business Wire*, August 15, 2006, at www.cairchicago.org (accessed August 25, 2006).

29. Tex Sample, *Blue-Collar Ministry: Facing Economic and Social Realities of Working People* (Valley Forge, PA: Judson Press, 1984), 177.

30. Monsignor George G. Higgins with William Bole, *Organized Labor and the Church: Reflections of a "Labor Priest"* (New York: Paulist Press, 1993), 5.

314. Gregory Baum, *The Priority of Labor: A Commentary on* Labor Exercens *Encyclical Letter of Pope John Paul II* (New York: Paulist Press, 1982), 69.

32. Pope John Paul II, *Labor Exercens*, 1981 Encyclical Letter, chapter 25.

33. A good one is www.biblegateway.com

34. Verna Dozier was quoted from *Confronted by God: The Essential Verna Dozier*,

ed. Cynthia Shattuck and Frederica Harris Thompsett (New York: Seabury Books, 2006), in *Initiatives* 160 (November 2006): 4

35. The National Center for the Laity can be found at www.catholiclabort/NCL.htm. Cited *Initiatives*'s issues were from January 2006 (no. 153), October 2005 (no. 151), September 2005 (no. 150), April 2005 (no. 147), March 2005 (no. 146), January–February 2005 (no. 145), December 2004 (no. 144), September 2004 (no. 142), March 2004 (no. 138), January 2004 (no. 136), September 2003 (no. 133).

36. The National Jewish Labor Committee publishes a directory of readings on traditional Jewish texts on Labor and Worker Rights at www.jewishlaborcommittee.org.

37. Michael Perry, *Labor Rights in the Jewish Tradition* (New York: National Jewish Labor Committee, n.d.), 1.

38. Ibid., 10–11.

39. "Jewish Federation Host Labor Seder," in *Faith Works*, National Interfaith Committee for Worker Justice, May 2004, 5.

40. *The Qur'an and Worker Justice*, an educational booklet published by the National Interfaith Committee for Worker Justice, n.d., 3.

41. Tonya Maxwell, "Churches Warned of Labor's Slide," *Chicago Tribune*, September 5, 2005, Section 2, 3.

42. For background information on the National Interfaith Committee for Worker Justice and to examine copies of their publication, *Faith Works*, go to www.nicwj.org.

43. A few prominent examples of twentieth-century faith-inspired movements to address America's social problems were the Protestant Social Gospel, Catholic Worker Movement, and Labor Forward Movement.

44. Two outstanding and comprehensive analyses of the logic of unrestrained global capitalism are William Greider, *One Word Ready or Not* (New York: Simon & Schuste, 1998), and Thomas Frank, *One Market under God: Extreme Capitalism, Market Populism and the End of Economic Democracy* (New York: Anchor Books, 2000).

45. "Lay Formation," in *Initiatives*, National Center for the Laity, no. 145 (January-February 2005): 2.

46. Spoto, *In Silence, Why We Pray*, 151.

APPENDIX

Roster of Interviews

CONGREGATION:
FAMILY IN FAITH LUTHERAN CHURCH

Name	Occupation	Race/Ethnicity	Age	Date of Interview
Donna Schiavone	Massage Therapist	Italian	41	8-10-04
John Schiavone	Data Entry Technician	Italian	46	8-10-04
George Gennardo	School Custodian	Italian	44	8-21-04
Todd Macdonald	Painter (u)	Scottish	42	8-27-04
Craig Rutz	Police Officer (u)	Polish	53	8-07-04
Gerry Vargas	Shipping Clerk	Mexican	41	8-21-04
Kim Vargas	Housewife	Russian	36	8-21-04
Patty Brown	Day-care Provider	English	36	8-21-04

(u) = union member

CONGREGATION:
CHURCH OF OUR LORD AND SAVIOR JESUS CHRIST EVANGELICAL

Name	Occupation	Race/Ethnicity	Age	Date of Interview
Josie Winston	School Social Worker	African American	55	9-26-04
Ron McCracken	Unemployed	African American	47	9-26-04
James Word	Customer Service Representative	African American	41	9-26-04
Lamont Harrison	Public Relations	African American	21	9-26-04
Florence Joseph	Bank Clerk	African American	62	9-26-04
Cheryl Lawrence	Customer Service	African American	46	9-26-04
Reginald Earle McCracken	Pastor/Project Assistant (u)	African American	51	9-26-04
Philip Blunt	Records Clerk	African American	26	9-26-04
Steve Kennedy	Store Clerk	African American	18	9-26-04
Jason Benoit	Store Clerk	African American	24	9-26-04
Angela Blunt	Customer Service Representative	African American	29	9-26-04

CONGREGATION:
NEW GARDEN COMMUNITY UNIVERSALIST-UNITARIAN CHURCH

Name	Occupation	Race/Ethnicity	Age	Date of Interview
Jean Darling	Computer Technician		55	6-2-05
Dave Karcher	School Teacher	German	50	6-2-05
Sharon Perry	Food Service Worker	African American	51	6-2-05
Owen Wagner	Dog Walker	German	58	6-2-05

CONGREGATION:
PARK LANE CHRISTIAN REFORM CHURCH

Name	Occupation	Race/ Ethnicity	Age	Date of Interview
John Dykstra	Computer Technician	Dutch	46	7-17-04
Linda Schutt	Registered Nurse	Dutch	49	7-10-04
Andy Schutt	Truck Driver (u-retired)	Dutch	75	7-10-04
Marvin DeVries	Electrician (u-retired)	Dutch	78	7-10-04
Sandra Aardsma	Registered Nurse	Dutch	49	7-10-04
Craig Doornbos	Truck Driver (u)	Dutch	45	7-10-04
Tim Goudzwaard	Special Ed Teacher	Dutch	38	7-17-04
William Kamp	Field Service Technician	Dutch	46	7-10-04
Marilyn VanderBout	Secretary	Dutch	53	7-11-04

CONGREGATION:
COMMUNITY MENNONITE CHURCH

Name	Occupation	Race/Ethnicity	Age	Date of Interview
Don Burklow	Maintenance	German	55	3-6-04
Edmund Mix	Store Clerk (u-retired)	African American	71	3-13-04
Ivorie Lowe	Rehab Counselor	African American	67	3-7-04
Doug Swartz	Home Remodeling	German	52	3-6-04
Martha Stinyard	Beautician (retired)	African American	69	2-28-04
Mertis Odom	Rehab Counselor (retired)	African American	70	2-28-04
Eric Shirk	Quality Control Inspector	Swedish	47	2-28-04
Karen Shirk	Nurse	Swedish	48	2-28-04
Shirley Havock	School Lunch Hostess (retired)	German	79	3-6-04
Kenneth Cook	Special Ed Teacher	African American	40	3-13-04
Chuck Kozlowsky	Postal Clerk (retired)	Lithuanian	68	2-28-04
Gwen Kozlowsky	Housewife	Lithuanian	67	2-28-04
Denis Wilson	Registered Nurse (u)	African American	42	3-13-04
Paul Mares	Carpenter (u)	Bohemian	45	2-28-04
Sandra McDowell	Social Worker (u)	English	45	2-28-04
Barbara Lee	Food Services (u-retired)	African American	68	2-28-04

CONGREGATION:
ST. DENIS ROMAN CATHOLIC CHURCH

Name	Occupation	Race/ Ethnicity	Age	Date of Interview
Thomas O'Connell	Laborer (u)	Irish	42	3-27-04
Theresa O'Connell	Office Assistant	Irish	38	3-27-04
Laura Dawson	ESL Teacher	English	47	4-3-04
Pat Glatz	Special Ed Teacher (u)	German	59	3-27-04
Ellen Kilmurry	Social Service Counselor	Irish	55	8-22-04
Ed Carrile	Carpenter (u)	French	43	4-3-04
Hank Schuberth	Telephone Installer (u-retired)	Irish	77	3-20-04
Carol Schuberth	Housewife/Artist	German	68	3-20-04
Tom Dahill	Typesetter (u- retired)	Irish	66	3-20-04
Renee Pletsch	Receptionist	German	51	3-20-04
Jim Pletsch	Truck Driver (u)	German	48	3-20-04
Larry Hill	Grave Digger	Irish	52	3-20-04

CONGREGATION:
IMMACULATE CONCEPTION B.V.M. CATHOLIC CHURCH

Name	Occupation	Race/Ethnicity	Age	Date of Interview
Caroline Garcia	Processing Clerk	Mexican	52	1-16-05
Rudy Ramirez	Food Service (u)	Mexican	62	1-23-05

CONGREGATION: ST. BRUNO ROMAN CATHOLIC CHURCH

Name	Occupation	Race/ Ethnicity	Age	Date of Interview
Barbara Bedus	Processing Clerk	Polish	58	1-24-04
Stephanie Baron	Police Academy	Polish	21	2-21-04
Donna Logisz	Rehab Counselor	Polish	51	2-21-04
Jerry Logisz	Computer Programmer	Polish	52	2-21-04
Bernice Feltz	Office Assistant	Polish	48	1-24-04
Margarita Tellez	Teacher	Mexican	41	1-24-04
Lisa Haugustyniak	Food Service	Polish	38	1-24-04
Jim Stewart	Insurance Agent (unemployed)	English	38	2-21-04
Susan Stewart	Client Service Representative	English	34	2-21-04
Sharon Aftab	Customer Care Representative (u)		41	1-31-04
Edward Bartoszek	Telephone Repair (retired)	Polish	65	1-31-04
Mira Sojka-Topor	Part-time Church Music Director	Polish	31	1-31-04
John Hindelewicz	Welder	Polish	44	1-31-04
Deborah Hindelewicz	Research and Development	Polish	38	1-31-04
Krystyna Bogdanowicz	Lab Technician	Polish	43	2-21-04

CONGREGATION: HOLY ANGELS CATHOLIC CHURCH

Name	Occupation	Race/Ethnicity	Age	Date of Interview
Virginia Coleman	Clerk (u)	African American	52	4-25-04
Katie Jordan	Garment Fitter (u-retired)	African American	76	4-25-04
Arthur Reliford	Teacher	African American	49	5-16-04
Eileen Foggie	Office Clerk (retired)	African American	73	5-30-04
Rosemary Sykes	Processing Clerk	African American	52	5-2-04
Vincent Washington	Certified Assessor	African American	42	4-25-04
Sandra Houston	Circuit Board Designer (u)	African American	57	4-25-04
June Sargent	Outreach Manager for Non-Profit	African American	52	5-2-04
Rebecca Danforth	Secretary (retired)	African American	65	5-16-04
Michael Morman	Bus Driver (u)	African American	42	5-16-04

CONGREGATION:
OUR LADY OF GUADALUPE CATHOLIC CHURCH

Name	Occupation	Race/Ethnicity	Age	Date of Interview
Jim Estrada	Bricklayer (u)	Mexican	40	1-22-06
Marisella Estrada	Housewife	Mexican	35	1-22-06
Jose Estrada	Salesman	Mexican	48	1-22-06
Manuel Murillo	Demolition (u)	Mexican	52	1-22-06
Jesus Flores	Factory	Mexican	35	1-22-06
Ana Valtierra	Housewife	Mexican	37	1-22-06
Javier Castro	Demolition	Mexican	35	1-22-06
Paula Castro	Teacher's Aide	Mexican	32	1-22-06
Mateo Reyes	Salesman	Mexican	42	1-22-06
Arturo Vega	Roofer (u)	Mexican	43	1-22-06
Gabriel Padilla	Scrapyard Worker	Mexican	38	1-22-06
Catalina Padilla	Housewife	Mexican	36	1-22-06
David Castillas	Demolition (u)	Mexican	43	1-22-06
Rosaria Morales	Secretary	Mexican	n/a	1-22-06
Nena Barajas	Teacher-aide	Mexican	n/a	1-22-06

CONGREGATION:
ISLAMIC/MUSLIM BELIEVERS

Name	Occupation	Race/ Ethnicity	Age	Date of Interview
Mohammad Hareed	Cab Driver	Somalia	29	5-10-05
Azmat Ali	Cab Driver	Pakistan	43	5-10-05
Hussein Ali	Cab Driver	Kenya	28	5-10-05
Mohammad Khan	Cab Driver	Somalia	54	5-10-05
Omar Ali	Cab Driver	Somalia	43	5-10-05
Mohammad Abdullah	Cab Driver	Sudan	35	5-10-05
Mohammad Hussein	Restaurant Manager	India	26	5-17-05
Mustafa Ali	Cab Driver	Somalia	37	5-17-05
Mohammad Saba	Cab Driver	Somalia	31	5-17-05

JEWISH BELIEVERS

Name	Occupation	Synagogue	Age	Date of Interview
Daniel Weinberg	Teacher	Temple Beth-El	23	1-3-05
Sherwin Epstein	Meatcutter (u)	n/a	58	3-1-06
Barry Blaustein	Mashgiach (u-kosher foods supervisor)	Sherith Yisroel	53	4-28-06
Jeffrey Goldberg	Electrician (u)	B' nai Yehuda Beth Sholom	38	4-1-06
Sarah Goldberg	PT Store Manager	B' nai Yehuda Beth Sholom	36	4-1-06
Sylvia Wald	Inventory Control Clerk (u)	n/a	53	2-28-06

OTHER INDIVIDUALS

Name	Occupation	Race/Ethnicity	Age	Date of Interview
Lori Landers-Rippy	Furnace Maker (u)	Welsh	45	6-15-06

WORKS CITED

Books

Agrell, Goren. 1976. *Work, Toil and Sustenance: An Examination of the Views of Work in the New Testament, Taking into Consideration Views Found in Old Testament, Intertestamental, and Early Rabbinic Writings*, translated by Stephen Westerholm. Lund: Verbum H. Olsson.

Armstrong, Karen. 1993. *Muhammad: A Biography of the Prophet*. New York: Harper Collins.

Arberry, A. J. trans. 1955. *The Koran Interpreted*. New York: Touchstone.

Ariel, David S. 1995. *What Do Jews Believe? The Spiritual Foundations of Judaism*. New York: Schocken Books.

Augustine, Gregory Pierce. 2003. *Spirituality @ Work: 10 Ways to Balance Your Life on-the-Job*. Skokie, IL: ACTA Publications.

Barrett, James R. 1987. *Work and Community in the Jungle: Chicago's Packinghouse Workers, 1894–1922*. Champaign: University of Illinois Press.

Baum, Gregory. 1982. *The Priority of Labor: A Commentary on* Labor Exercens *Encyclical Letter of Pope John Paul II*. New York: Paulist Press.

Berryman, Phillip. 1988. *Liberation Theology: Essential Facts about the Revolutionary Religious Movement in Latin America and Beyond*. Philadelphia: Temple University Press.

Best, Wallace. 2005. *Passionately Human, No Less Divine*. Princeton: Princeton University Press.

Beth, Laurie Jones. 1995. *Jesus CEO: Using Ancient Wisdom for Visionary Leadership*. New York: Hyperion Press.

Bigott, Joseph C. 2001. *From Cottage to Bungalow: Houses and the Working Class in Metropolitan Chicago, 1869–1929*. Chicago: University of Chicago Press.

Bogle, John. 2005. *The Battle for the Soul of Capitalism*. New Haven: Yale University Press.

Bonhoeffer, Dietrich. 1995. *The Cost of Discipleship*. New York: Touchstone Books.

Borg, Marcus J. 1995. *Meeting Jesus Again for the First Time*. San Francisco: Harper Collins.

Bruno, Robert. 1999. *Steel Worker Alley: How Class Works in Youngstown*. Ithaca: Cornell University Press.

Buber, Martin. 1956. *Hasidism and Modern Man*. Highland, NJ: Humanities Press International.

Buss, Terry F., and Steven F. Stevens. 1983. *Shutdown at Youngstown: Public Policy for Mass Unemployment*. Albany: State University of New York Press.

Byers, David. 1985. *Justice in the Marketplace: Collected Statements of the Vatican and the United States Catholic Bishops on Economic Policy, 1891–1984*. National Conference of Catholic Bishops, United States Catholic Conference.

Candeloro, Dominic. 2003. *Chicago's Italians: Immigrants, Ethnics, Americans*. Aurora: Arcadia Publishing.

Carlyle, Thomas. 1965. *Past and Present*. Boston: Riverside Press.

Chaves, Mark. 2004. *Congregations in America*. Cambridge, MA: Harvard University Press.

Ciulla, Joanne. 2000. *The Working Life: The Promise and Betrayal of Modern Work*. New York: Three Rivers Press.

Cohen, Abraham. 1995. *Everyman's Talmud: The Major Teachings of the Rabbinic Sages*. New York: Schocken Books.

Coleman, John, ed. 1991. *One Hundred Years of Catholic Social Thought*. Maryknoll, NY: Orbis Books.

Crossan, John Dominic. 1995. *Jesus: A Revolutionary Biography*. New York: HarperCollins.

Cutler, Irving. 1996. *The Jews of Chicago: From Shtetl to Suburb*. Champaign: University of Illinois Press.

Dollinger, Marc. 2000. *Quest for Inclusion: Jews and Liberalism in Modern America*. Princeton: Princeton University Press.

Dreyer, Elizabeth. 1994. *Earth Crammed with Heaven: A Spirituality of Everyday Life*. New York: Paulist Press.

Eastwood, Carolyn. 2002. *Near West Side Stories: Struggles for Community in Chicago's Maxwell Street Neighborhood*. Forest Park: Lake Claremont Press.

Egon Mayer, Barry A. Kosmin, and Ariela Keysar. *The American Jewish Identity Survey: An Exploration in the Demography and Outlook of a People*. Graduate Center of the City University of New York, 2001.

Evans, Christopher H. 2004. *The Kingdom Is Always But Coming: A Life of Walter Rauschenbusch*. Grand Rapids, MI: Wm. B. Eerdmans Publishing.

Fraser, Steven. 1993. *Labor Will Rule: Sidney Hillman and the Rise of American Labor*. Ithaca: Cornell University Press.

Fox, Matthew. 1994. *The Reinvention of Work: A New Vision of Livelihood for Our Time*. New York: Harper Collins.

Frank, Thomas. 2000. *One Market under God: Extreme Capitalism, Market Populism and the End of Economic Democracy*. New York: Anchor Books.

Fuechtmann, Thomas, and Robin Lovin. 1989. *Steeples and Stacks: Religion and the Steel Crisis in Youngstown, Ohio*. Cambridge: Cambridge University Press.

Genie, Al. 2000. My *Job, My Self: Work and the Creation of the Modern Individual*. London: Routledge Press.

Ghanea Bassiri, Kambiz. 1997. *Competing Visions of Islam in the United States: A Study of Los Angeles*. New York: Greenwood Press.
Glasmeirer, Amy. 2005. *An Atlas of Poverty in America: One Nation, Pulling Apart 1960–2003*. New York: Routledge Press.
Greider, William. 1998. *One Word Ready or Not: The Logic of Global Capitalism*. New York: Simon and Schuster.
Gutierrez, Gustavo. 1988. *A Theology of Liberation: History, Politics and Salvation*. Maryknoll, NY: Orbis Books.
Gutterman, David S. 2005. *Prophetic Politics: Christian Social Movements and American Democracy*. Ithaca: Cornell University Press.
Harrington, Michael. 1997. *The Other America*. New York: Scribner.
Hart, Stephen. 1996. *What Does the Lord Require? How American Christians Think about Social Justice*. New Brunswick, NJ: Rutgers University Press.
Higgins, Monsignor George G., with William Bole. 1993. *Organized Labor and the Church: Reflections of a "Labor Priest."* New York: Paulist Press.
Hillman, Os. 2005. *9 to 5 Window*. Ventura, CA: Regal Books.
Hochschild, Arlie. 2003. *The Second Shift*. New York: Penguin Books.
Holi, Melvin G., and Peter D. Jones. 1995. *Ethnic Chicago: A Multicultural Portrait*. Grand Rapids, MI: Wm. B. Eerdmans Publishing.
Hunter, Albert. 1974. *Symbolic Communities: The Persistence and Change of Chicago's Local Communities*. Chicago: University of Chicago Press.
Jirasek, Rita Arias, and Carlos Tortolero. 2002. *Mexican Chicago*. Aurora: Arcadia Publishing.
Keil, Hartmut, and John Jentz, eds. 1988. *German Workers in Chicago: A Documentary History of Working-Class Culture from 1850 to WWI*. Champaign: University of Illinois Press.
Kostarelos, Frances. 1995. *Feeling the Spirit: Faith and Hope in an Evangelical Black Storefront Church*. Columbia: University of South Carolina Press.
Kurzman, Charles. 1998. *Liberal Islam: A Sourcebook*. Oxford: Oxford University Press.
Lagrand, James B. 2002. Indian *Metropolis: Native Americans in Chicago, 1945–75*. Champaign: University of Illinois Press.
Larive, Armand. 2004. *After Sunday: A Theology of Work*. New York: Continuum Press.
Le Gai Eaton, Charles. 1986. *Islam and the Destiny of Man*. Stony Brook: State University of New York Press.
Lewis, C. S. 1961. *A Grief Observed*. New York: Bantam Books.
———. 2001. *The Problem of Pain*. New York: HarperCollins Books.
———. 1995. *Surprised by Joy*. New York: Harcourt, Brace Jovanovich.
Livezey, Lowell, ed. 2000. *Public Religion and Urban Transformation: Faith in the City*. New York: New York University Press.
Luther, Martin. 1909. "The Method and Fruits of Justification." In *The World's Great Sermons, Volume I*, compiled by Grenville Kleiser, 113–44. New York: Funk and Wagnalls Company.
Lynd, Staughton. 1983. *The Fight against Shutdowns: Youngstown's Steel Mill Closing*. California: Singlejack Books.
Mason, Mike. 2002. *The Gospel According to Job: An Honest Look at Pain and Doubt from the Life of One Who Lost Everything*. Wheaton, IL: Crossway Books.

Meilaender, Gilbert. 2006. "Friendship and Vocation." In *Leading Lives That Matter: What We Should Do and Who We Should Be*, edited by Mark R. Schwehn and Dorothy C. Bass. Grand Rapids, MI: Eerdmans Publishing Company.

McLaughlin, John Gerard. 2003. *Irish Chicago*. Aurora: Arcadia Publishing.

McMahon, Eileen M. 1996. *What Parish Are You From? A Chicago Irish Community and Race Relations*. Lexington: University Press of Kentucky.

Meeks, Douglas. 2000. *God the Economist: The Doctrine of God and Political Economy*. Minneapolis: Augsburg Fortress Publishers.

Miles, Jack. 1995. *God, a Biography*. New York: Vantage Books.

Mishel, Lawrence, Jared Bernstein, and Sylvia Allegretto. 2005. *The State of Working America 2004/2005*. Ithaca: Cornell University Press.

Murphy, James Bernard. 1993. *The Moral Economy of Labor: Aristotelian Themes in Economic Theory*. New Haven: Yale University Press.

Niebuhr, H. Richard. 1957. *The Social Sources of Denominations*. New York: New Meridian Books.

Nasr, Seyyed Hossein. 2000. *Ideals and Realities of Islam*. Chicago: Kazi Publications.

Pacyga, Dominic A. 2003. *Polish Immigrants and Industrial Chicago: Workers on the South Side, 1880–1922*. Chicago: University of Chicago Press.

Pagels, Elaine. 2003. *Beyond Belief: The Secret Gospel of Thomas*. New York: Vintage Books.

Pattillo-McCoy, Mary. 2000. *Black Picket Fences: Privilege and Peril Among the Black Middle Class*. Chicago: University of Chicago Press.

Pope, Liston. 1942. *Millhands and Preachers*. New Haven: Yale University Press.

Prothero, Stephen. 2003. *American Jesus: How the Son of God Became a National Icon*. New York: Farrar, Straus and Giroux.

Roof, Wade Clark, and William McKinney. 1987. *American Mainline Religion: Its Changing Shape and Future*. New Brunswick, NJ: Rutgers University Press.

Rumi. 1991. *One-Handed Basket Weaving*, translated by Coleman Barks. Athens, GA: Maypop.

Russo, John, and Sherry Linkon. 2002. *Steel-Town USA: Work and Memory in Youngstown*. Lawrence: University Press of Kansas.

Safi, Omid, ed. 2003. *Progressive Muslims: On Justice, Gender, and Pluralism*. Oxford: One World Publications Ltd.

Sample, Tex. 1984. *Blue Collar Ministry: Facing Economic and Social Realities of Working People*. Valley Forge, PA: Judson Press.

Sayers, Dorothy. 2006. "Why Work?" In *Leading Lives That Matter: What We Should Do and Who We Should Be*, edited by Mark R. Schwehn and Dorothy C. Bass. Grand Rapids, MI: Eerdmans Publishing Company.

Schor, Juliet. 1991. *The Overworked American: The Unexpected Decline of Leisure*. New York: Basic Books.

Scott, Lindy. 1980. *Economic Koinonia within the Body of Christ*. Mexico City: Editorial Kyrios.

Shapiro, Mark Dov, and Neil Waldman. 1991. *Gates of Sabbath: A Guide for Observing Shabbat*. New York: Central Conference of American Rabbis.

Shattuck, Cynthia, and Frederica Harris Thompsett, eds. 2006. *Confronted by God: The Essential Verna Dozier*. New York: Seabury Books.

Sherman, Douglas, and William Hendricks. 1987. *Your Work Matters to God*. Colorado Springs: Navspress.

Sobrino, Jon. 1978. *Christology at the Crossroads: A Latin American Approach*. Maryknoll, NY: Orbis Books.

Spoto, Donald. 2004. *In Silence, Why We Pray*. New York, New York: Penguin Group.

Terkel, Studs. 1972. *Working*. New York: Avon Books.

The New Oxford Annotated Bible, Revised Standard Version. 1973. New York: Oxford University Press.

Volf, Miroslav. 2001. *Work in the Spirit: Toward a Theology of Work*. Portland, OR: Wipf and Stock Publishers.

Wade, Louise Carroll. 2003. *Chicago's Pride: The Stockyards, Packingtown, and Environs in the Nineteenth Century*. Champaign: University of Illinois Press.

Wallis, Jim. 2000. *Faith Works: Lessons from the Life of an Activist* Preacher. New York: Random House.

Wallis, Jim. 1995. *The Soul of Politics: Beyond "Religious Right" and "Secular Left."* New York: Harcourt, Brace.

Warner, Steven C. 2003. *Christ Has No Body Now But Yours*. Franklin Park, IL: World Library Publications.

Weber, Max. 1958. *The Protestant Ethic and the Spirit of Capitalism*. New York: Scribner's Press.

Wedam, Elfriede. 2000. "God Doesn't Ask What Language I Pray." In *Public Religion: Faith in the City and Urban Transformation*, edited by Lowell W. Livezey. New York: New York University Press.

White, Ronald C., and C. Howard Hopkins. 1976. *The Social Gospel: Religion and Reform in Changing America*. Philadelphia: Temple University Press.

Whitman, Walt. 1986. *Leaves of Grass, The First (1855) Edition*, edited by Malcolm Crowley. New York: Penguin Classics.

Williams, Peter W. 2002. *America's Religions: From Their Origins to the Twenty-First Century*. Urbana: University of Illinois Press.

Wolfe, Alan. 2003. *Transformation of American Religion: How We Actually Live Our Faith*. Chicago: University of Chicago Press.

Wolff, Edward N. 2001. *Top Heavy: A Study of the Increasing Inequality of Wealth in America*. New York: New Press.

Wood, Darren Cushman. 2004. *Blue Collar Jesus: How Christianity Supports Workers' Rights*. Santa Ana, CA: Seven Locks Press.

Wuthnow, Robert, and J. H. Evans, eds. 2002. *The Quiet Hand of God: Faith-based Activism and the Public Role of Mainline Protestantism*. Berkeley: University of California Press.

Wurthnow, Robert. 1994. *God and Mammon in America*. New York: Free Press.

———. 1988. "Mobilizing Civic Engagement: The Changing Impact of Religious Involvement." In *Civic Engagement in American Democracy*, edited by M. Fiorina and Theda Skocpol. Washington, DC: Brookings Institution.

Zwick, Mark and Louise. 2006. *The Catholic Worker Movement: The Intellectual and Spiritual Origins*. New York: Paulist Press.

Zweig, Michael. 2001. *Working Class Majority: Americas Best Kept Secret*. Ithaca: ILR Press.

Journal Articles and Unpublished Papers

Almeida, Beth. "Weathering the Perfect Storm: Defined Benefit Pensions Plans in the Airline Industry." *Labor and Employment Relations Association Series, Proceedings of the 57th Annual Meeting, 2005*.

Bruno, Robert. "USWA-Bargained and State-Oriented Responses to the Recurrent Steel Crisis." *Labor Studies Journal* 30.1 (Spring 2005): 67–91.

Curry, Evan, Jerome R. Koch, and Paul Chalfant. "Concern for God and Concern for Society: Religiosity and Social Justice." *Sociological Spectrum* 24 (2004): 651–66.

Domhoff, G. William. "Who Rules in America?: Wealth, Income and Power." www.sociology.ucsc.edu/whorulesamerica/power/wealth. February 2006.

Freeman, Richard, and Morris Kliener. "Employer Behavior in the Face of Union Organizing Drives." *Industrial Relations Review* 36.4 (1990): 351–65.

Gaede, Stan. "Religious Participation, Socioeconomic Status, and Belief-Orthodoxy." *Journal for the Scientific Study of Religion* 16.3 (September 1977): 245–53.

Goode, Erich. "Class Styles of Religious Socialization." *British Journal of Sociology* 19. 1 (March 1998): 1–16.

———. "Social Class and Church Participation." *American Journal of Sociology* 72.1 (July 1966): 102–11.

Hout, Michael, and Claude Fischer. "Religious Diversity in America, 1940–2000." Paper presented at the America Sociological Association Annual Meeting, Chicago. August 2001.

Ladd, K. L., and B. Spilka. "Inward, Outward, and Upward: Cognitive Aspects of Prayer." *Journal for the Scientific Study of Religion* 41 (2002): 475–84.

Logan, John. "Consultant, Lawyers, and the 'Union Free' Movement in the USA since the 1970s." *Industrial Relations Journal* 33.3 (2002): 38–51

McVeigh, Rory, and David Sikkink. "God, Politics, and Protest: Religious Beliefs and the Legitimation of Contentious Tactics." *Social Forces* 79.4 (June 2001): 1425–58.

Orr's, Douglas V. "Strategic Bankruptcy and Private Pension Default." *Journal of Economic Issues* 32.3 (1998): 669–87.

Pope, Liston. "Religion and the Class Structure." *Annals of the American Academy of Political and Social Sciences* 256 (March 1948): 84–91.

Shureen, D. Douglas. "What Is 'Religion' for Purposes of Employment Discrimination Cases?" *Employees Relations Law Journal* 29.4 (Spring 2004): 34–43.

Smith, Christian, and Robert Faris. "Socioeconomic Inequality in the American Religious System: An Update and Assessment." *Journal for the Scientific Study of Religion* 44.1 (2005): 95–104.

Wolff, Rick. "The Fallout from Falling Wages." *Monthly Review*, June 12, 2006, at mrzine.monthlyreview.org, December 6, 2006. Accessed April 21, 2008.

Wuthnow, Robert. 2003. "The Changing Nature of Work in the United States: Implications for Vocation, Ethics, and Faith." *The Cresset*, Michaelmas.

———. "Overcoming Status Distinctions? Religious Involvement, Social Class, Race, and Ethnicity in Friendship Patterns." *Sociology of Religion* 64.4 (Winter 2003): 423–42.

Popular Articles

Bornas, Amy, et al. 2003. "Business Gets Religion." *Business Week*, February 3, 40–41.

Condon, Bernard. 2004. "The Coming Pension Crisis." *Forbes Magazine*, August 12.

Conlon, Michelle. 1999. "Religion in the Workplace." *Business Week*, November 1, 151–58.

Crutsinger, Martin. 2006. "Average American Family Income Declines." Associated Press, February.

Dalia, Martinez. 2003. "Say Amen Boss!" *Newsweek*, August 25, 8–10.

Drew, Douglas. "Couple Convicted of Drug, Other Violations of Labor Camps in Florida, North Carolina." *Daily Labor Report*. 2006. Bureau of National Affairs, Washington, DC, 168 (August 30): A–7.

Glantz, William. 2006. "Labor Objects to 'Super Pensions.'" *The Washington Times*, April 7, n. pag.

Gunther, Marc. 2001. "God and Business." *Fortune Magazine*, July 9, 58–80.

Harrop, Froma. 2006. "Why the Minimum Wage Wins." www.TomPaine.com, April 13.

Irvin, Helen. 2004. "Proselytizing in the Workplace Carries Risk of Religious Harassment Disputes." *Daily Labor Report*, Bureau of National Affairs, Washington, DC, 151 (August 6): C1–C4.

Jackson, Derrick Z. 2005. "As Goes GM, so Goes the Nation." *Chicago Tribune*, October 24, 19.

Kass, John. 2007. "Decency Drives Cabbie to do the Right Thing." *Chicago Tribune*, February 15, Section 1, 2.

Lowenstein, Roger. 2005. "The End of Pensions." *New York Times*, October 30, 56.

Maxwell, Tonya. 2005. "Churches Warned of Labor's Slide." *Chicago Tribune*, September 5, Section 2, 3.

Perry, Michael. N.d. *Labor Rights in the Jewish Tradition*, published by the National Jewish Labor Committee.

Ramirez, Margaret. 2006. "As Activist Rally, Priests Show Support by Fasting." *Chicago Tribune*, April 11, 8

Reuters News Service. 2006. "United Airlines Emerges from Bankruptcy." February 1.

Rose, Barbara. 2005. "Religious Faith Finding Place in Workplace." *Chicago Tribune*, October 23, 1.

Sasseen, Jane, and David Polek. 2006. "White-Collar Crime: Who Does Time?" *Business Week online*, www.businessweek.com, Special Report, February 6.

Shorto, Russell. 2004. "Faith at Work." *New York Times Magazine*, October 31, 40.

Sloan, Allan. 2006. "Ford Takes a Tax Holiday for 'Job Creation.'" *Washington Post*, January 24, D2.

Teather, David. 2006. "Four Years On, Enron Men Face their Day of Reckoning." *The Guardian*, January 26, n. pag.

Toomey, Shamus. 2006. "Our Lady of Guadalupe Home to Nation's First St. Jude Shrine." *Chicago Sun-Times*, May 5, A11.

Union Labor Report. 2006. "'Working Poor' Number 7.8 Million." Bureau of National Affairs, Washington, DC, 60.12, (June 16): 91.

Flyers/Newsletters/Web Stories

"City Worker Charged in Cab Driver's Death." 2005. CBS2 News Report, February 7, at cbs2chicago.com.

Initiatives. 2006. National Center for the Laity, October, 159; April, 155. 2005. January, 153; October, 151; September, 150; April, 147; 2005, 146; January–February, 145. 2004. December, 144; September, 142; March, 138; 2004, 136. 2003. September, 133.

"Jewish Federation Host Labor Seder." In *Faith Works*, National Interfaith Committee for Worker Justice, May 2004.

"Key Religious Leaders Launch Coalition with Chicago Hotel Workers (UNITE HERE); Crucial support comes on eve of Hilton, Hyatt strike votes." *Business Wire*, August 15, 2006, at www.cairchicago.org.

The Qur'an and Worker Justice, an educational booklet published by the National Interfaith Committee for Worker Justice, n.d.

"Update on Haroon Paryani Case." The Council of Islamic Organizations of Greater Chicago at www.ciogc.org.

Reports/Data Archives

American Federation of State County and Municipal Employees Council 31. 2005. "The High Price of Growth at Resurrection Health Care: Corporatization of Quality Care." November, at www.afscmeorganizers.org.

American Religion Data Archive. 2005. Survey Report. Pennsylvania State University, at www.thearda.com.

American Religious Identity Survey (ARIS). 2001. The Graduate School of the City University of New York, at www.gc.cuny.edu.

Archdiocese of Chicago, Joseph Cardinal Bernardin Archives and Records Center. Chicago.

Barna Poll on U.S. Religious Belief. 2001 at www.adherents.com/BarnaPoll.

Bonfenbrenner, Kate. 2000. *Uneasy Terrain: The Impact of Capital Mobility on Workers, Wages and Union Organizing*. Cornell University, September 6.

Bureau of Labor Statistics. 2005. "The Employment Situation: September 2005." United States Department of Labor. Washington, DC.

Centers for Disease Control and Prevention. 1996. *Morbidity and Mortality Report*. Washington, DC: U.S. Government Printing Office, March 15.

Congressional Budget Office. 1992. *Factors Contributing to the Infant Mortality Ranking of the United States*. Washington, DC: U.S. Government Printing Office, February.

Egon Mayer, Barry A. Kosmin, and Ariela Keysar. 2001. *The American Jewish Identity Survey: An Exploration in the Demography and Outlook of a People*. Graduate Center of the City University of New York.

General Social Survey. 2006. National Opinion Research Center, University of Chicago.

Kaiser Family Foundation and Health Research and Educational Trust. 2004. *Employer Health Benefits 2004 Survey*, at www.kff.org/insurance.

Kennickell, Arthur. 2006. *Currents and Undercurrents: Changes in the Distribution of Wealth, 1989–2004*. Washington, DC: Federal Reserve Board, 20551, January 30.

Lenz, Thomas J. 1998. "Building a Force for the Common Good: United Power for Action and Justice." *Shelterforce Online* 101, September/October, at www.nhi.org.

National Coalition for the Homeless. 2005. "How Many People Experience Homelessness?" NCH Fact Sheet #3, June.

National Conference of Catholic Bishops. 1989. *Economic Justice for All: Pastoral Letter on Catholic Social Teaching and the U.S. Economy*. Washington, DC: United States Catholic Conference.

National Jewish Population Survey. 2000–2001. "Strength, Challenge and Diversity in the American Jewish Population." United Jewish Communities, at www.ujc.org.

National Law Center on Homelessness and Poverty. 2004. "Homelessness in the United States and the Human Right to Housing." January.

National Opinion Research Center's General Social Survey. 2004. The University of Chicago.

National Surveys of Religion and Politics. 2004. The Bliss Institute of Applied Politics at the University of Akron.

The Pew Forum on Religion and Public Life. 2006. The Pew Research Center for the People and the Press, at www.people-press.org/reports.

Urban Institute. 1996. *National Survey of Homeless Assistance Providers and Clients*. Accessed October 23, 2006, at http://www.urban.org/publications/410496.html.

United States Census Bureau. 2004. *Income, Poverty, and Health Insurance Coverage in the United States*. Department of Commerce, Washington, DC.

United States Census Bureau, Census of Population. 2005. Washington, DC: United States Department of Commerce.

United States Department of Health, Education, and Welfare. 1973. *Work in America: Report of a Special Task Force to the Secretary of Health, Education, and Welfare*. Cambridge, MA: MIT Press.

United States Conference of Mayors. 2004. *A Status Report on Hunger and Homelessness in American Cities*. Washington, DC: U.S. Conference of Mayors.

World Health Organization. 2005. *Infant Mortality Rates and Rankings, World Health Report*, at www.who.int.

Work and Faith (and Other) Websites

Chicago Port Ministries, at www.theportministries.org.

Citizen Works, at www.citrizenworks.org.

"The Diversity Project: Stories and Practical Learning's about the Origins of Multicultural Urban Churches," at www.newlifetimeministries-nlm.org.

"Faith in Action." *Hospitality Accountability Project, Report No. 5*, Service Employees International Union, at www.hospitalmonitor.org.

Faith and Work Project, at faithandwork@improvemnet.co.uk.

Marketplace Leaders: Helping You Fulfill God's Calling, at www.icwm.net.

The National Center for the Laity, at www.catholiclabort/NCL.htm.
National Interfaith Committee for Worker Justice, at www.igc.org/nicj.
National Jewish Labor, at www.jewishlaborcommittee.org.
The Professional Association for People Involved with Spirituality in the Workplace, at www.spiritatwork.
Spirituality @ Work Dialogue, at gpierce@actpublkications.com.
United Power for Action and Justice, at www.united-power.org.

INDEX

A

B

C

T

U

V

W